RETIREMENT PLANNING

RETIREMENT PLANNING

Savvy Strategies
and Practical Advice
for a Secure
Financial Future

by Lita Epstein

Adams Media Corporation
Avon, Massachusetts

A Streetwise® Publication.
Streetwise® is a registered trademark of Adams Media Corporation.

Published by Adams Media Corporation
57 Littlefield Street, Avon, MA 02322 U.S.A.
www.adamsmedia.com

ISBN: 1-58062-772-2

Printed in the United States of America.

J I H G F E D C B A

Library of Congress Cataloging-in-Publication Data
Epstein, Lita.
Streetwise retirement planning / Lita Epstein.
p.   cm.
Includes index.
ISBN 1-58062-772-2
1. Retirement–United States–Planning. 2. Retirement–United States–Finance.
3. Social security–United States–Management. 4. Bank investments–United States.
5. Finance, Personal–United States. I. Title: Retirement planning. II. Title.
HQ1063.2.U6 E67 2002
646.7'9'0973–dc21
2002009991

This publication is designed to provide accurate and authoritative information with regard to the subject matter covered. It is sold with the understanding that the publisher is not engaged in rendering legal, accounting, or other professional advice. If legal advice or other expert assistance is required, the services of a competent professional person should be sought.
— From a *Declaration of Principles* jointly adopted by a Committee of the American Bar Association and a Committee of Publishers and Associations

This publication is intended to provide current and prospective business owners with useful information that may assist them in preparing for and obtaining business capital loans and investment funding. This information is general in nature and is not intended to provide specific advice for any individual or business entity. While the information contained herein should be helpful to the reader, appropriate financial, accounting, tax, or legal advice should always be sought from a competent professional engaged for any specific situation regarding your enterprise.

Cover illustration by Eric Mueller.

This book is available at quantity discounts for bulk purchases.
For information, call 1-800-872-5627.

Visit our exciting small business Web site: www.businesstown.com

CONTENTS

PART I: ASSESSING YOUR NEEDS

PART II: YOUR RETIREMENT GAP

PART III: RETIREMENT PLAN TYPES

CONTENTS

PART III: RETIREMENT PLAN TYPES (CONTINUED)

PART IV: PUTTING IT ALL TOGETHER

CONTENTS

PART V: RETIREMENT PLAYBOOK

Introduction

Everyone has a dream of what his or her ideal retirement life should be. Yours may be visions of lying on a beach somewhere, reading a book, and sipping Margaritas. Or, your ideal retirement could be to live in a private retirement community with a golf course that you can use daily. Or, maybe you prefer a quiet home along a mountain stream. Or, you may have a passion for starting your own business.

Whatever your dream, are you taking the steps you need to employ now to make sure that dream becomes a reality? Do you even know what the costs of living in that dream world will be? You've probably discussed your retirement dreams many times around the water cooler at work, but if you are like most people you have never even tried to develop a retirement budget.

We're going to take a journey together to help you develop a plan that can make your retirement dreams a reality. It's not easy. It will require a lot of thought and a good deal of number crunching, but it can also be fun to draw up a roadmap for your senior years.

Don't get discouraged if some of the initial calculations seem to make your dream impossible. You may just need to reorder some priorities and shift some of your current spending to make that future dream come true. Let's get started by assessing your needs.

PART I

Assessing Your Needs

This part helps you:

- Discuss the economic and demographic trends that sometimes get in the way of successfully funding your retirement goals.

- Look at the possible reductions to your anticipated retirement benefits.

- Come up with goals for your dream retirement.

- Review the key living costs in retirement: food, shelter, and health care.

- Develop a retirement budget.

- Create comprehensive inventories of your assets and liabilities.

- Calculate your net worth.

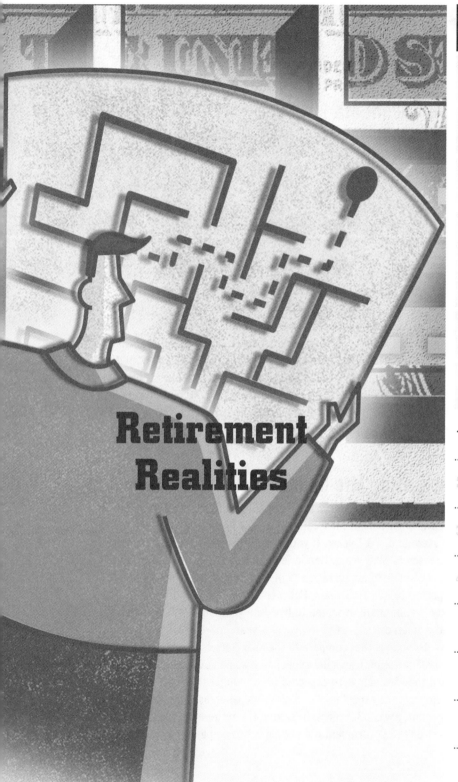

Retirement
Realities

The Recent Market Slide

Economic realities changed dramatically after the terrorist attacks on the World Trade Center on September 11, 2001. The world will never be the same and our futures will be permanently changed by this attack, even if we didn't know anyone directly affected by the events.

I'm sure you noticed your retirement portfolio took a nosedive after these events, and it probably was already hurting from the bursting of the tech stock bubble in 2000. We just lived through one of the most dramatic changes of economic fortunes, second only to the Great Depression of the 1920s, but most economists believe our economy is in much better shape and will recover more quickly than it did in the 1930s. Hopefully they are right. The stock market took about twenty-five years to recover from the stock crash of 1929. It wasn't until 1954 that the stock market rose above its peak of 1929.

We can't go back and change our investing decisions before this market slide happened, but we can modify how we plan to rebuild the lost ground. There are many things that haven't changed. Let's take a look at some of those realities.

Gender makes a difference.

Increasing Life Spans

There is no doubt: People are living longer. In its most recent study, the National Center for Health Statistics found that Americans live an average of 76.7 years. If you make it to sixty-five, that average increases to 82.8 years. Gender also makes a difference. Men can expect to live to an average age of 73.8 years, and women are expected to live 79.5 years. For men and women who make it to sixty-five, men are expected to live 15.9 years more (80.9 years old), and women are expected to live 17.8 years more (82.8 years old).

How does that compare to the year Social Security became law? In 1935, an American's life expectancy was an average of 61.7 years. Even then women were expected to live longer than men. Men had an average life expectancy of 59.9 years, whereas women's life expectancy was 63.9 years. In setting the retirement age at sixty-five, it's clear the government did not expect to be paying most people any

Social Security benefits. Today that's no longer true; Social Security estimates one in six people will not live to collect full benefits.

The first year that average life expectancy topped seventy years was 1962. Improvements in health care and lifestyles are the greatest contributors to these increasing life span numbers.

Calculating Life Expectancy

Why is life expectancy important for retirement planning? The only way you can determine how much you will need for retirement is to "guesstimate" how long you will be around to enjoy it. How long you will live is a crucial number in the formula.

I'm sure your first question is, "How do I do this?" You could take the simple route and just use the averages above, but you would be much wiser to use a life expectancy calculator, which can personalize the number for you. These calculators take lifestyle, family history, health, diet, and exercise into account to come up with a more realistic number. You can find an excellent one at MSN Money: *http://moneycentral.msn.com/investor/calcs/n_expect/main.asp*.

Making Ends Meet

Were you surprised to find out how long you are expected to live? Many people are living twenty to thirty years in retirement—longer than the number of years spent in childhood. During childhood years your parents paid your bills. Who will pay them during retirement if you haven't set aside enough money?

Unfortunately, for many retirees or near retirees the answer is to continue working to make ends meet. Some decide to work because they want to, but too many people are working because they have to in order to eat and pay their housing and medical costs. Others are lucky enough to have children or other family members who are able to take them in. But, do you want to live off your children and burden them financially while at the same time they may be sending their kids to college and saving for their own retirement?

Age is not the only retirement reality you must face. Let's take a look at some of the economic and demographic trends that are affecting people's ability to save for retirement.

> Many people are living twenty to thirty years in retirement.

Economic and Demographic Trends

You've probably heard this many times, but baby boomers will have the greatest impact on your future retirement finances even if you aren't in that generation. First, who are the baby boomers? About 78 million Americans who were born after World War II, between 1946 and 1964, make up the baby boomer generation.

This population mass has challenged economic and governmental systems since the beginning. As they moved through the various stages of life, they have thrown financial and governmental services out of whack: first, by forcing a major buildup to provide for their needs and then by causing a drain on the system as they passed through that stage. Their impact will be no different when they start retiring in the 2010s.

> Most baby boomers will start their retirement between 2010 and 2030.

Social Security Drain

Just for starters, let's take a look at how baby boomers will drain the foundation of most people's retirement funds: Social Security. Most baby boomers will start their retirement between 2010 and 2030. Rather than paying payroll taxes toward retirement, baby boomers will begin collecting their hard-earned benefits. Social Security is primarily a pay-as-you-go system, which means that 85 percent of current benefits are paid by current tax revenues. Only 15 percent is drawn from the Social Security Trust Fund.

What does this mean for Social Security? In 2000, there were 3.4 workers for every retiree. You will see that number fall dramatically. The trustees of the Social Security fund expect it to go as low as 1.9 workers per retiree in 2075. To make ends meet, Social Security is expected to start using the Social Security Trust Fund more extensively in 2020.

Unless there is some kind of fix, the Social Security Trustees expect the funds to be fully exhausted by 2038. Payroll taxes are projected to cover only 73 percent of Social Security's costs in that year. By 2075, without a solution for the ailing system, payroll taxes will be able to cover only 67 percent of promised benefits. What will happen when Social Security taxes no longer cover program costs? Benefits will have to be cut, taxes will have to be raised, or other governmental programs will have to be cut to pay for Social Security. Regardless of the chosen solution it will impact you financially, whether you are a retiree hoping to collect the benefits you paid toward all your life or a worker strapped with additional taxes or fewer government services.

Medicare, which is the key health care insurance program for people ages sixty-five and up, is even in worse shape than Social Security. We'll take a closer look at these programs in Part 3 of this book.

Being Sandwiched

While you've probably heard that Social Security is in trouble, are you aware that an even larger problem is cutting a huge hole in many people's ability to save for retirement? It's called the "sandwich generation." Many baby boomers are now adding this new generation nametag to their credentials. People stuck in the sandwich generation are faced with the financial pressures of paying for their kids' college, trying to save for their retirement, and helping their aging parents with their living and health-care costs.

People facing demands of the sandwich generation are estimated to total about 15 to 25 million baby boomers already and more are added to their ranks monthly. The National Council on Aging found that 70 percent of people taking care of their aging parents are women. Many women are being forced to balance the demands of care for their children and their elderly parents at the same time their careers are reaching their peaks. While women realize there is pressure to increase their savings so they will have enough to retire, many cannot act on this reality because of these multigenerational financial strains.

These financial realities are compounded by the heavy debt many families are carrying. Americans, on average, are incurring debt at a rate that is 4½ times greater than their savings rate.

For many baby boomers, their own life choices placed them in this squeeze. While many expected to be facing the types of challenges their parents faced when they reached their forties and fifties—trying to redefine their lives as empty nesters and rediscovering

Not Saving Enough

The Radcliffe Public Policy Center conducted a study in 2000 that found less than one-third (29 percent) of all respondents, both male and female, earned "enough to save for the future" and one-quarter (27 percent) said they earn "just enough to get by." Many folks who responded to the survey said they plan to retire early, but half of the respondents (48 percent) said they were only "somewhat confident" of their ability to fulfill that dream. Surveys conducted at the end of 2001 by other sources indicate that the number of people who believe they will now have to delay their retirement plans has increased because of the poor performance of the stock market in 2000 and 2001.

their relationships with their spouse—they didn't live their lives before their forties the same way their parents did. Many delayed having children until they got their careers off the ground, until their mid-thirties or later. Just as the couple sends off their last child to college, many find that an older child returns home because of a job loss or divorce, frequently bringing with them children of their own.

These new family realities are compounded by the successes medicine has had in extending people's lives. But, this has left many elderly people with the need for assistance with daily living, as they get older and cannot always care for themselves. Relatives, mostly daughters, care for four out of five elderly people who become at least partially disabled.

If you are already faced with this new reality, you'll need to incorporate all your creative skills to be sure this does not derail your own retirement plans. Here are some pointers for dealing with the challenges of the sandwich generation:

> Relatives, mostly daughters, care for four out of five elderly people who become at least partially disabled.

1. Find ways to share. Don't allow all the duties of care for your elderly parents to fall on your shoulders. If you do have adult children living at home, be sure they take on some of the responsibility of caring for their grandparents. Your first step will be to call all the generations together and discuss how everyone can help each other. Encourage independence as much as possible.

2. Organize your finances. Needless to say, you'll find it difficult to balance the needs of so many different generations financially. If you're not able to come up with a reasonable plan, you may want to contact a financial planner to help assess your needs, as well as the needs of your elderly parents, to develop a long-range solution that won't hamper your own long-term retirement plans.

3. Decide on legal moves. You may find this difficult to do, but it is time to discuss your parents' legal needs. There could come a time when your parents will not be able to make their own decisions. You should talk with your parents and work out the legal documents jointly with an attorney, while

they are still able to be part of the decision-making. You will need to execute powers of attorney for financial and health-care decisions, a living will with instructions regarding things such as life support, and a will for distributing assets after death.

4. Find out what your community offers. You may have more help available within your community than you realize. One of the first stops to find out more about resources is the National Aging Information Center (*www.aoa.dhhs.gov/ naic/default.htm*). If you don't have Internet access, you can reach them at: National Aging Information Center, Administration on Aging, 330 Independence Avenue, SW, Room 4656, Washington, DC 20201; tel: 202/619-7501; fax: 202/401-7620. You also may find that your local religious and civic organizations have programs that will help you meet the challenges of being "sandwiched."

5. Reorder your priorities. If you are someone who has always been very active in volunteer organizations, you may need to reconsider your involvement. You may find it is time to con-centrate on your family and put off your outside commit-ments to make more time for yourself and your family.

6. Consider telecommuting. While telecommuting still hasn't become mainstream, it still may be an option you want to dis-cuss with your employer. Or, you may decide it's time to start that home business you always dreamed about. Working at home may just give you the flexibility you need to get through the difficult times, allowing you to more easily man-age medical appointments and care for your parents. Advancements in technology make it much easier today to work from home. Even if you are stuck in a doctor's office with family members, you can still stay in touch with cus-tomers using the technological tools available today.

The challenges of the sandwich generation can be even more taxing as families face the other realities that threaten to derail their retirement future. For instance, divorce can really throw a wrench into the works.

> You may find it is time to concentrate on your family and put off your outside commitments.

Women Save Less Than Men

The National Center for Women and Retirement Research (NCWRR) found that one year after divorce the average mid-life woman is still single and earning only $11,300. More than 58 percent of female baby boomers have less than $10,000 saved toward their retirement, while male baby boomers have saved three times that amount. In a 2000 survey conducted by Employee Benefits Research Institute, 86 percent of women said they were confident they will have enough money for basic expenses, but fewer have confidence they'll have enough money for other critical expenses. Only 64 percent believe they will have enough to pay for medical expenses and 47 percent expect to be able to foot the bill for long-term care.

Divorce Epidemic

You may think that divorce is one of those things that could never happen to you. Well don't be so sure. The U.S. Bureau of Census reports that divorce is the fastest growing marital category. In 1970, there were 4.3 million divorced people. The number of divorced people jumped to 18.3 million in 1996.

The U.S. National Center for Health Statistics reported in May 2001 that 43 percent of first marriages end in separation or divorce within fifteen years. That reality can be particularly difficult on women. While divorced men may have significant financial burdens after a divorce, their earning power is much higher, especially if their ex-wives had stayed home to care for the family.

The big mistake women make is that they do not save for retirement during the years they are raising a family. Instead, the couple's retirement funds are built solely through the husband's workplace. Even if you are not working outside the home, it is critical that you build your own retirement nest egg. We'll look more closely at this issue in Chapter 17.

Facing Widowhood

Divorce is not the only way women are financially challenged. The average age for widowhood in the United States is fifty-six. In 1996, 71 percent of the 4 million elderly women were poor. Of this group 48 percent were widowed. The median income for women over sixty-five in 1996 was $8,189.

Women's Unique Retirement Challenges

Based on the NCWRR 1996 baby boomer study, women born between 1946 and 1964 are expected to be stuck in the workforce until at least the age of seventy-four because of their inadequate savings and pension. Otherwise, they will be unable to maintain the same standard of living they enjoyed prior to age sixty-five.

Over the next forty years, researchers estimate that the number of women over eighty-five will triple or quadruple and three fourths of those women will be single, divorced, or widowed. Many are expected to be living at or under the poverty level.

Why are women so heavily impacted? We've already discussed that women live longer than men so they need to save more to avoid outliving their savings. But other reasons exist. Women are still earning just 74 cents versus each dollar that men make. Even if they do start on equal footing, women tend to be the ones that take off to raise a family. When they return to work, they are no longer on the same career path as the men who have worked steadily. The NCWRR estimates that for every year a woman stays home to care for a child, she must work five years to recover the lost income, pension coverage, and career setbacks.

Fortunately, women are aware of the problem, according to findings of the Employee Benefits Research Institute's (EBRI) 2000 Women's Retirement Confidence Survey. Here are some key findings:

- Eighty-six percent of women are confident they will have enough money for basic expenses, but fewer express confidence in having enough money to pay for medical expenses (64 percent) or long-term care (47 percent).
- Sixty-five percent of women expect to work in retirement, an increase from 57 percent in 1998. This makes women as likely as men (68 percent in 2000) to think they will work for pay in retirement.
- Fifty-eight percent of working-age women say they have not received retirement planning information from an employer within the past year. Those who are saving for retirement are more likely than those who are not saving to say they have received this information.
- Sixty-seven percent of women believe that anyone can have a comfortable retirement if he or she is disciplined and saves. Most feel they are disciplined savers (62 percent), but they are undecided about whether to risk these savings. Twenty-eight percent report that they are unwilling to take any type of financial risk no matter what the gain, while 33 percent say they are willing to take substantial risks for substantial financial gains.

Women do tend to be more conservative about their investments and are more likely to put their savings in guaranteed or

> Every year a woman stays home to care for a child, she must work five years to recover the lost income, pension coverage, and career setbacks.

insured investment vehicles. Many don't understand this strategy also carries risk—the risk that the growth will be totally eaten up by inflation and they will not be able to meet their retirement goals. We'll talk more about investing risks and how to minimize those in Chapter 16.

How do all these challenges impact retirement dollars? Not surprisingly, women get significantly lower benefits. At the beginning of 2000, a woman's monthly Social Security retirement benefit averaged $697, whereas a man's average monthly benefit was $904. EBRI found a similar pattern with pension benefits. Only 28.8 percent of women over age sixty-five have a pension, while 45.7 percent of men earned pension benefits. In 1999, males aged sixty-five and older had annual pensions of $14,046; women's average pension was only $8,224.

All these numbers are in current dollars. As we all know, these current dollars will not be worth the same amount by the time we reach retirement. Even if you are already in retirement, the dollars will still get eaten away by inflation. Let's take a quick look at how inflation affects your retirement planning.

Inflation and Interest Rates

The number one enemy to saving for retirement is inflation. The key is to find a way to save your money that will beat inflation and help you grow those assets beyond the price increases that inflation fuels. While you might enjoy seeing interest rates rise so your savings earn more, those interest rate increases just help to fuel inflation and the cost to produce the products you use. Inflation can also slow spending and throw the country into recession.

To show you how inflation may impact your savings, let's practice using the mathematical formula called the Rule of 72. Mathematicians use this formula to calculate the power of compounding. They have found that dividing the number 72 by the rate of inflation will give you the number of years it will take for your expenses to double.

Inflation historically runs about 3 percent annually. At this rate your expenses double in twenty-four years (72 / 3 = 24). If that number jumps just one percent, your expenses will double in eighteen years (72 / 4 = 18).

This rule can also be used to figure out how long it will take your investments to double. Historically, savings accounts have a return of 2 to 3 percent, bonds have averaged 5 to 6 percent, and stocks have averaged 10 to 12 percent over a period of twenty years. Let's use the Rule of 72 to see how long it will take to double the money you have saved.

If you are earning 3 percent, it will take twenty-four years for your money to double (72 / 3 = 34). If you are earning 6 percent, it will take twelve years (72 / 6 = 12). If you are earning 12 percent, it will take six years (72 / 12 = 6). Obviously, we'd all like to earn 12 percent, but the stock market doesn't always cooperate. To get the highest earnings rate, you'll need to take a lot of risk with your portfolio. We'll take a closer look at this in Chapter 16.

Disability

Even if you do all the right things, you still can get hit with an unexpected roadblock to retirement: disability. Social Security estimates that three in ten twenty-year-olds today will become disabled before their full retirement age. Yet many people don't have private disability insurance.

You can depend on Social Security disability, but in order to collect you will have to be so severely disabled that you are unable to work in any capacity. In order to protect your rights to work only in the field for which you are trained, you will need to pay for your own disability insurance coverage.

Benefits Reduction

We've talked a lot about the things that can go wrong personally, but another obstacle in reaching your retirement goals is the threat to your hard-earned retirement benefits at work. Each year we hear about more and more companies shifting their guaranteed retirement benefits to plans based on cash balances. Only about 10 percent of workers today will have the type of pension their parents

> Social Security estimates that three in ten twenty-year-olds today will become disabled before their full retirement age.

had–a guaranteed monthly amount paid by their company for life after they retire.

Today you are more likely to have a 401(k) account if you work in the private for-profit sector, a 403(b) account if you work in the private non-profit sector, or a Section 457 account if you work in the public sector. To build a decent retirement, in most cases, you will need to contribute to these plans to even qualify for the company matching contribution. Retirement benefits have become a partnership between companies and employees, with employees assuming all the risks of having enough funds for retirement.

Most companies no longer take any responsibility to be certain your savings at the time of retirement last throughout your retirement years. This situation is compounded by the concerns that Social Security benefits also will be cut to keep the program solvent. Part 3 will cover these topics in greater detail.

> Retirement benefits have become a partnership between companies and employees.

Phased Retirement

Workers planning to retire today and in the future will no longer just be concerned about where they want to spend their retirement years, or what leisure activity they want to engage in; rather, their transitions will also include greater concerns about how to get there financially. One option that is quickly taking hold is "Phased Retirement." There isn't a clear picture of what this will look like, but companies and their employees are experimenting with numerous options.

EBRI published a report in September 2001, "Phased Retirement: Leaving the Labor Force," that reviews the development of this new phenomena. Generally, phased retirement is a "flexible work option" that gives employees the option to reduce their work hours or move through a succession of jobs as they prepare to leave the work force permanently.

EBRI found there are basically two types of Phased Retirement:

1. A formal or structured program. Employers initiate or permit the creation of a phased retirement arrangement for one or more employees. EBRI found formal phased retirement programs are still in their infancy, especially in the private

sector. In fact, most of these programs begin as ad hoc arrangements that allow workers to continue employment, but in a reduced work capacity, and are gradually structured into formal arrangements.

2. Ad hoc or informal arrangements. These arrangements tend to involve a continued relationship with the same employer beyond the expected retirement age. A related practice could entail employer retention of retirees as consultants or the rehiring of retirees on a part-time or part-year basis. Other routes can include employees who leave a primary employer to work elsewhere through a series of "bridge jobs" until final retirement.

Now that we are living longer, people are finding there is only so much time that they want to spend taking adult-learning classes, playing golf, or pursuing other interests. Going back to work or never fully stopping is becoming a more popular choice for potential retirees.

Phased Retirement was made much more attractive when former President Bill Clinton signed the "Senior Citizens Freedom to Work Act" into law in 2000. In signing the bill, President Clinton said, "Today, one in four Americans between sixty-five and sixty-nine has at least a part-time job. Eighty percent of the baby boomers say they intend to keep working past age sixty-five." The bill removed penalties for working after you reach full retirement age.

Prior to the bill's passage, a portion of your Social Security benefit could be reduced up to the age of seventy if you continued working. Now once you reach full retirement age you can still collect 100 percent of your Social Security benefits and continue to work. There is still a benefit reduction if you start your Social Security benefits early. We'll look at the work rules more closely in Chapter 8.

> Going back to work or never fully stopping is becoming a more popular choice for potential retirees.

The Ball Is in Your Court

The bottom line is that the ball is in your court. You must decide how you want to spend your retirement years and how you will pay for them. How successful you will be at meeting your goals is solely dependent on how carefully you plan and how well you stick to that plan.

Before we get into all the hard work of figuring out how to come up with the money, let's start with the fun part. In Chapter 2, you'll get to design your dream retirement. Then we'll work hard to figure how you can pay for it.

For more information on this topic, visit our Web site at www.businesstown.com

Chapter 2

Your Dream Retirement

What Do You Want in Retirement?

Now it's time to dream. If money were no object, how would you like to spend your retirement years? If you are married, sit down with your spouse and brainstorm your ideal retirement together. Most importantly, have fun with this task.

Would you like to take a trip around the world? Maybe you'd like to buy a cabin in the woods to get away from it all. Or, you may enjoy living at the beach. Whatever strikes your fancy, add it to the list of your dreams. Don't edit as you go along. Put everything down at this point.

If it's easier or less pressure for you, post the list in a convenient place and add to it throughout the week as ideas pop into your head. Remember this should be fun, not work. Don't get stressed trying to think of everything. We're not etching this in stone. You can revise the plan later in life as your priorities change.

Once you have your list, put a number next to each item. Place a five next to the things you absolutely must do. Put a one next to the things that you would not miss terribly if you were not able to get them done. Use numbers two, three, and four for items in between those two points.

Here's a sample of what your list should look like:

Dreams	Rankings
Alaskan Cruise	5
Mountain Cabin	4
Start My Own Business	5
Buy a Boat	2
Retire at 55	3

Now reorder your list, placing the "5s" on top, next the "4s", then the "3s", then the "2s", and finally the "1s." That wasn't so hard. Now you have a list of your retirement dreams and how important each one is to you and your spouse.

Why did I put you through this exercise? Before you can even start to develop a plan you need to know the critical items for which you want to plan. How can you develop a budget for retirement if you don't have some idea of how you want to live during that time period? Of course, as you grow older and get closer to retirement

How would you like to spend your retirement years?

your dreams and desires could change. That's not a problem, just step through the planning process again and revise your needs based on the new goals. In fact, as you'll read often in this book, it's best to revisit your plans yearly to be certain you are still on track and there aren't any major changes in your life that could have an impact on your retirement goals.

Each of these goals will have a different impact on your planning process. We'll take a look at some questions you must answer. Your answers will affect your money needs during retirement.

When Do You Want to Retire?

The first big question: When do you want to retire? Your financial needs will vary greatly once you figure out the answer to this question. You may even want to develop budgets based on all three options—retire early, retire on time, or delay retirement as long as possible—to see what you can afford to do.

Retire Early

Retiring early sounds great to many people until they consider what it will mean financially. Unless you are entitled to some kind of early retirement package from your place of work, you will have to drain your savings to meet all costs. Rather than your hopefully sizeable portfolio building steam, its growth will stall as you begin draining it.

Social Security isn't even a possibility until age sixty-two for most people. (We'll talk about the few exceptions in Chapter 8.) If you do decide to start your Social Security benefits before your full retirement age, they will be significantly reduced, and this reduction is a permanent one throughout your retirement years.

So, how much of your Social Security benefit is at risk if you decide to retire at age sixty-two? If you were born before 1937, the reduction in benefits would be:

- At age 62: Your benefits would be reduced 20 percent.
- At age 63: Your benefits would be reduced about $13^1/_3$ percent.
- At age 64: Your benefits would be reduced about $6^2/_3$ percent.

> Retiring early sounds great to many people until they consider what it will mean financially.

For people born after 1937, the reductions are higher; how much depends on your year of birth. We'll delve into this much in Chapter 8. I just wanted to give you an idea of what is at stake if you retire early.

Medical costs can be one of the biggest deterrents to early retirement, even if you think you have enough saved to live on otherwise. Retiring before age sixty-five means you will have to pay all the costs of your medical insurance, unless you are one of the lucky few with medical coverage included in your private or government retirement plan. Not only are private medical insurance plans very costly, frequently topping $1,000 per month, if you have any significant medical problems you may have trouble even getting coverage. Or, you may find that some medical conditions could be excluded from coverage completely, increasing your out-of-pocket expenses dramatically.

> Your full retirement age according to Social Security will vary depending on when you were born.

Retiring on Time

This may sound strange to you, but your full retirement age according to Social Security will vary depending on when you were born. In an attempt to fix Social Security's financial woes in the 1980s, the full retirement age was adjusted to rise gradually from sixty-five to sixty-seven. Only those born in 1937 or earlier can still retire at sixty-five and get full benefits.

Here's a chart from Social Security that lays out the full retirement age by year of birth:

Year of Birth	Full Retirement Age
1937 or earlier	65
1938	65 and 2 months
1939	65 and 4 months
1940	65 and 6 months
1941	65 and 8 months
1942	65 and 10 months
1943–1954	66
1955	66 and 2 months
1956	66 and 4 months
1957	66 and 6 months
1958	66 and 8 months
1959	66 and 10 months
1960 and later	67

If you qualify for Social Security, you will also automatically qualify for Medicare at age sixty-five. There is no plan to raise that age, at least at this time. Furthermore, a lot of holes in Medicare coverage still exist. You may still want to carry a private Medigap insurance policy to pay the full costs of medical coverage over the age of sixty-five, but that is cheaper than having to pay for medical insurance entirely out-of-pocket. Medigap policies (which cover what Medicare doesn't) have many options, which we'll cover in greater depth in Chapter 14.

This stuff does get complicated. I just want you to get an idea of the things you must budget for in addition to your dreams.

Delayed Retirement

Waiting to retire may be just what you need to stretch your retirement savings. Not only does your money get to grow for a longer period of time before you start drawing it down, your Social Security benefits will be permanently increased as well.

There is a point, however, where it makes no sense to wait any longer to begin collecting Social Security. Once you turn seventy, your benefits won't increase any more if you wait and there is no penalty if you want to keep working anyway. In fact, as I mentioned earlier, you can continue working once you reach full retirement age without risking a benefit reduction.

Just like we saw with early retirement, the year of your birth affects how much your benefits will increase if you delay collecting them. In the chart below from the Social Security Administration, you will see how benefits are impacted each year you delay applying for Social Security.

> Once you turn seventy, your benefits won't increase any more if you wait and there is no penalty if you want to keep working anyway.

Increase for Delayed Retirement			
Year of Birth	Yearly Rate of Increase	Year of Birth	Yearly Rate of Increase
1930	4.5%	1937–1938	6.5%
1931–1932	5.0%	1939–1940	7.0%
1933–1934	5.5%	1941–1942	7.5%
1935–1936	6.0%	1943 or later	8.0%

Persons born on January 1 of any year should refer to the rate of increase for the previous year.

Now you understand why the date for retirement is so critical to budget planning. The next most critical decision is where you want to live.

Where Do You Want to Live?

The first big question is whether you will want to continue living in your current home or you will definitely want to move out of it. You may wish to stay in the same general location, but simply find something smaller that will be less costly and easier to maintain, especially since you hopefully will be providing living arrangements for only you and your spouse.

Another option will be to move into a retirement community and use the assets from your home to buy into that community. If your children have relocated, you may choose to move closer to them. Or you may just want to move to a warmer climate. Whatever your choice, there are many financial options to consider.

Your Home

First, of course, you must decide whether to keep or sell your home. For many people, their home is their largest asset. Sometimes, its value is even more than what they have saved in their retirement portfolio.

Even if you decide to keep your home, you may want to consider accessing some of the assets you've built up in that home in order to afford your retirement plans.

Be certain you understand the implications if you choose to take any kind of equity loan or reverse mortgage on your property. Remember, you won't get much in the way of raises in retirement. You'll essentially be living on a fixed income. If an emergency comes up and you can't make a loan payment, you could risk losing the home.

Home Equity Line

A home equity line is actually a type of revolving credit for which your home serves as the collateral. You get approval for a loan

Tapping Your Home's Equity

To gain access to your home's assets at retirement, you can do one of three things:

1. Sell your home and move into something smaller or to a location you prefer. This will free up the cash to buy that smaller home. You can bank whatever is left over for future use. You may also decide to rent and avoid the hassles of home ownership. That way you can put all the profits into your retirement portfolio for future use.
2. Take an equity line of credit or a new mortgage to free up the cash. This will give you a set amount of cash to live on.
3. Use a reverse mortgage that will pay you a set amount per month. Again, this will generate instant cash for your expenses.

amount and can borrow the money as you need it. Many equity lines are set up so you can just write a check from your checking account. If there isn't enough money available, the bank automatically takes some money from the equity line. Other plans are set up with a credit card that you can use to take out the money. Another option is to transfer funds from the equity line to one of your bank accounts.

These loans can be very convenient, maybe even too convenient. You do add risk to the security of your home. You will need to make monthly payments on the loan amount and, if you can't pay them, foreclosure is a possibility.

The amount of credit for which you can qualify will depend on the value of your home, the amount of equity you have in the home (in other words, how much your home is worth above the existing loans on it), and your ability to repay the loan. Your income, debts, and other financial obligations, as well as your credit history, will be reviewed when you apply for the loan.

Most home equity lines are taken for a fixed period of time, frequently ten years. Throughout the period of the loan you can borrow using the equity line, repay what you borrowed, and then borrow again. Some equity lines end after the fixed period and must be repaid in full at the end of that time. Others are set up with an automatic renewal possibility.

Reverse Mortgage

Reverse mortgages may sound too good to be true. Rather than paying down on a mortgage by sending money into a mortgage company, *you* can end up receiving a monthly payment. I'll bet that sounds great, but don't get excited too quickly.

Basically, a reverse mortgage is a loan taken out with your home as collateral that you won't have to pay back during your lifetime. You can get the money in a lump sum, in monthly installments, or you can draw from the funds whenever you choose as you would with an equity line. You, and any other co-borrowers, must be at least sixty-two years old to qualify for a reverse mortgage.

The loan is repaid with interest when you die, if you sell the home before you die, or if you move to another home. Since you don't make loan payments while you are alive, the loan amount

> A reverse mortgage is a loan taken out with your home as collateral that you won't have to pay back during your lifetime.

grows larger each time you draw out some money. The good news is that you or your heirs can never owe more than your home's value when the loan is repaid. If the bank errs in computing the home value or you live longer than the bank expects when the loan is established, it will take the loss at the time of sale. You do continue to have the responsibilities of home ownership while you live there. You will have to pay property taxes (unless you are in one of the states that exempt retirees), insurance, and for any necessary repairs.

Who offers reverse mortgages? Your state or local government may offer them. Most of these public sector loans are taken so that recipients can pay for home repairs or property taxes. The more common place to get a reverse mortgage loan is from a bank or mortgage company. These private sector loans don't have any strings attached that stipulate how the money can be used. The amount you will be able to borrow will depend on your age, your home's value and location, and the cost of the loan (interest rate and loan origination costs are the key costs to watch). The older you are and the greater your home value, the more funds you will qualify for with a reverse mortgage.

You probably should not plan this as your first choice, but it may be a good option if you suffer severe financial difficulties in retirement. If you want to learn more about reverse mortgages, the American Association of Retired Persons (AARP) has an excellent collection of articles about reverse mortgages at *www.aarp.org/revmort*.

Retirement Living Choices

If you do decide you want to move, your next choice will be where you want to live. This might be an easy decision, if you already know the exact city or town you wish to live in. Or, you may first need to pick the place. Whatever part of the decision process you are in, there is an excellent Web site you can visit to begin exploring your options called Retirement Net: *www.retirenet.com*.

It may be too early to decide exactly which type of retirement living arrangement you'll want. A big variable is how healthy you are when you get there. If you can live completely independent of others, your choices are unlimited. As you lose your ability to care for yourself independently, other hard choices will need to be made.

Many people hope to stay in their home as long as possible. They can offset their need for assistance by paying for in-home services, such as lawn care, cooking, shopping, personal care, or skilled nursing care. This choice can get expensive as your needs for assistance increase.

There are basically three levels of care and services for seniors once they start to need help:

1. Living independently in your own home or a retirement community with meals provided, activities, housekeeping, and maintenance
2. Living in an assisted living facility where housing is provided along with other support services to aid with personal care services and medication management
3. Living in a nursing home setting for seniors who become temporarily ill or who need long-term health care

One of the most popular choices for active seniors is the independent living retirement community. In these complexes, seniors live on their own, but can make arrangements for a comprehensive service package. Meals, housekeeping, activities, transportation, and security can be provided for a monthly fee, if you desire. Monthly fees vary dramatically, depending on what you need, but usually range from $350 to $1,500 per month. There are also government facilities that offer subsidized senior housing. They are not as luxurious as the private communities, but costs are usually adjusted based on your personal financial situation.

The next level of care is called the assisted living facility. In these facilities, residents get additional housekeeping services, receive assistance with managing their medications, and usually get help with bathing, grooming, and dressing. Many also provide group activities for the residents. Assisted living facilities have complicated fee structures based on the level of care you need. Monthly bills average between $3,000 and $5,000 per month.

Plan for Getting Help with Daily Living Needs

Estimates are that 85 percent of people will find a need for at least some assistance with daily living at some point in their retirement years. About 60 percent of these people will get the help they need from their family and friends, while others will end up needing institutional support. The more carefully you plan before retirement, the greater control you will have over these decisions. If you save enough and protect your assets with necessary insurance in case of a catastrophic illness or loss, you will have a much better chance of living according to the standards you desire and without the risk of running out of money.

CCRC Fee Schedules

Often you will find three different types of fee schedules:

- An extensive contract will include unlimited long-term nursing care at little or no increase in monthly fee. These are the most expensive.

- Modified contracts will limit the amount of nursing care included. After that time you pay all the costs of the nursing care.

- Fee-for-service contracts require you to pay daily rates for long-term nursing care. These will usually be the cheapest because you take all the risks.

In exchange for these fees you get a place to live, meals, and health-care services up to the nursing home level. The only type of health care not included is critical care in a hospital setting. These communities offer the independence of retirement home living with the security of long-term care. The drawback is that they are very expensive. Contracts for CCRCs are also very complicated. If you do decide to consider this option, be certain you have an attorney look over the documents to be sure you are getting the long-term security you are seeking.

Lastly, nursing homes are for individuals whose disability requires regular skilled nursing care. For most people and their families, these facilities are the option of last resort. Their costs are high, usually averaging about $200 per day or $6,000 per month and can go as high as $10,000 per month.

Some people are making the choice to live in Continuing Care Retirement Communities (CCRC), also known as Life Care Communities. These communities combine all three levels of care—independent living, assisted living, and nursing home care—within the walls of one community. The big advantage of this choice is that as you move through the stages of retirement, you will continue to be close to the same set of friends. This can be a wonderful support network in your later years.

Most CCRCs have a sizeable entry fee, plus monthly maintenance fees. Their costs vary greatly. On the low end you may find entry fees of $20,000, but in this case the monthly costs will probably be higher than the high-end entry fees. On the higher end, the entry fees can be as great as $400,000. Monthly fees for these CCRCs range from $200 to $2,500.

Other housing options are also available for seniors. There are group homes, which provide independent, private living but in a house shared with several seniors who split the rent, housekeeping services, utilities, and meals. Some homeowners who want to share their house with others offer shared housing. Many times the homeowner is a widow or widower who is looking for companionship as well as for someone to help with expenses.

Another option available in some communities is adult foster care, where a family will care for a dependent person in their home. Meals, housekeeping, and help with dressing, eating, bathing, and other personal care are provided. You can check with the local social services department to find out if adult foster care is available in an area you are considering for retirement.

I'm sure you've figured out by now that choosing a retirement location requires a lot of research. A popular book about the best places to retire is *Retirement Places Rated* by David Savageau (Hungry Minds, 1999). You may also want to take a year's subscription to the magazine *Where to Retire* for location ideas.

Your flexibility during retirement increases in communities that provide a greater choice of living options for seniors. Making the right choice up front can not only save you a lot of money, but will also prevent your having to move a great distance as your needs change or if you find out you just hate the place you chose.

Retirement Stages

As we've talked about the different types of living arrangements and health-care needs, I'm sure you've begun to realize that your life in retirement will not be one long stage in which all your needs will remain exactly the same. Planners have found that, in general, there are actually three stages of retirement.

1. *Active Stage.* This is the time you really get to enjoy all the money you so carefully socked away. Your health will be in good shape and you'll be able to travel and do things you dreamed about. Living costs will probably be nearly the same as they were when you were working.
2. *Passive Stage.* During this stage, you will find that you need to slow down, but will still be healthy enough to remain independent and in your own home. Living costs will probably be the cheapest in this stage because your medical bills will not be that high and your travel, transportation, clothing, and entertainment costs will probably decrease.
3. *Dependent Stage.* Unless you are one of the lucky few, you will get to a stage of your life where you are dependent on others in order to meet your daily needs of life. You may even need to move to a facility that can offer you more intensive care. Living costs in this stage can sometimes be the highest because of your intensive need for services and skilled nursing care.

When we start on budget planning in the next chapter, we'll take a closer look at the key issues you'll need to consider as you plan for these various stages of retirement.

> Retirement will not be one long stage in which all your needs will remain exactly the same.

Keeping Fit

Whatever you decide to do, don't forget the essentials of keeping yourself fit and healthy. You'll find it is even more important to plan exercise regularly and eat smart. Exercise can be a fun part of your day, depending on how you plan. A daily long walk with a close friend can be the best exercise and keep you fit, as well as give you an opportunity to get support emotionally for various challenges you may face.

Travel and Leisure Goals

Now we'll move on to the fun stuff! I hope all this talk of varying living needs hasn't been too depressing. Unfortunately, they are the realities of the retirement phase of life.

Hopefully, you will have entered retirement without having to work full time to make ends meet and with enough money to do the things you never had time for while you were working. If you have, the possibilities are limited only by your imagination and what you want to do with your time.

Let's revisit the dream list you created at the start of this chapter. How many of those items fit in the category of travel and leisure goals? In addition to the goals you have already identified, retirement can be a time to learn new things and try things you've never tried before. Don't get too rigid about your dreams and forget to enjoy things that just happen to come your way.

One big advantage during retirement is that you don't have to travel during prime vacation times. This allows you to take advantage of travel bargains because of your increased time flexibility.

Seniors also have some interesting new ways to travel and can do it at a very low cost. One creative travel idea that is catching on is trading homes. Other seniors are taking in travelers and then enjoying being guests in their homes. Not only do seniors enjoy the benefits of free hospitality, but they also get a chance to meet other senior travelers.

There are two successful sites on the Internet to explore this new travel phenomenon:

- Elder Travelers (*www.eldertravelers.com*) gears its services to people over fifty who like to travel and meet other people. Their members stay in homes of fellow senior travelers and provide hospitality in their own home in exchange. The site also has links to travel bureaus in each of the fifty states in the United States, as well as links for world travel.
- Seniors Vacation and Home Exchange (*www.seniorshome exchange.com*) takes this a step further. People actually exchange their homes in order to lower their travel costs.

The group also arranges hospitality vacations in which you visit someone and then return the favor by letting them visit you.

Finding new ways to learn is another popular alternative for seniors. Elderhostel (*www.elderhostel.org*) is the first such organization that formed in the United States and is the world's largest educational and travel organization for adults aged fifty-five and older. The not-for-profit organization was founded in 1975 and now offers learning opportunities around the globe. Frequently, Elderhostel trips are organized with the help of local universities to offer learning and travel opportunities.

Once you start exploring the alternatives, you'll find organizations that cater to whatever your individual desires might be. Here are a few examples:

- Travel with Grandchildren (*www.grandtrvl.com*) helps you plan vacations for you and your grandchildren.
- Skiers over 50 have an active organization called the Over the Hill Gang (*www.skiersover50.com*).
- If you enjoy hiking and walking, WebWalking (*www.webwalking.com/hiking.html*) will help you find the best places worldwide.

As you can see, your dream retirement is only limited by your imagination and your initiative to find out what might be available. Many options are available for free or nearly free so that even if you haven't saved all the money you had hoped you can still travel the world.

Charity and Gift Goals

Another important question to ask as you develop your retirement budget is whether you want to leave anything behind? You may want to help your grandchildren with their college expenses or donate money to your favorite charity or alma mater.

Whatever your money goals, don't forget to include these as part of your retirement planning. If you expect to have a substantial

> Your dream retirement is only limited by your imagination.

amount that may end up being subject to inheritance taxes (and who knows what they will be after the 2001 tax bill crafted by Congress), you probably should seek help from an estate planner to be sure you are doing things just right to meet your goals.

Overall Living Standard

We've covered a lot of ground here to begin planning your dream retirement. You may have more questions now than you did before we started this chapter. Retirement is a big part of your life. If you take the time to plan, it can be the most enjoyable time of your life, when you finally have the time to concentrate on your needs and what you want to accomplish rather than answering to the needs of your boss or your family. It also gives you a second chance to do the things you might not have done quite right, but would like to try again.

Hopefully by this stage of life, your children are grown and out of the house. Your overall living standard is what you and your spouse set for yourselves. You don't need to worry about saving for your child's education or figuring out how to pay for your child's braces.

Whether you want to live in a small cabin in the woods, stay in your current home, or find a beach house along the coast, your choice is no longer based on where you have to live to find work. Your possibilities are a blank page and you get to draw the roadmap. You choose the standard of living you would like to have and find ways to get there.

> Your overall living standard is what you and your spouse set for yourselves.

For more information on this topic, visit our Web site at www.businesstown.com

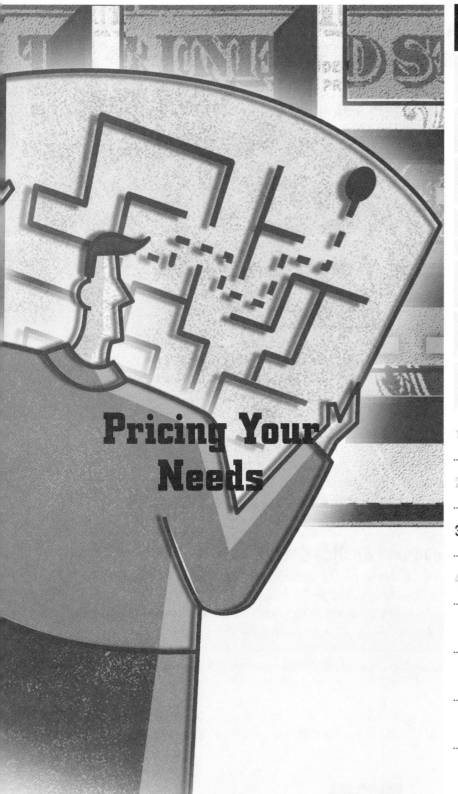

Pricing Your Needs

Crunching Numbers

We're ready to start crunching some numbers. Unless you're someone who loves working with figures, you may have to push yourself to work through this chapter. The time will be well spent, though, because you'll have a much better idea of what you need financially to make your retirement dreams happen. Use the information you gathered in Chapter 2 to start thinking about your retirement budget needs.

When we're done figuring out your expenses, we'll then move on to estimating your current assets and liabilities. Once we've got all these numbers together, we'll be able to use them to figure out how close you are to reaching that golden ring–your dream retirement.

We're going to review the possible costs in great detail, so you'll know what you need to think about when actually planning a retirement budget. However, you can decide how deeply you want to explore the costs. If you want to simply make ballpark guesses, that's okay. Unless you are just a few years away from retirement, you probably aren't ready to take such a microscopic look at your possible expenses. Just use the information to develop a ballpark estimate at today's costs. Obviously, inflation and other economic forces will affect the numbers greatly by the time you are ready to retire. When we start to figure the retirement gap, we'll do an inflation-adjusted budget. For now, don't worry about it.

> Inflation and other economic forces will affect the numbers greatly by the time you are ready to retire.

Food and Shelter Costs

Let's start with food and shelter costs. Whether you decide to rent, buy a new home, or remain in a home that's already paid off, you will have monthly expenses. To come up with this number, you'll need to estimate a monthly housing number. In addition to rent or a mortgage payment, you may need to include a homeowner's association fee, condominium fee, or maintenance fee; retirement community membership and/or services fee; costs for various types of utilities; costs of maintenance and repairs; and household supplies.

Other monthly housing costs could vary, depending on personal lifestyle. If you are a computer buff, you'll certainly need to budget for an Internet connection. Most folks will also want to budget for a cable TV connection as well. You also may have some one-time costs when you first move to your new retirement place, such as furniture and moving costs. We'll develop a separate lump-sum figure for all the one-time costs later.

These estimated costs could also change dramatically during the three phases of life we discussed earlier. In the active phase, you may have a vacation home in addition to your residence, especially to escape the cold winter months if you live up north. Of course, you will need to budget for that as well if this is in your plans. In the passive phase, you'll stop moving around and choose to live in your permanent residence or make your vacation residence a permanent home. That could lower your living costs considerably and possibly even free up some additional cash when you sell one of your residences.

> You also may have some one-time costs when you first move to your new retirement place, such as furniture and moving costs.

Budgeting for Food

You know what you are paying for groceries now, but will you be eating the same way in retirement? That's a hard thing to know now. You may need to change eating habits based on various medical conditions. Your best bet is to use an average monthly figure of what you are spending now on food, so we have something to use as we develop this budget.

One thing to consider though is that you'll probably go out to eat more, especially if you live in an active retirement area. Many restaurants offer early-bird specials for seniors to keep their establishments busy during the slow hours. Who wants to cook anyway?

Budgeting for Personal Care Items

You'll also want to budget for toiletries, cosmetics, hair care, and other personal care items you use now. You may cut back on some of that because you don't need to go to work each day, but probably won't save that much at least in the active phase of retirement. Once you get to the dependent phase your costs for personal care items will be different, but likely as high if not higher because of additional needs and services.

Clothing costs will probably drop a bit because you won't have to worry about buying new suits and dresses for work. However, you may need some new leisure outfits, so you'll still have clothing costs. You'll probably want to avoid buying clothes for which you'll need dry cleaning to save some money and the hassle of running to the cleaners all the time, but that's a personal choice. You'll also need to consider other costs for laundering, mending, and repairing clothes.

▶ FOOD AND SHELTER ESTIMATES

Jot down an estimate for your food and shelter costs in each phase of retirement.

Active Phase: ....

Passive Phase: ....

Dependent Phase: ....

Health-care Costs

Aside from housing and food, health-care costs are the biggest drain for most seniors. In fact, you've probably heard many stories about seniors having to decide between eating and paying for medications. It's shocking to hear, but unfortunately true. Seniors' annual out-of-pocket costs for health care average about $3,000.

> Medicare is broken into two parts. Part A covers inpatient costs and Part B covers other medical needs.

Let's take a look at some of the detail for budgeting purposes, but you may want to simply use the average number I mentioned above for your estimate. We'll explore costs in greater detail when we talk about health-care issues in Chapter 14. The first thing you need to learn about is the foundation of health-care coverage once you reach age sixty-five: Medicare. Medicare is broken into two parts. A very simplified view is that Part A covers inpatient costs and Part B covers other medical needs. Part A carries no monthly costs if you paid long enough into Medicare through taxes (about ten years), and Part B (in 2002) is $54 per month.

On top of those costs there are costs for deductibles, co-payments, and exclusions or items not covered. Just in case you aren't familiar with those terms, we'll define them here. *Deductibles* are the minimum amount you must pay before health insurance starts to pay its share of the costs. *Co-payments* represent the cost sharing of health care between you and the insurer; for example, you pay 20 percent for a doctor's appointment and your health insurance pays 80 percent. No health plan pays everything, therefore the *exclusions* are things not covered at all. For Medicare the biggest exclusion is coverage for medication, which can be a huge chunk of your medical budget.

You also may need to plan for vitamins and supplements. If you are taking them now, you know the approximate costs. If not, stop by a drugstore or the pharmacy section of your food store and take a look at the supplements recommended for seniors. Most seniors will take at least a vitamin supplement and others will take supplements regularly for ailments such as arthritis or osteoporosis. You'll probably need the least amount for health care in the active phase and the most in the dependent phase.

▶ HEALTH CARE ESTIMATES

Jot down your health care cost estimates below.

Active Phase: ....

Passive Phase: ....

Dependent Phase: ....

Medigap

Since living on a fixed income makes it difficult to absorb unexpected costs, many people find it wise to take a health insurance policy that will cover the gaps in Medicare called Medigap. There are many variables to this type of insurance, which we will cover in greater detail in Chapter 14, but for budgeting purposes the monthly costs can range from $200 to $1,000, depending on where you live and how much coverage you want. If you'd like to explore the possibilities for your state as part of the budgeting process, go to the Medicare Personal Plan Finder at *www.medicare.gov/ MPPF/home.asp*.

Transportation Costs

Another budget item is transportation. In the active and passive phases of retirement you will probably still be driving yourself around, if you drive now. In the dependent phase you are likely to pay for some form of assisted transportation.

Hopefully, your car will be paid off and you won't have to worry about car payments. You will have to worry about auto maintenance costs, parking fees, and tolls. You may want to use public transportation as well. Of course, you can't forget the usual costs of gasoline, car registration, taxes, and any other governmental fees that may be common in your state.

▶ TRANSPORTATION ESTIMATES

Jot down your transportation cost estimates below.

Active Phase: ....

Passive Phase: ....

Dependent Phase: ....

Insurance Costs

Now we'll take a look at the things you probably hate to pay for, but know they are necessary to protect yourself and your family from catastrophic occurrences. Your need for insurance doesn't go away in retirement, it just changes to different types of insurance.

Some of the insurance you will maintain you are probably already carrying, such as homeowner's or renter's insurance and auto insurance. One insurance policy you'll probably be able to cut back on is life insurance. You shouldn't cut it out completely because it can help with funeral costs and, if you have a sizeable estate, it is frequently used to help pay the taxes.

Health insurance will differ considerably, as we previously discussed, and since we included it with other health-care costs you don't need to include it here. Dental insurance and vision care are optional, and if you do want to carry them, then budget for those out-of-pocket costs. Most dental and vision-care policies are essentially prepaid insurance. They rarely cover more than your actual outlays for the year because of their coverage limits.

One type of insurance you definitely won't need in retirement is disability. If you already have it in your budget, it will give you some room to find the money for the new types of insurance that we've addressed here.

▶ INSURANCE ESTIMATES

Jot down your estimates for insurance costs below.

Active Phase: ....

Passive Phase: ....

Dependent Phase: ....

Leisure and Travel Costs

Leisure and travel costs will vary greatly depending on personal preferences. I can't give you any definite figures to work with, but will review the types of things you should include in this section of the budget.

First, of course, are any vacation or travel plans you might wish to make room for in your budget. You also may need certain types of equipment, such as scuba gear if you are a diver or new golf clubs, as well as for the maintenance of any equipment. You also may have membership costs attached to your desired leisure activities, such as for fitness clubs or country clubs. Be sure you don't forget to estimate those.

> Leisure and travel costs will vary greatly depending on personal preferences.

Entertainment

Next you should think about tickets for entertainment activities you enjoy, such as movies, concerts, plays, or sporting events. You may be an avid music or film collector, so you'll have to set aside some money for purchasing those CDs, videotapes, or DVDs you might want to add to your collection. If you're a computer buff, you will definitely want to budget money so you can add to your systems. If you enjoy entertaining folks at home or you have a big family that you expect will come for frequent visits, you'll need to figure that into the entertainment section of the budget, too.

Hobbies

Hobbies could take up a big chunk of your time in retirement. You may finally have the time to learn various crafts, but to do so costs money, whether it's woodworking, ceramics, or any other activity that strikes your fancy.

Pets and Plants

Pets and plants can add a lot to your life in retirement. Many studies have shown seniors are healthier and happier when they have another living creature to take care of in the house. Pets can give a lot of love and even calm your nerves. Plants can make a room feel alive. Both can give you something to talk to if you are feeling lonely. It's a lot better than talking to the four walls!

Reading Materials

Finally, you can't forget to make room in your budget for reading, especially as you slow down in the later phases of retirement. You'll probably want to add to your books, have a subscription to at least the local paper, and continue your subscriptions to your favorite magazines.

> Many studies have shown seniors are healthier and happier when they have another living creature to take care of in the house.

▶ LEISURE AND TRAVEL ESTIMATES

Jot down your leisure and travel estimates below.

Active Phase: ....

Passive Phase: ....

Dependent Phase: ....

Debt/Credit Obligations

Hopefully, by the time you get to retirement you'll have gotten rid of most of your debt. If you regularly carry balances on your credit, make a plan to work these down as much as possible before retirement. However, if you are sure you'll have some payments to make, include them in this section.

You may want to purchase and pay off what hopefully will be your last car just before retirement to avoid car loans, but you may not be able to do that. With good planning, you will have paid off any 401(k) loans you may have taken before retirement; if not, you will most likely have to pay those off before you leave the job. Few companies allow people to continue paying their loans after they quit.

Also review any other debts you currently hold and figure out if they will be gone before retirement. If not, be sure to budget for them here. These can include a stock-secured loan (such as a margin account), unsecured loans (such as revolving credit cards), and investment or vacation real estate mortgages.

If you are divorced, you may need to plan for alimony or child support, or your ex-spouse may get a portion of your retirement assets. If that is the case, budget for them in this section.

▶ DEBT/CREDIT OBLIGATIONS ESTIMATES

Add your calculations for debt/credit obligations below.

Active Phase: ....

Passive Phase: ....

Dependent Phase: ....

> If you are divorced, you may need to plan for alimony or child support, or your ex-spouse may get a portion of your retirement assets.

Religious and Other Charitable Donations

Many people will cut back on their charitable donations once they live on a fixed income. Whether you do or not, of course, depends on your personal preference. If you are a member of a religious institution, you'll almost certainly want to continue that membership.

The support of a community of which you have been a part for many years is definitely not something you want to give up in your retirement years, if you are staying in your current location. If you are moving to another location and have been active in a religious community, you will most likely want to join again wherever you live, so be sure to budget for that here.

You also may be active in a charity for many years to come. You'll certainly want to continue that relationship, but may change how much you donate in dollars and how much you donate in time or even household items you'll no longer need. You may find it easier to donate time rather than money.

Whatever you plan, you'll probably have higher charitable donations in your active phase and will need to cut them down in size or cut them out completely as you shift into the passive and dependent phases.

▶ RELIGIOUS AND OTHER CHARITABLE DONATIONS ESTIMATES

Write down your estimates for religious and charitable donations here.

Active Phase: ....

Passive Phase: ....

Dependent Phase: ....

> A professional planner can help you decide how to withdraw your hard-earned retirement savings.

Professional Services

Your need for professional services will vary depending on how many assets you have. It is a good idea to work with a financial planner or accountant who specializes in financial planning just before you make your final choices for how you will draw down your retirement assets.

A professional planner can help you decide how to withdraw your hard-earned retirement savings. Some choices you make just before retirement are critical and cannot be changed, such as whether you will draw down on a pension plan only for yourself or for you and your spouse. Most couples will take their pension plans with something called right-of-survivorship. In other words, the amount of the pension withdrawal is set up so that whomever lives the longest will continue to get a payment. This does lower your monthly payment, but gives security to both you and your spouse.

You'll also need to work with your attorney to be certain your will reflects how you want any leftover assets to be divided among your survivors. If you haven't already set up a living will that states your wishes should you be unable to participate in medical care decisions at some point, be sure to develop one before retirement.

You may also want to leave room for professional dues or other memberships so you can stay involved with your friends even after you stop working. You may decide to drop this in the later phases as you become more established within your new retirement community and find new friends.

> **Work with your attorney to be certain your will reflects how you want any leftover assets to be divided among your survivors.**

▶ PROFESSIONAL SERVICES COSTS ESTIMATES

Jot down your calculations for professional services here.

Active Phase: ....

Passive Phase: ....

Dependent Phase: ....

Savings and Investments

Savings and investments is another area in which you will probably budget a lot less in retirement than you do now, but you may still find that you have some room in the budget for these items, especially if you want to help your grandchildren through college or need to shore up your retirement savings.

Unless you are working at least part time, you will no longer have employer retirement plans to which you can contribute, such as a 401(k) or 403(b), but you could still add to Individual Retirement Accounts (IRAs) or other investment vehicles.

▶ SAVINGS AND INVESTMENT ESTIMATES

Add your savings and investment estimates here.

Active Phase: ....

Passive Phase: ....

Dependent Phase: ....

Taxes

Some seniors don't pay any taxes on their Social Security payments.

Taxes are certainly something you wish you never had to make room for in a budget, but even in retirement they won't go away. They should be considerably reduced, however. You will no longer have to pay into Social Security and Medicare and your federal taxes should be significantly reduced. Some states exempt seniors completely from state taxes and local property taxes. At the very least, you will be able to take some additional tax write-offs as a senior.

Some seniors don't pay any taxes on their Social Security payments, while others have to pay taxes on about 50 percent of their Social Security. Those with the highest incomes could be stuck with taxes on as much as 80 percent of their Social Security benefits. How much you pay in taxes is based on how much your total income is in retirement.

Most of your private retirement income will be taxed. Money from pensions and from employer defined-contributions plans—401(k) and 403(b)—is taxable. Any retirement savings that you deposited tax-deferred will be taxed at retirement. You may have delayed paying taxes until then, but you will finally have to pay them as you use the money.

The only type of retirement savings that is completely tax-free at retirement is the Roth IRA. To get this benefit, you pay the taxes on the money deposited before making the investment. What makes the Roth IRA such a great alternative is that you don't have to pay taxes on your capital gains. The Roth IRA is one of those rare gifts from Congress designed to encourage retirement savings.

We'll take a much closer look at your possible tax bite in Chapter 22. In order to estimate your taxes, you'll need to guess what your tax bracket will be.

▶ TAX ESTIMATE

Jot down your best tax estimate below.

Active Phase: ....

Passive Phase: ....

Dependent Phase: ....

Other Budget Items

Now we've come to the tricky miscellaneous category. If you have ever budgeted before, you know there are always items you just didn't think about. You'll probably want to plan for some unexpected expenses by guessing at a number for this category:

▶ OTHER BUDGET ITEMS ESTIMATE

Jot down your best other budget items estimate below.

Active Phase: ....

Passive Phase: ....

Dependent Phase: ....

Developing a Total Budget

You've done the hard part. Now all you have to do is transfer the numbers and you'll have your retirement budget. If you don't have a budget currently, you may want to create a column to put down your current needs as well.

▶ RETIREMENT BUDGET

BUDGET ITEM	ACTIVE PHASE	PASSIVE PHASE	DEPENDENT PHASE
Food and Shelter	....	....	....
Health Care	....	....	....
Transportation	....	....	....
Insurance	....	....	....
Leisure and Travel	....	....	....
Debt/Credit Obligations	....	....	....
Religious and Charitable Donations	....	....	....
Professional Services	....	....	....
Savings and Investments	....	....	....
Taxes	....	....	....
Other Items	....	....	....
Total Budget	....	....	....

PRICING YOUR NEEDS

You'll also want to make a list of one-time costs that you expect to incur when you finally get to retirement. This can include:

▶ Furniture: ....

▶ Moving: ....

▶ Entry Fees: ....
(For retirement community)

▶ Loan Fees: ....
(If you think you may want to take out a loan to get access to your home equity or for any other purpose.)

▶ Loan Payoffs: ....
(If you think you will want to set aside money for lump-sum payoffs of existing loans, such as your mortgage or car loan.)

▶ Miscellaneous: ....
(Any costs you expect that we haven't already included.)

Great work! Now we have a budget figure to work with as we begin our path toward developing your retirement plan. You'll certainly want to review this number annually because your needs and desires will change. I guarantee it. But, now that you've done the hard part, it will just be a matter of minor adjustments to the line items you want to change. Now we'll move on to take a look at where you currently stand on your path to retirement.

> You'll certainly want to review this number annually because your needs and desires will change.

For more information on this topic, visit our Web site at www.businesstown.com

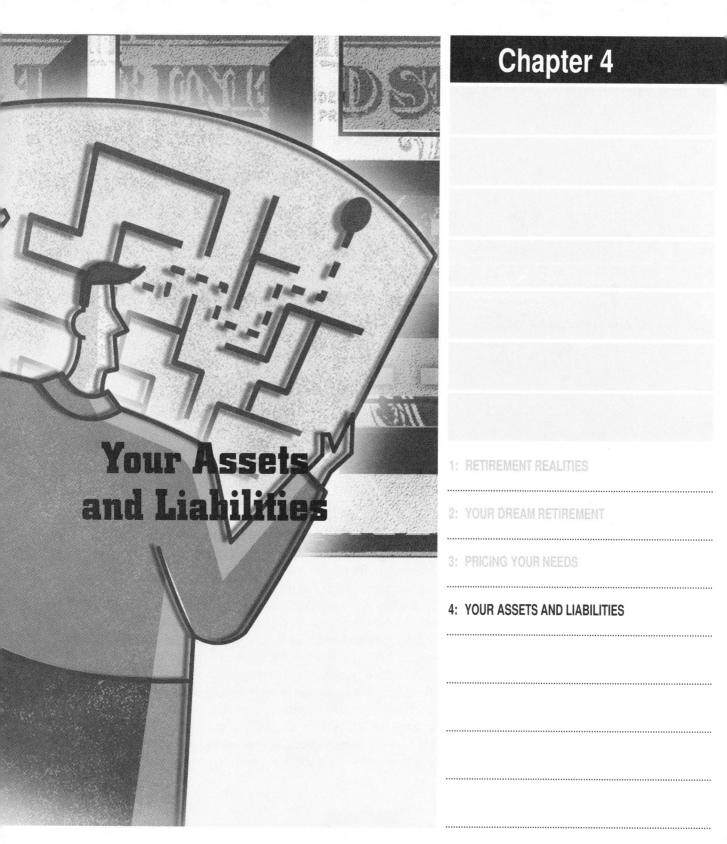

Chapter 4

Your Assets and Liabilities

Gather Your Financial Documents

Now that we've figured out your retirement goals and what financial resources you will need to live your dream retirement, let's see how close you are to getting there. Our first step is to figure out how much you currently are worth. We'll need to look at two things: your assets (how much you have) and your liabilities (how much you owe).

Before we get started, you'll need to do some preparation. Pull out all your bank statements, loan statements, credit card statements, retirement savings statements, and any other financial documents you may have on hand. At this point, we just want to do an inventory. We'll explore each type of retirement asset more closely in Part 3.

Various Types of Assets

If you are like most of us, you have worked in numerous jobs throughout your lifetime. If you have done the prudent thing, each time you took a new job you rolled over any retirement savings from the previous one into another retirement plan. What happens when you do this is that you can have retirement savings sitting in various types of assets, such as 401(k) plans (for profit company retirement plans), 403(b) plans (for non-profit company retirement plans), Section 457 (state and local government retirement plans), and various types of IRAs. There are also traditional pension plans and cash-balance pension plans. We'll get into specifics for all these types of investments in Part 3. For now, we simply wish to compile all documentation for the funds you have.

You may also have additional savings in employee stock option plans and stock or mutual fund accounts where you save outside of a retirement plan umbrella. Just because your savings is outside the umbrella, don't leave it out of the equation. You may decide not to include it as we progress through the planning if you plan to use it for something before you get to retirement, but it's best to take a snapshot of your entire financial picture. That way you may decide to shift some current spending plans so you can meet your retirement goals. That will be your choice, but we need to have all the information in one place to help you make that decision.

> If you have done the prudent thing, each time you took a new job you rolled over any retirement savings from the previous one into another retirement plan.

Finding Market Values

In addition to jotting down the numbers, we're also going to estimate what their true value is if were you to sell them today. This computation will not include an adjustment for taxes you may owe. For now, we'll just concentrate on assets without complicating the equation with tax considerations. For one thing, tax rules vary greatly depending on the type of asset. We'll cover tax impacts in much greater detail when we explore the individual asset types.

In Chapter 6, we'll discuss how to use this information to figure out your retirement savings gap. For now, just write down the following information:

- Asset type
- Asset name
- Market value (how much you can sell it for today)
- Any dividends or interest that you were paid
- Estimated costs to sell the asset
- Your cost basis (how much you paid to get the asset) and the date purchased
- The number of years you've held the investment

If you hold the assets in a retirement account and automatically reinvest all dividends and interest, you may find that you have to go through each of your annual statements to get a total of dividends and interest. For the purpose of this inventory, just leave the column blank if you cannot easily find your total of dividends and/or interest.

I'll leave it up to you to decide how timely you want this plan to be. If you do decide to use the figures on your statements, be sure to jot down the date indicated on the statement for the market value. For example, if you have a statement that was sent in July or August, it most likely reflects the market value as of the end of the second quarter—June 30. When you've completed this inventory, you can see how outdated your market values are and then decide which ones you want to update.

Finding Accurate Numbers

If you are working with quarterly or annual statements from your retirement plans or other assets, the market value on those statements will reflect that of the end of a quarter or year and not necessarily today's value. The market value could be much higher or much lower, depending on what's happened in the stock or bond markets since you received your statement.

Of course, to get the most accurate number, look up your funds online at one of the financial Web sites—Yahoo Finance (*http://finance.yahoo.com/?u*) and Morningstar (*www.morningstar.com*) are two of my favorites. If you don't have easy access to the Internet, you can find the information in the financial pages of your local newspaper.

Creating an Inventory Worksheet

If you use a spreadsheet program, such as Excel or Lotus 1-2-3, to build this inventory, it will help you tremendously as we try to analyze all this information. These programs can also save you a lot of time because they will do all the calculations for you, which helps you avoid silly calculations errors.

Here's how you should set up the worksheet, even if you are doing this on paper:

▶ ASSETS INVENTORY

Asset Category	Asset Name	Market Value/ Date	Dividends or Interest	Cost to Sell	Basis/ Date Purchased	Years Held
....	....	....	....	....	....	....
....	....	....	....	....	....	....
....	....	....	....	....	....	....
....	....	....	....	....	....	....
....	....	....	....	....	....	....
....	....	....	....	....	....	....
....	....	....	....	....	....	....
....	....	....	....	....	....	....

Add to this worksheet as you read through the chapter. When we're done you'll know exactly what you have and what you owe.

Cash-Equivalent Savings

First, let's start with the easiest stuff: what you have in cash-equivalent accounts. These are the assets you own whose value will not change when the market goes up and down. You should also only include in this section money held outside of a retirement account.

The obvious candidates for this category are your checking, savings, and money market accounts. If you are holding savings in Certificates of Deposit (CDs) there could be penalties for cashing in those assets early. We will assume for now that you're not planning to cash these in early and incur the penalties. If you do think you may want to make an early withdrawal, you can note in the cost-to-sell column the rules of early withdrawal. Your cost basis for all these accounts should be the same as your market value.

Another type of cash-equivalent savings can be bonds, provided you don't sell them before they mature. Bonds are sold with a face value that is guaranteed, that is if you hold the bond for its full term. For example, a $10,000 five-year bond will be worth $10,000 at the end of the five years. At the end of the five-year period the bond has matured. If you sell the bond prior to that time you will get less than that value. We'll cover bonds in much greater in Chapter 16. As with the CDs, we will assume you are planning to hold onto any bonds until their maturity dates.

There are other miscellaneous items you might have here. For example, if you have loaned a family member or friend some money and expect to get it back, you should add it to the list. You may also be expecting a major payment from an insurance company, court settlement, or major contract project; if so, add that information here too.

Market and Insurance Investments

Now it's time to move onto investments you hold outside of your retirement accounts. These could include stocks, mutual funds, employee stock purchase plans, or annuities. We included the bonds above, but if you do trade bonds frequently and do not plan to hold them until maturity, you may want to include them here instead. As mentioned above, we're reviewing the basics here to be sure you

Life Insurance Cash Value

Some life insurance policies have a cash value. If you have term life insurance, that means you are only paying for the cost of the life insurance. These types of policies have no cash value. Most other types of insurance, which can include whole life insurance and variable life insurance, could have a cash value. The cash value is not the same as the death benefit, which is the amount that would be paid to your beneficiaries at the time of your death. You can find this information on the annual statement from your insurance company. If you are not sure what you have, call your agent or financial advisor. This definitely should not be a mystery to you.

understand how to develop your inventory of assets, but we'll explore investing basics more fully in Chapter 16.

Stocks

Most of these assets will have costs associated with selling them. If you hold stock, you most likely paid a commission or a set fee to buy the shares and you will have a similar cost to sell them. Your market value for these investment vehicles fluctuates throughout the day. Your best bet is simply to include the stock price from the market close the day before. When you add these to your worksheet, estimate your cost to sell based on your current broker. For example, if you pay a set fee per transaction, include that fee. If your fees are based on a percentage, estimate the dollar amount using that percentage of the asset. Your basis should be the cost of the asset when you purchased it.

Mutual Funds

Mutual funds work a bit differently. They have what is called a Net Asset Value (NAV), which you can find in the newspaper or on a financial Web site, such as Yahoo Finance (*http://finance.yahoo.com*) or Morningstar (*www.morningstar.com*). Basically, this Net Asset Value reflects the total assets held by the mutual fund minus any costs of operations divided by the number of shares held by investors. The NAV for most funds changes once a day after the market closes.

The cost of selling and buying mutual funds depends on how you got them. You can buy some mutual funds directly from a mutual fund company and pay no fees to buy or sell the funds. These are called no-load funds. You can also end up paying a fee to both buy and sell the funds. These are called load funds. When you are filling out your inventory, include the cost of buying the fund in the basis amount. If you have a no-load fund, you probably won't have selling costs unless you sell the shares through a broker. If you have a load fund, you will need to look at your prospectus to find out what fees may be involved in selling the fund or you can call your broker, mutual fund company, or financial planner to learn more about selling costs.

> The NAV for most funds changes once a day after the market closes.

Employee Stock Purchases

You may also hold shares of company stock in an employee stock purchase plan. These plans typically allow employees to purchase stock at a price lower than market value. Many times employee discounts are 10 to 15 percent below what they would have had to pay for the stock if they bought it through a broker. This stock is usually purchased through a deduction from your salary to buy shares each month.

If you do have an employee stock purchase plan, look at your statement to find out how many shares you hold. You can use that information to figure out a current market value. For the basis, you'll need to use the total that has been taken from your paycheck to buy the shares. If you are not sure how they should be sold and what the stipulations are, now is a good time to find out how it works so you can add the most accurate figure into the cost-to-sell column.

Annuities

The last asset you'll want to add to this section is the cash value of an annuity if you have one. An annuity is a product usually sold by insurance companies that allows you to save money and then get the money back in future monthly payments. Insurance agents love these because they make lots of money on the commissions they generate, but they don't make sense for most people. They only make sense as a tax avoidance investment vehicle if you have put the maximum allowable amounts into all other possible tax-deferred retirement savings and want to put the money somewhere so that it can grow tax-deferred until you begin to collect it.

These vehicles usually have high costs and penalties if you decide to take the money out early. If you want to value them here, you'll need to figure out what their cash value would be if you wanted to get the money out. This is called the surrender value, which is the current value of the annuity minus any penalties for withdrawing or "surrendering" it. You can put the current value in the market value column, your costs of purchasing it in the basis column, and your costs for surrendering it in the cost-of-sale column.

> You'll need to figure out what their cash value would be if you wanted to get the money out. This is called the surrender value, which is the current value of the annuity minus any penalties for withdrawing or "surrendering" it.

Employer Retirement Benefits

Your largest retirement asset is probably your employer retirement plan unless you are self-employed and have contributed to an individual account that you started. We're not going to cover this in great depth here, but will be exploring them in detail in Part 3 of this book.

Basically, what you'll need to complete the inventory here is the statement for your current employer's retirement plans and statements from retirement plans you still own from past jobs. You may have rolled over your holdings from retirement plans of former employers into individual retirement accounts; if so we'll include them in the next section.

You probably hold your 401(k), 403(b), Section 457, or other employer retirement savings in a number of investment vehicles. To simplify our listing here, let's just use the market value of the portfolio from your most recent statement. You can, of course, look up all the current market values to be even more accurate in your inventory. If you're lucky, you may have an employer that allows you to access the information online where current market values are available.

All of this money most likely went into the account before you paid taxes, so it will all be taxed on the way out. You only need to keep track of the basis on these accounts if some of the money went in after you paid taxes. Money already taxed will not be taxed again at retirement. We'll cover this more carefully as we discuss each asset type in detail.

If you work for a small employer, they may have opened a SIMPLE IRA or SEP-IRA for you. These accounts have some similarity to 401(k)s, but there are significant differences as well. We'll describe these further in Chapter 10.

Most likely, you and your spouse have separate retirement plans if you both work. Keep those accounts separate here as you fill out the inventory.

Individual Retirement Accounts

You may also hold retirement assets in Individual Retirement Accounts (IRAs). These accounts allow you to save money tax-deferred until you

> Money already taxed will not be taxed again at retirement.

retire. One of these, called the Roth IRA, even allows you to save money completely tax-free. We'll look at all the IRA options more closely in Chapter 13.

Again, in order to complete the inventory, use the market value from your most recent statement. If you want to be the most accurate, get your current values for the assets held in these accounts online or on the financial pages of your daily newspaper. If you have put the money into the IRAs before paying taxes, all the money that you take out will be taxed at retirement. If you have put already taxed money into a traditional IRA or Roth IRA, be sure to total all your assets that have already been taxed and put those in the basis column. In later chapters, when we start delving more deeply into tax issues, these already-taxed funds will be subtracted before we estimate taxes. In fact, for the Roth IRA even the gains are tax-free in most cases.

Social Security Benefits

You may be asking, "Will Social Security even be around when I get to retirement?" While I have no doubt that there will be considerable changes to the benefits that will be available, I'm sure something will still be there. The Social Security trustees in their most dire predictions expect that even when the trust funds run out of money and there is no fix between now and then, the Social Security Administration will still be able to pay about 70 percent of current benefits. If you want to be the most cautious about what you can expect, use that 70 percent figure (though there is little doubt in my mind that some fix will be in place before then).

Many plans out there suggest a fix that will reduce the amount that benefits increase, but does not actually cut the dollar figure. Since inflation will most likely eat away at today's current value, Social Security could be worth less. The actual dollar figure will still most likely increase from today's amount.

Social Security is not like your traditional retirement savings. You don't have a lump sum in your account. You have a guaranteed monthly benefit that you will get at retirement based on your

Defined-Benefit Plans

We have primarily been talking about retirement plans that build up a cash value in your name, also known as defined-contribution plans. About 10 percent of the population has what are called defined-benefit plans, in which companies will guarantee you a payment for life. These types of plans are also common if you are a government worker. For these plans you don't have a cash value, but instead an estimated monthly benefit at retirement. The benefit of these types of accounts is that the risk of not having enough to make that monthly benefit payment is on the shoulders of your employer instead of you.

Most companies will provide you with a yearly statement that estimates your monthly benefit at retirement. Jot that amount down at the bottom of this section and we'll use it later when we're figuring out your retirement gap.

earnings and the amount of time you paid into Social Security. You can get an estimate of that monthly figure three different ways:

1. You can use the online calculators at the Social Security Administration site (*www.ssa.gov/retire2/calculators.htm*).
2. You can call the Social Security Administration at 1-800-772-1213 and request an "Earnings and Benefits Statement."
3. You can request an "Earnings and Benefits Statement" and get more information about what is in a statement online at *www.ssa.gov/mystatement/*.

Basically, these statements will tell you how much you can expect to collect if you retire early, on time, or late. They will also give you information about family benefits and disability benefits. We'll review this all in greater detail in Chapter 8.

▶ SOCIAL SECURITY BENEFITS

For the purpose of this inventory, just write down at the bottom or top of your inventory the expected monthly benefits:

Early Retirement Monthly Benefit (at age 62): ....

On-Time Retirement Monthly Benefit (at age 65): ....

Late Retirement Monthly Benefit (at age 70): ....

On-time retirement or full retirement is gradually rising to age sixty-seven. As previously discussed, it depends upon when you were born. See Chapter 8 for more details.

Home Equity and Real Estate

For many future retirees, their home equity is one of their largest asset categories. You may also own a vacation property or, possibly, you could be someone that makes extra money by buying and renting properties. In this section, we'll include the actual asset values.

> On-time retirement or full retirement is gradually rising to age sixty-seven.

If you have an extensive rental property business, you may want to include a calculation for those revenues and value in the next section on business value. If you are certain you will cash out on all the real estate you own, just list it here.

For market value, include the current value of the property you own. In the cost-to-sell column, include any real estate commissions, loan expenses, or other sales costs you expect to pay and an estimate of fix-up costs if you think you will need to do some major repair work before you can sell the property or properties. Your basis should be a total of all other costs you put into the property, including initial purchase price, loan fees, and major fix-up costs over the years.

You will have to worry about taxes on any other gains in your real estate holdings that are not your primary residence. You can minimize those taxes by carefully tracking all costs you put into the home. If you have carefully tracked all this, filling out the inventory should be easy. You may already have a total of your basis. If not, try to pull together what you can to save yourself taxes later.

Property, Collectibles, and Business Value

This will be your miscellaneous area for anything else you own that you think will have significant value at retirement. When you fill out the inventory, be realistic about value. Lean toward a conservative estimate rather than an optimistic one. Remember, the only people who will see this are you and possibly your spouse or other family member. If you overstate what you have, you'll only be hurting your chances of meeting your retirement goals when the money is not truly available.

You know the drill. Estimate what you think the current market value is of the asset, which can include jewelry, boats, computers, camera equipment, luxury cars, or anything else you think you will be able to sell for cash at retirement. If you own a business, think about whether it is something you can truly sell and make a profit on the sale.

Exclusion from Taxes

Any profit on your primary residence will be excluded from taxes up to $250,000 if you are single or up to $500,000 if you are married. It's important to keep track of your basis and what you put into the home so you can avoid paying taxes later by carefully calculating any profit you may make on the sale of the property. You won't need to use all this paperwork if the market value of your home is below the levels at which taxes are excluded, but do keep track just in case your property appreciates above those levels.

Many small-business people will run a successful business that is not easily transferable to another owner. If you are not sure how to start valuing your business, you may want to read up on how to do it. Two good books that can help get you started are: *A Basic Guide for Valuing a Company* by Wilbur M. Yegge and *The Small Business Valuation Book* by Lawrence W. Tuller.

Potential Gifts and Inheritance

You may or may not be aware of how much money to expect in the way of gifts and inheritances. If you are sure you will be getting some money, make a conservative estimate of how much you think that will be.

Again, as with the section on collectibles and business value, any overstatement will only hurt your chances of meeting your goals. It is much better to be surprised with extra funds than to find out you don't have enough and have to go back to work or live below the standard you are used to living.

Know Your Liabilities

We just finished putting together the good news side of the equation. Now it's time to move on to the bad news: a reality check on how much you actually do have once you subtract out all your debt.

If you haven't already done so, pull out all your paperwork related to any money you owe. This should include mortgages, credit cards, revolving credit loans, home equity loans, car loans, and any other major bills. You don't need to include your utilities and other routine bills. We've got those covered in the retirement budget that we worked up in Chapter 3.

We'll use a different type of inventory worksheet for debt. In this worksheet, we'll include the type of debt, the total amount you owe, monthly payment, interest rate, and loan terms and payoff debt. The worksheet should look like the following.

> It is much better to be surprised with extra funds than to find out you don't have enough.

Your Assets and Liabilities

Type of Debt	Amount Owed	Monthly Payment	Interest Rate	Terms/Payoff Date
....	....	....	....	....
....	....	....	....	....
....	....	....	....	....
....	....	....	....	....
....	....	....	....	....
....	....	....	....	....
....	....	....	....	....
....	....	....	....	....
....	....	....	....	....
....	....	....	....	....
....	....	....	....	....
....	....	....	....	....

Hopefully, you'll be debt-free when you enter retirement. You certainly want to get as close as possible to that goal when you are living on a fixed income. You may not be able to pay off your house, but as we discussed in the previous chapter, there are numerous options for using those assets.

There is one other group of liabilities you will want to think about here, even though they will hopefully not be a factor in retirement. The money you will need for these liabilities will certainly decrease the amount you can save.

The greatest amount of money you spend before retirement will most likely be on your children. If your dream is to build a business, you may also need to consider using much more of your current money on business expenses than you normally spend when you work for someone else.

> The greatest amount of money you spend before retirement will most likely be on your children.

Jot down major expenses, such as college tuition for your children, business start-up and maintenance costs, and any other major item that you think will be a drain on the money that you can save for retirement. Include any major debt or planned expense not already mentioned.

Calculating Your Net Worth

We're done collecting information. Now it's time for the moment of truth. We'll calculate your net worth. This is going to be a quick and dirty number just so you have an idea of where you stand.

Using the Assets Inventory, total your market-value and cost-to-sell columns. Subtract your selling costs from your market value. These are your net assets before taxes. Using the Liabilities Inventory, total your amount-owed column. You may also want to total your monthly-payment column to get a good handle on how much you pay out each month if you don't already know it. Now subtract the amount owed from your market value. This answer is your net worth.

Great job! You've done a lot of hard work getting here. We'll be using all the budget figures and the assets and liability inventory figures throughout the book as we work on your plan. You now know where you stand, and we'll work on getting you to where you want to be as we continue our journey into the world of retirement planning.

For more information on this topic, visit our Web site at www.businesstown.com

PART II

Your Retirement Gap

This part helps you:

- **Learn how to use basic finance techniques to monitor your investments and determine whether they are helping you meet your goals.**

- **Calculate your retirement needs.**

- **Learn the basics of after-tax cash flow.**

- **Calculate your retirement gap.**

- **Look at investment alternatives.**

- **Consider what tax moves you might make to help you save more money.**

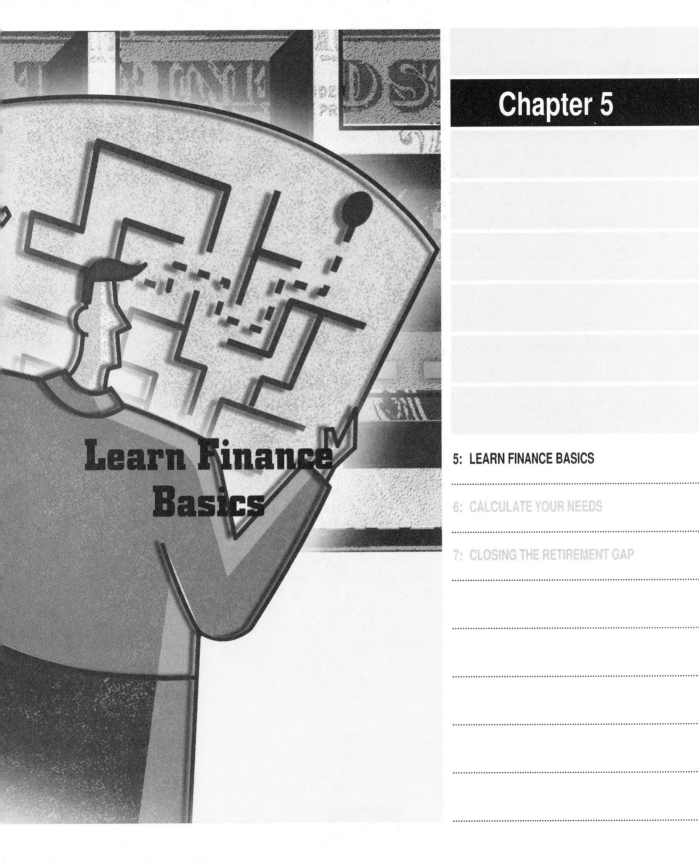

Chapter 5

Learn Finance Basics

Levels of Money Supply

The Fed monitors:

1. Currency—This is the money outside of banks, the U.S. Treasury, and the Federal Reserve. There is no control of this money, and it usually represents the smallest share of the money pie.
2. M-1—This includes some currency, travelers' checks, and checking account balances. This money flows easily into and out of banks.
3. M-2—This includes M-1 plus savings accounts, savings deposits under $100,000, money market mutual funds, some overnight deposits between banks and other financial institutions, and some deposits in foreign offices of U.S. banks.
4. M-3—This includes M-2 plus large-denomination savings deposits and deposits of financial institutions.
5. L—This includes M-3 plus non-bank holdings of U.S. savings bonds and short-term Treasury securities, and commercial paper.
6. D—This includes outstanding debt incurred by nonfinancial parts of the economy.

Impact of Inflation and Interest Rates

In Chapter 1, we mentioned that inflation could be a major impediment to saving enough for retirement. We reviewed the Rule of 72 to look at the impact that inflation could have on both expenses and savings.

Now we'll take a closer look at inflation and the attempts made to control it by the Federal Reserve (the Fed) and its chairman, Alan Greenspan. First, we need to look at how our money supply works. Since 1913, in the United States money has been printed and distributed by the federal government. (Prior to that time there were a number of different arrangements for printing money.) This power to print money gives the government control over the money supply.

Let's take a simplified look at what fuels or stops inflation. Think about what you do when interest rates are high. You tend to spend less and pay down debt or save more. This reduces the amount of money you—and everyone else doing the same thing—put into the economy. This decrease in spending usually creates a drop in the prices of goods sold because there is less demand, thereby reducing inflation.

The exact opposite happens when interest rates are low. People see little value in saving money when credit is cheap. In this scenario, spending increases, which tends to reduce the supply of goods, making prices eventually rise.

The Fed uses its ability to change interest rates to either encourage or discourage spending in an attempt to control inflation. What the Fed is actually controlling is the money supply.

Each week the Fed distributes a report about the state of the money supply within each of these levels. The Fed tweaks these levels when it makes changes in interest rates. M-1 and M-2 are the levels most sensitive to these interest changes. By changing the rate the Fed charges banks to borrow money, it can affect interest rates for all other kinds of borrowing. When the Fed raises the cost of borrowing, then banks will in turn increase the interest rates they charge their customers.

Economic Factors

In addition, the Fed monitors numerous economic factors. The key factors include:

1. Consumer Price Index (CPI)—This measures the changes in price of key consumer goods and services, such as food, clothing, gasoline, and housing.
2. Producer Price Index (PPI)—This measures the price changes faced by sellers and manufacturers.
3. Gross Domestic Product (GDP)—This measures the total value of what is produced in the economy.
4. Commodities Prices—These measurements track the prices of individual commodities, such as oil, gold, and silver.

The Fed meets periodically to look at all these economic statistics to decide whether to increase interest rates, decrease interest rates, or not to act at all. During 2001, the Fed cut interest rates eleven times, trying to encourage spending and help pull the country out of a recession. Short-term interest rates fell below 2 percent for the first time in forty years.

The decision to cut rates is made by the Federal Open Market Committee chaired by Alan Greenspan. These rate reductions push down rates for mortgages, car loans, and business loans. Interest rate cuts are the most powerful tool the Fed has to stimulate the economy.

Impact on Retirement

So, what does all this have to do with retirement? In 2001, inflation was not a concern of the Fed, rather it was the opposite problem—recession. If you are saving for retirement this can hurt too. Interest you are earning on cash assets is low and stock and bond holdings are probably also down. In fact, some people have lost more than 50 percent of their retirement savings because of the bursting of the bubble in technology stocks in 2000.

> The decision to cut rates is made by the Federal Open Market Committee chaired by Alan Greenspan.

Right now we are in a down cycle, but it is only a matter of time before things will again head in the other direction. The worst period of inflation in recent history was the period between 1973 and 1982. Inflation topped 5 percent throughout that period and during four of those years topped 10 percent. Imagine what that did to people's retirement savings! Few could find ways to grow their money significantly faster than inflation.

Many people make the mistake of seeking safety in their retirement accounts over all other considerations. This hunt for safety can actually be more risky—you are taking the risk that your money will grow more slowly than the inflation rate, which is known as "inflation risk." Inflation risk can be very harmful to meeting your retirement goals. In Chapter 16, we'll look at the different types of risks and how to balance those when managing your portfolio.

Time Value of Money

When you are trying to figure out how much you need to save now so you will have what you need in the future, the question to answer is, "What is the *time* value of money?" You want to know how much the amount of money you currently hold will be worth at some point in the future based on the rate of growth you are able to get on your money. That rate of growth will depend on how you choose to invest your money.

You can put it in a safe haven, such as an insured savings account, but may only earn an average of 2 to 3 percent on your money. You can put it in bonds that earn an average of 5 to 6 percent on your money. Or you can put it into stocks that traditionally earn an average of 10 to 12 percent on your money. Let's take a look at what that means if you have $10,000 to invest over twenty years. We want to test how much money you will have twenty years from now in each of these three scenarios.

Compounding

Before doing that, I need to explain one of the key concepts related to the time value of money—compounding. Essentially, what

You Must Beat Inflation

The trick in retirement savings is to grow your money faster than inflation so you will have enough when it comes time to retire. Just to give you an idea of what that means historically, here are some statistics from the Fed:

- Since 1960 inflation has averaged 4.5 percent per year.

- Since 1982 inflation has averaged 3.5 percent per year.

- When inflation averages 3.5 percent per year for twenty years, consumer prices nearly double.

Today inflation levels are even lower, but you can't be sure they will stay this low until you are ready to retire.

happens with compounding is that provided you leave your profits in the account, both your original investment and your profits earn more money.

Here's how it works:

You deposit $100 in a savings account that earns 2 percent per year. At the end of the first year you will have $100 plus $2 in interest. If you leave all the money in the account, the next year you will have $102 plus $2.04 in interest or $104.04. We certainly don't want to manually calculate how that money will grow over a thirty-year period. Instead we'll use a financial calculator.

If you don't already own a financial calculator you can buy one for under $50. They are very useful not only for retirement planning, but also to calculate how much various types of loans will cost you when you are considering a major purchase. Two popular calculators are the Hewlett Packard HP10B and the Texas Instruments BAII.

Hopefully, you have one on hand. If you do, practice these time-value-of-money calculations along with me. With these calculators you need to know a number of factors:

- N = The number of years or months you expect to leave the money on deposit if you are looking at an investment opportunity. If you are considering a loan, it would equal the number of months you expect to have that loan.
- I = The interest rate you expect to earn on that money or, for a loan, the interest rate you expect to have to pay to borrow that money.
- PV = The present value of the money or the loan amount.
- PMT = The amount of money you expect to add to the savings each month or year. Or, it can be the amount you will have to pay each month or year to pay off the loan.
- FV = The future value of the money for an investment. If you are considering a loan, you want the future value to be 0, which would mean you paid off the loan.

Now let's get back to the question of what $100 will be worth in thirty years in a savings account that pays 2 percent interest.

Calculate how much various types of loans will cost you when you are considering a major purchase.

1. Enter 30 as your N (number of interest payments).
2. Enter 2 as your I (interest rate).
3. Enter $100 as your PV (present value).
4. Enter 0 as your PMT (payment, we won't make any additional deposits).
5. Hit FV (future value) to find out what the money will be worth.

In thirty years that $100 will be worth $181.14. This is a simplified view of compounding. Most banks pay interest monthly, so the future value would be even higher since the compounding would happen on a monthly rather than yearly basis.

Testing Investment Options

Now let's get back to the question of what $10,000 would be worth in twenty years. We'll use 2 percent as the interest factor for a savings account. We'll use 5 percent for a bond investment, and we'll use 11 percent for a stock investment.

Let's walk through the first calculation for a savings account together. Before we start, be sure to clear your calculator. We'll keep it simple. Set your calculator for one payment per year:

1. Enter 20 as your N (number of interest payments).
2. Enter 2 as your I (interest rate).
3. Enter $10,000 as your PV (present value).
4. Enter 0 as your PMT (payment, we won't be making any additional deposits in this example).
5. Hit FV (future value) to find out what the money will be worth.

You should find that $10,000, saved in an account for twenty years that earns 2 percent interest, will be worth $14,859.47. You will see a negative sign in front of the number. We'll ignore that for these calculations. It becomes a more critical factor when you work with more complex financial calculations, but won't be important for us to deal with now.

Most banks pay interest monthly, so the future value would be even higher since the compounding would happen on a monthly rather than yearly basis.

Now repeat the steps for $10,000 at 5 percent. Your answer should be $26,532.98. Now repeat the steps once more for $10,000 at 11 percent. Your answer should be $80,623.12. Now we're getting somewhere. You can easily see from this example how important the concepts of the time value of money and compounding interest are to your retirement planning success.

Adding to Your Account Annually

We're now going to make this a bit harder to practice what you can save by adding to your retirement account each year. Let's use the same investments—a savings account that earns 2 percent, a bond that earns 5 percent, and a stock that earns 11 percent. Instead of a lump-sum investment for twenty years, we're going to deposit $2,000 a year for twenty years. We'll do the first calculation together:

1. Enter 20 for N (number).
2. Enter 2 for I (interest).
3. Enter 0 for PV (no present value).
4. Enter $2,000 for PMT (payment).
5. Hit FV (future value) to find out what the investment will be worth.

For $2,000 a year, saved at 2 percent per year for twenty years, the answer is $29,566.63. Repeat the same steps for the bond and stock investments. A payment of $2,000 per year toward a bond investment would be $69,438.50. A payment of $2,000 per year toward a stock investment would be $142,530.29.

In actuality, things get more complicated than this because some investments pay out interest on a monthly basis, while others pay out quarterly, and still others pay out annually. In the case of stock, you only get a payout if your stock pays dividends. If not, you are dependent on the stock you select going up in value.

I'm not trying to turn you into a financial analyst. I just want to give you an idea of how to calculate the time value of money. We'll be working with simpler calculations to figure out your retirement

> Some investments pay out interest on a monthly basis, while others pay out quarterly, and still others pay out annually.

gap, but the tools we just reviewed will help you figure out how to look at various investments options and see whether they will let you save enough to meet your goals.

Making Investments Work for You

What should certainly be clear to you after working through those calculations is how important earning a good return on your money is in order to meet your retirement savings goals. You must be able to figure out how much your investments are earning in order to determine whether you will have enough money ten, twenty, thirty, or forty years down the road.

In order to calculate your investment return you need four components:

1. Initial investment (I)
2. Market Value (MV)–The amount at which the asset could be sold
3. Periodic Earnings (E)–The interest or dividends that may be paid on the investment
4. Costs to Buy and Sell (C)

Using a Formula to Calculate Investment Returns

Once you've collected that information about an investment, you first need to calculate the total dollar gain or loss of the investment. In order to do that, you total the value of any interest or dividends you received. Then subtract your original cost of investing (C) from the current market value (MV) minus any costs to sell that asset to find your capital gain. Add to that capital gain your total interest and dividends. Divide this number by the original cost value and you will have your rate of return.

Here is what it looks like in a formula:

Gain (MV - I + E - C)

[R] = Return on Investment

I

> You must be able to figure out how much your investments are earning in order to determine whether you will have enough down the road.

Let's practice using this formula. Let's say you purchased ten shares of stock at $10 per share two years ago. You earned 25 cents per share each of the two years for a total of $5 in dividends. Two years later you can sell the stock for $11 per share. You paid $10 to buy stock and will have to pay $10 to sell the stock using a discount broker who charges per transaction. What is the return on this investment?

I = $10 x 10 shares = $100

MV = $11 x 10 shares = $110

E = 25 cents x 10 shares x 2 years = $5

C = $10 to buy + $10 to sell = $20

Your formula would then look like this:

110 – 100 + 5 – 20 = –$5

[R] = –5%

100

You can see, in this case, that the stock had a negative return on investment. The costs of buying and selling the stock ate up all the gain. A critical thing to remember when you are selecting an investment is how long you will hold the investment and how the costs of buying and selling that investment will affect your rate of return.

Let's look at the same investment held for twenty years. Now the market value of the stock has jumped 300 percent. You can sell the stock for $30 per share. To make it simple, we'll assume dividends stayed the same at 25 cents per share, which will make it easier to compare the two time frames. We'll assume the costs of buying and selling the stock stayed the same as well.

Your formula would then look like this:

300 – 100 + 50 – 20 = 230

[R] = 230%

100

> A critical thing to remember when you are selecting an investment is how long you will hold the investment.

That's a nice profit for twenty years. In order to look at this as an investment for retirement though, you need to calculate an average annual return. To do that you would divide the investment return by the number of years to find the annual rate of return. Here's what that would look like:

230%

[R] = 11.5 percent per year.

20 years

The 11.5 percent is an annual rate of return before taxes. If you assume a 27 percent tax rate, the return after taxes is 8.4 percent (11.5 x (27 percent – 100 percent)). In addition to taxes you need to consider the impact of inflation. If we use the average inflation rate of 3.5 percent, the rate of return after inflation and taxes is about 8.1 percent (8.4 x (3.5 – 100 percent)).

> In addition to taxes you need to consider the impact of inflation.

Using Your Assets Inventory

Now take some time to practice calculating your return on investment and rate of return for some of your assets in your Assets Inventory. If you are working with a spreadsheet program, you can plug in the formula to calculate these numbers for you.

Remember, the columns of your inventory should look like the following chart.

▶ ASSETS INVENTORY

ASSET CATEGORY	ASSET NAME	MARKET VALUE/DATE	DIVIDENDS OR INTEREST	COST TO SELL	BASIS/ DATE PURCHASED	YEARS HELD
....	....	....	....	....	....	....
....	....	....	....	....	....	....

If you completed all columns of the inventory, you can use these numbers to calculate your return on investment and annual rate of return rather quickly. If you have a number of long-term investments in which you regularly reinvest dividends, interest, and capital gains, it will be a bit more difficult to come up with these numbers. To do these calculations you will need to collect statements from each of the years you had these investments and separate out the dividends, interest, and actual costs of investment.

You may not want to take the time to do this. This becomes a more critical thing to do if you are trying to decide whether to keep or sell the investment. If you suspect that your return on an investment may not be good enough, definitely take the time to go through this exercise. Depending upon who holds your investment, it is possible your statements will show an annual rate of return for the investment.

You may be wondering what a good annual rate of return is for your investments. That will depend on the type of investments you hold. In the 1990s people got used to double-digit returns, some even triple digit, but in reality this time period was a bubble in the market and not representative of what you can truly expect to earn on your investments.

Let's take a look at a sample portfolio. A portfolio balanced for growth would likely have 60 percent stock, 20 percent bonds, and 20 percent cash. Using these returns as the average, the portfolio would likely earn 8.4 percent before taxes and inflation. This is what is called a weighted average. Let me show you how it works:

> 60 percent stock at 11.3 percent:
> 11.3 x .60 = 6.78 percent
>
> 20 percent bonds at 5.1 percent:
> 5.1 x .20 = 1.02 percent
>
> 20 percent cash at 3 percent:
> 3.0 x .20 = .60 percent
>
> *Total* = 8.40 percent

You can group your portfolio into these types of baskets and get a weighted average of the return you might expect from the

Rates of Return

Historically, the rate of return for large company stocks has averaged 11.3 percent between 1925 and 2000. During that same period, bonds averaged a 5.1 percent return and cash savings averaged a 3 percent return. Rates of return are even higher for small company stocks, but they are also much more volatile. While you may want to add a small percentage of small company stocks to your portfolio, be ready for a lot of ups and downs with that type of investment.

Tax Law Changes

The new tax laws get more complex with each new round of tax legislation. Before selling any investment, be sure you understand the tax consequences of the sale and find out if holding it for just a bit longer could save you more on taxes. If you find the tax laws just too hard to decipher, don't hesitate to sit down with a tax specialist to be sure you are making the right choice.

portfolio. If you have mutual funds, they should calculate what percentage of stock, bonds, and cash are held within the fund. You can use those percentages when you want to compare this in your portfolio.

If you assume a 20 percent long-term capital gains tax rate and a 3.5 percent inflation rate, the real rate of return for this portfolio after taxes and inflation would be 6.4 percent. As you get closer to retirement you would be wise to shift to a more conservative investment, which would earn even less than 6.4 percent. The most aggressive growth portfolio would be 100 percent stock. This portfolio would also be the riskiest.

Taxation Basics

Now that we've started to discuss the impact of taxes, let's take a look at how investments are taxed and how you can at least delay the impact of taxes on your retirement savings. The Roth IRA is the only way you can avoid paying taxes on your retirement savings entirely. The money is taxed, however, before it gets deposited in the IRA.

All other retirement savings, whether you put it in before paying taxes on it or after the money was already taxed will face taxation when you take it out at the time of retirement.

First, let's look at how investments outside of the shelter of a retirement plan are taxed. There are three types of taxation on investments: long-term capital gains, short-term capital gains, and taxes on dividends and interest. Short-term capital gains are gains you make after the sale of an asset that you held for less than one year. The gains, dividends, and interest are all taxed at whatever your current tax rate is.

Long-term capital gains, which are gains you make on an investment held longer than a year, are taxed at 20 percent if your tax rate is above 26 percent. This rate drops to 18 percent for investments purchased after January 1, 2001. The 18 percent tax rate is also available as a super long-term gain rate if stock purchased before 2001 is held at least five years.

People in a lower tax bracket are taxed only 10 percent on long-term capital gains. This amount drops to 8 percent for people in a lower tax bracket if the investment is held for more than five years. The 8 percent rate will be available for this group for any investment purchased after January 1, 2001.

Never base an investment decision solely on the tax impact. Obviously, if you no longer have faith that it is a good investment, you would want to sell it before it loses even more money. You could also decide that the company's growth rate is going to slow considerably and you have a better choice for your investment dollars. While taxes should be a consideration in the sale of assets, it should never be the only factor you consider when deciding whether to hold or sell the investment.

One common assumption is that you will likely be in a lower tax bracket when you start withdrawing your funds in retirement, so you will then be able to take advantage of the reduced tax rates. As you work through your retirement plans, keep these tax rates in mind. Some folks who have been very frugal find that their investment income actually puts them in a higher tax bracket in retirement.

Tax-deferred savings, such as employer retirement plans and IRAs, help you delay paying taxes on gains. In fact, some employer retirement plans and IRAs let you avoid even paying taxes when you first receive the money. We'll review the variety of tax-deferred savings plans and how they work in Part 3.

Aside from avoiding paying the government taxes early, you may be asking what the other benefits of tax-deferred savings are. The most critical benefit is that your money grows without being taxed each year. **Figure 1** illustrates the results of a $1,000 investment held for thirty years:

> One common assumption is that you will likely be in a lower tax bracket when you start withdrawing your funds in retirement.

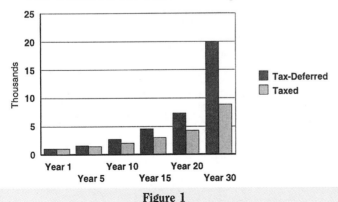

Tax-Deferred vs. Taxed Savings

Figure 1

As you can see from this chart, the initial tax savings on a tax-deferred investment are not significant. But, the tax-deferred investment benefits increase dramatically beginning in year 15. The primary reason is that as the compounded interest, dividends, and capital gains grow unhindered by taxes, their benefit becomes even greater.

After-Tax Cash Flow

Unfortunately, for all investments but the Roth IRA you will be liable for paying taxes. As you begin planning how to use your retirement savings, you can't count on all the money being there for you. Some will have to go back to the government.

The after-tax cash flow is calculated using two different formulas depending upon whether your assets are being held within a qualified retirement account or in an account not sheltered by the retirement rules.

If you want to estimate an after-tax cash flow for the money you expect to have at retirement in a tax-deferred plan you first need to calculate the estimated taxes. This is a relatively simple calculation:

Estimated Tax (ET) =
Annual Income Estimate (AIE) x Expected Tax Rate (ETR)

After you estimate your taxes, then calculate your after-tax cash flow:

After-Tax Cash Flow = AIE – ET.

It's a bit more difficult for investments not in sheltered accounts. You first must calculate the capital gains or losses as I showed you above and use either the long- or short-term capital gains rate to find your after-tax cash flow. These calculations can get even more complex if you are looking at a windfall, such as a large inheritance. As your tax questions become more complex, never hesitate to seek expert advice. The amount you'll save in taxes will most likely pay for the advisor.

> For all investments but the Roth IRA you will be liable for paying taxes.

Estimation and Assumption

As we move through the planning process, you'll be making many guesses about money and lifespan in order to come up with at least a ballpark estimate. You'll have to pick a rate of return you expect your money will earn ten, twenty, or thirty years down the road. Unless you have a good crystal ball or time machine, it can be no more than an educated guess.

You'll have to assume the number of years you need the money based on a guess about your lifespan. You'll estimate budgets based on currently known costs without a true idea of what lies ahead. Try to make your estimates based on what you know today, but realize that because there are so many unknowns, you'll need to review your plans and revise them regularly as more information becomes certain.

You can't plan without estimates and assumptions, and it's not wise to avoid planning completely, just because you were afraid to risk a mistake. The only true mistake is not planning for your retirement at all. Any other mistake in your estimates or assumptions can be fixed the next time you review the plan. If a major life change occurs, you can always review your plan sooner than scheduled to be sure you are not thrown way off track.

> You can't plan without estimates and assumptions, and it's not wise to avoid planning completely.

For more information on this topic, visit our Web site at www.businesstown.com

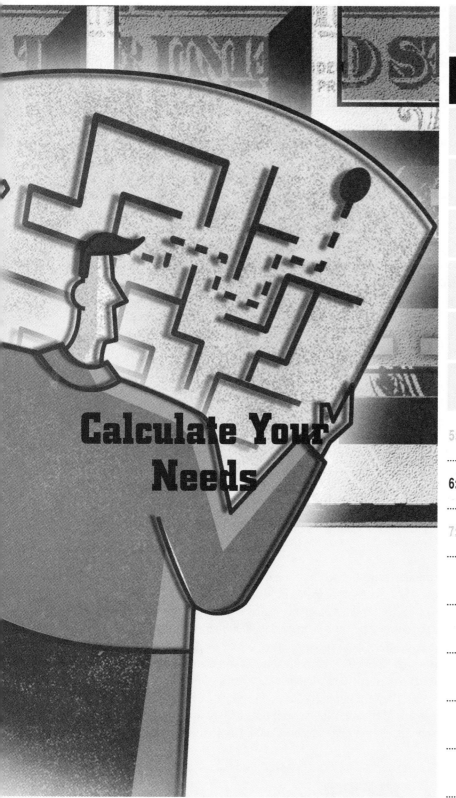

Calculate Your Needs

Chapter 6

Using the Ballpark E$timate

We're now ready to take the plunge. Let's estimate how much more you need for retirement and how much you will need to save each year to get there. To show you how all this works, we're going to step through the calculations with three different fictitious couples. Then we'll tackle your own numbers.

To make it easier for you to compare, we'll make believe all three couples are thirty-five years old. The husband earns $40,000 and the wife earns $20,000. Not to sound sexist here, but it's usually true that the husband makes more than the wife. In this case, we'll assume the wife is working part time and raising her family. As a part-time worker, the wife has no retirement benefits at work and it is up to her to finance her own retirement savings.

We'll use the American Savings Education Council's Ballpark E$timate worksheet to see how well each of these couples are doing in meeting their retirement savings goals. We'll estimate how much they need to save each year to reach their retirement dream. To save space in this chapter, I am using an abbreviated form of the wording. You can find a complete copy of the worksheet in the back of this book, published with the permission of the council, or you can use an interactive version of the worksheet at *www.asec.org/ballpark*. Once we're finished with this comparison, we'll start crunching the numbers for you.

Introducing the Couples

First, I'll introduce you to the couples. Sally and Sam Spender are the live-for-today types. They aren't worried about their retirement future and just want to enjoy what they have now. Neither of them participates in an employer-sponsored retirement savings program. They spend everything they have and have accumulated significant debts, so they can't save even if they wanted to do so. All their extra money goes toward paying down these debts.

Sheri and Scott Shoestrings live week to week on their paychecks. They do realize the need for savings, and Scott participates in his company 401(k). Scott puts in 6 percent of his salary, or $2,400, and his company matches 50 percent of that, or $1,200, for a total of $3,600. His current 401(k) balance is $50,000. Sheri, as a part-timer, has no retirement benefits, but she does deposit 6 percent of her earnings or $1,200 in an IRA each year. Her IRA is worth $25,000. Their total annual retirement savings is $4,800.

Cindy and Seth Savers cut corners wherever they can and put retirement savings as a number one priority. They are hoping to retire five years early at age sixty-two. Both are saving 10 percent of their earnings. Seth puts $4,000 in his company 401(k) and receives a company match of 50 percent or $2,000. His 401(k) is worth $110,000.

Cindy puts $2,000 into her IRA, but there is no company match. Her IRA is worth $40,000. Their total annual retirement savings is $8,000.

Average Budget Needs

We're going to make a number of assumptions for each of the couples about their retirement needs. We're going to assume a retirement age of sixty-seven, which is when they will be eligible for full retirement under Social Security. Their active phase of retirement will be five years until age seventy-two. Their passive phase of retirement will be ten years until age eighty-two, and their dependent phase of retirement will be five years until age eighty-seven. In the active phase they will spend 90 percent of their current budget, in the passive phase they will need only 50 percent, and in the dependent phase they will need 80 percent.

Let's compute a weighted average for their budget needs in retirement:

- Active Phase—5 of 20 retirement years = 25 percent of 90 percent budget needs, which is 22.5 percent.
- Passive Phase—10 of 20 retirement years = 50 percent of 50 percent budget needs, which is 25 percent.
- Dependent Phase—5 of 20 retirement years = 25 percent of 80 percent budget needs, which is 20 percent.

Adding these three weighted averages: 22.5 percent + 25 percent + 20 percent = 67.5 percent.

In other words, the couples will need 67.5 percent of their current budget in order to have enough for their retirement plans. Since their current budget is based on total income of $60,000, for the purpose of this worksheet, we'll assume they need an average of $40,500 per year in retirement ($60,000 x 67.5 percent). For the husbands, 67.5 percent of $40,000 is $27,000, and for the wives 67.5 percent of 20,000 is $13,500.

Estimating Social Security

For Social Security, we will use the estimates on the Ballpark E$timate worksheet. For the husbands who are making $40,000 per year, their Social Security benefit would be $12,000 per year in retirement. For the wives who are making $20,000 per year, their Social Security benefit would be $8,000 in retirement. Remember, our sample couples will all be retiring at their full retirement age of sixty-seven. When working with the worksheet, we'll be using age sixty-five, since that is the full retirement age behind these calculations. Remember, retirement savings is the one thing you must do separately, even as a married couple.

The Spenders

We don't even have to do the calculations for the Spenders to know they are way behind in their savings, but let's see how far behind they are. Let's go through the steps of the worksheet together:

▶ SAM SPENDER'S WORKSHEET

1. Annual income needed $27,000
2. Subtract annual income you expect to receive in retirement:

   Social Security $12,000
   Employer pension $0
   Part-time income $0
   Other $0

   How much you will need annually $15,000

3. Multiply this amount by the factor depending on retirement age. (The worksheet does not have a factor for age 67, but we'll use the factor for age 65 since that is the full retirement age for someone who is 35 today.) Looking at the worksheet the factor is 16.4 for age 65.

   Multiply $15,000 x 16.4 . . . . $246,000

4. Early retirement factor $0
5. Multiply savings to date depending upon number of years to retirement. All are age 37 and retiring at 67 in 30 years. The factor will be 2.4.

   Multiply $0 x 2.4 . . . . $0

   Total additional savings needed for retirement $246,000

   This number looks high, but the Ballpark E$timate worksheet does show you how to break this down into yearly savings, which takes compounding of your investment into account. The worksheet is based on a 3 percent real rate of return after inflation.
6. Since our couples are retiring in 30 years, the factor for them will be .020, so we calculate their annual savings by multiplying the total needed by .020. Sam Spender's needed annual savings would be:

   $246,000 x .020 = ... $4,920

CALCULATE YOUR NEEDS

Now we'll take a look at Sally Spender's savings needs.

▶ SALLY SPENDER'S WORKSHEET

1. Annual income needed $13,500
2. Subtract annual income you expect to receive in retirement:

   Social Security $8,000
   Employer pension $0
   Part-time income $0
   Other $0

   How much you will need annually $5,500

3. Multiply $5,500 x 16.4 . . . . $90,200
4. Early retirement factor $0
5. Multiply $0 x 2.4 . . . . $0

   Total additional savings needed for retirement $90,200

6. Multiplying the total needed by .020, Sally Spender's annual savings
   needed would be:

   $90,200 x .020 = ... $1,804

Combined, the Spenders need to save $6,724 a year to be able to meet their retirement budget needs or 11.2 percent of their current income. They would need to change their spending habits dramatically to meet these goals. They do have two other options. One is to consider working part time in retirement and the second is to retire at age seventy. Let's take a look at how each of these options would have an impact on their savings needs.

▶ **SAM SPENDER'S WORK IN RETIREMENT WORKSHEET**

1. Annual income needed....................................... $27,000
2. Subtract annual income you expect to receive in retirement:

   Social Security... $12,000
   Employer pension $0
   Part-time income $10,000
   Other.. $0

   How much you will need annually $5,000

3. Multiply $15,000 x 16.4.................................... $82,000
4. Early retirement factor.................................... $0
5. Multiply $0 x 2.4... $0

   Total additional savings needed for retirement.............. $82,000

6. Multiplying the total needed by .020, Sam Spender's
   annual savings needed would be:

   $82,000 x .020 = ... $1,640

If Sam were able to earn $10,000 per year in retirement, it would reduce his savings needs by $3,280. You do have to ask though whether it is realistic to think a person could earn $10,000 per year through the age of eighty-seven. Some eighty-seven-year-olds may be active and able to do that, but they are probably in the minority. Of course, Sam could decide to earn more in his active years and then cut back.

Another option for Sam would be to retire later. Let's look at how much help that would be. In this scenario, we will change the numbers to reflect a delayed retirement to age seventy.

CALCULATE YOUR NEEDS

1. Annual income needed.................................... $27,000
2. Subtract annual income you expect to receive in retirement:

    Social Security.. $12,000
    Employer pension $0
    Part-time income $0
    Other... $0

    How much you will need annually $15,000

3. Multiply $15,000 x 13.6................................ $204,000
    (Note the factor for age 70 is 13.6)
4. Early retirement factor.................................... $0
5. Multiply $0 x 2.4... $0

    Total additional savings needed for retirement...... $204,000

6. Multiplying the total needed by .016 (this is the factor for retirement
    in 35 years), Sam Spender's annual savings needed would be:

    $204,000 x .016 = ... $3,264

Sam Spender can reduce his retirement savings requirements by $1,656 per year by deciding to retire later. The Spenders can reduce their savings needs even more if Sally decides to either work longer or work part time in retirement. As you can see, deciding not to save for retirement has a significant impact on whether you will be able to retire comfortably.

The Shoestrings

Now, let's take a look at our folks living check-to-check, but still making some effort to save for retirement. We'll now work through Sheri and Scott Shoestrings' retirement worksheets.

▶ SCOTT SHOESTRING'S WORKSHEET

1. Annual income needed $27,000
2. Subtract annual income you expect to receive in retirement:

   Social Security $12,000
   Employer pension $0
   Part-time income $0
   Other $0

   How much you will need annually $15,000

3. Multiply $15,000 x 16.4 . . . . $246,000
4. Early retirement factor $0
5. Multiply $50,000 x 2.4 . . . . $120,000

   Total additional savings needed for retirement $126,000

6. Multiplying the total needed by .020, Scott Shoestring's
   additional annual savings needed would be:

   $126,000 x .020 = ... $2,520

Since Scott is saving $2,400 per year and his company matches another $1,200 per year, he is slightly ahead of his target for retirement.

CALCULATE YOUR NEEDS

1. Annual income needed $13,500
2. Subtract annual income you expect to receive in retirement:

   Social Security $8,000
   Employer pension $0
   Part-time income $0
   Other $0

   How much you will need annually $5,500

3. Multiply $5,500 x 16.4 . . . . $90,200
4. Early retirement factor $0
5. Multiply $25,000 x 2.4 . . . . $60,000

   Total additional savings needed for retirement $30,200

6. Multiplying the total needed by .020, Sheri Shoestring's
   additional annual savings needed would be:

   $30,200 x .020 = ... $604

Sheri's $1,200 per year also puts her slightly ahead of her retirement savings requirement. You may be wondering why Sheri is in such good shape even through she saves less. Social Security benefits are a higher percentage of current earnings for people earning in the lower brackets. We'll discuss how this works in greater depth in Chapter 8.

The Savers

Now, let's move on to our savers, Cindy and Seth Saver. First, we'll look at whether they are saving enough for retirement at age sixty-seven. You can probably answer this with a yes without crunching the numbers after seeing the results of our first two couples. We'll crunch the numbers anyway for practice, and then we'll see whether the couple can consider retiring early at age sixty-two.

▶ SETH SAVER'S WORKSHEET

1. Annual income needed $27,000
2. Subtract annual income you expect to receive in retirement:

   Social Security $12,000
   Employer pension $0
   Part-time income $0
   Other $0

   How much you will need annually $15,000

3. Multiply $15,000 x 16.4 . . . . $246,000
4. Early retirement factor $0
5. Multiply $100,000 x 2.4 . . . . $240,000

   Total additional savings needed for retirement $6,000

6. Multiplying the total needed by .020, Seth Saver's additional annual savings needed would be:

   $6,000 x .020 = ... $120

Seth is well ahead of this savings rate already. As expected, things are looking very good for him to be able to retire early.

CALCULATE YOUR NEEDS

▶ CINDY SAVER'S WORKSHEET

1. Annual income needed $13,500
2. Subtract annual income you expect to receive in retirement:

   Social Security $8,000
   Employer pension $0
   Part-time income $0
   Other $0

   How much you will need annually $5,500

3. Multiply $5,500 x 16.4 . . . . $90,200
4. Early retirement factor $0
5. Multiply $50,000 x 2.4 . . . . $120,000

   Total additional savings needed for retirement $0

Cindy Saver's annual savings needed would be $0; she doesn't need to save another penny if she wants to retire at sixty-seven. So the Savers are well ahead of what they need to meet their retirement goals. Let's see how much more they would need to save if they want to retire early at age sixty-two.

▶ SETH SAVER'S EARLY RETIREMENT WORKSHEET

1. Annual income needed..$27,000
2. Subtract annual income you expect to receive in retirement:

   Social Security..$12,000
   Employer pension $0
   Part-time income $0
   Other...$0

   How much you will need annually $15,000

3. Multiply $15,000 x 18.9....................................$283,500

   To retire at age 62 the new factor would be 18.9. (The worksheet factor is set at age 60, but we're adjusting all factors to reflect the two additional years for full retirement for 35-year-olds.) More money is needed because you will be spending more time in retirement.

4. Early retirement factor (which offsets the reduction in Social Security benefits for early retirement).

   $12,000 x 4.7 ....$56,400

5. Multiply $100,000 x 2.1...................................$210,000
   (The factor for current savings also needs to be changed because you will be saving for a shorter time period.)

   Total additional savings needed for retirement..............$129,900

6. Multiplying the total needed by .027 because he will now be retiring early in 25 years. Seth Saver's additional annual savings to retire earlier would be:

   $129,900 x .027 = ...$3,507

Seth is saving $4,000 per year and his company is matching another $2,000. He can definitely meet his goal of retiring early and even have some extra to help Cindy if her savings falls short.

Calculate Your Needs

▶ CINDY SAVER'S EARLY RETIREMENT WORKSHEET

1. Annual income needed $13,500
2. Subtract annual income you expect to receive in retirement:

   Social Security $8,000
   Employer Pension $0
   Part-time income $0
   Other $0

   How much you will need annually $5,500

3. Multiply $5,500 x 18.9 . . . . $103,950
4. Early retirement factor

   $8,000 x 4.7 . . . . $37,600

5. Multiply $50,000 x 2.1 . . . . $105,000

   Total additional savings needed for retirement $36,550

6. Multiplying the total needed by .027. Cindy Saver's additional annual savings for early retirement would be:

   $36,550 x .027 = ... $986.85

Cindy's $2,000 per year savings is definitely enough as well. There is no question the Savers could retire at age sixty-two. If all continues to go as planned, they will probably be able to consider retiring even earlier.

To plan for early retirement, the Savers will have to save extra to cover medical costs from the time they retire until they can qualify for Medicare. Medical insurance costs outside of an employee group policy will be very high and could be a budget buster. Living expenses during the early retirement years could actually be higher than their work expenses, especially if they have travel and other entertainment plans to fill those years.

Now that we have practiced with these fictitious couples, it's time to use what we have learned to figure out your own retirement needs. We'll look at how much you currently have saved toward those needs and how much you still need to save to fill your retirement gap.

Calculate Retirement Needs

Our first step will be to revisit your budget planning numbers. In Chapter 3 you should have completed a budget for the three phases of retirement that looks like this:

▶ RETIREMENT BUDGET

Budget Item	Active Phase	Passive Phase	Dependent Phase
Food and Shelter	....	....	....
Health Care	....	....	....
Transportation	....	....	....
Insurance	....	....	....
Leisure and Travel	....	....	....
Debt/Credit Obligations	....	....	....
Religious and Charitable Donations	....	....	....
Professional Services	....	....	....
Savings and Investments	....	....	....
Taxes	....	....	....
Other Items	....	....	....
Total Budget	....	....	....

Know Your Annual Budget Needs

If you do plan to retire early, be sure you are fully aware of the annual budget you will need. Once you start collecting your Social Security and other pension plans, you are stuck with that decision even if you may not have enough money to make it through retirement. Also, if you retire before you can start collecting Social Security and depend on Medicare for health coverage, your only choice will be to drain your savings. You will need to build a considerably larger nest egg if you plan to retire early.

If you are married, a portion of your budget needs to be covered by your retirement income and a portion needs to be covered by your spouse's. It is important to do a retirement estimate worksheet for each of you separately. The most logical way to calculate the budget figure for each is to total your current family income and determine the percentage of that income that is derived from each person's salary.

▶ Put your budget percentage figure here: ....

▶ Put your spouse's budget percentage figure here: ....

To make use of this budget, you'll also need to make a few other decisions about when you want to retire and how long each of you expect each of the retirement phases to last. Remember we're estimating lifespan and how healthy you think you will be in retirement. It's only a guess, but one you must make in order to go forward.

In Chapter 1, we pointed you to an excellent Web site to find out your expected lifespan. If you have not already done that, you should go to the life expectancy calculator now at *http://moneycentral.msn.com/investor/calcs/n_expect/main.asp.*

Now that you have an estimated lifespan, let's calculate your weighted average budget figure for the Ballpark E$timate worksheet:

▶ At what age do you anticipate retiring? ....

▶ To what age do you expect to live? ....

▶ How many years do you expect to spend in retirement? ....

▶ How many of those years will be spent in the Active Phase? ....

▶ How many of those years will be spent in the Passive Phase? ....

▶ How many of those years will be spent in the Dependent Phase? ....

Now, we'll use these estimates to figure the proportion of the retirement years you expect to spend in each phase. To do that, divide the number of years in each phase by the total number of years in retirement to get the percent of retirement.

Do this calculation for each of the three phases of retirement. Next, we'll use the percentages you calculated for your portion of the budget and for your percentage of time in each phase of retirement to compute your budget needs:

▶ Percentage of Active Phase:
phase budget x budget x percent of retirement = ...

▶ Percentage of Passive Phase:
phase budget x budget x percent of retirement = ...

▶ Percentage of Dependent Phase:
phase budget x budget x percent of retirement = ...

▶ Now, total these three numbers and you will have an
estimate of the annual income you will need in retirement   ....

Repeat these same steps for your spouse:

▶ At what age does your spouse anticipate retiring?   ....

▶ To what age does your spouse expect to live?   ....

▶ How many years does your spouse expect to spend in retirement? ....

▶ How many of those years will be spent in the Active Phase?   ....

▶ How many of those years will be spent in the Passive Phase?   ....

▶ How many of those years will be spent in the Dependent Phase?   ....

Now, we'll use these estimates to figure the proportion of the retirement years your spouse expects to spend in each phase. To do that, divide the number of years in each phase by the total number of years in retirement to get the percent of retirement.

Do this calculation for each of the three phases of retirement. Next we'll use the percentages you calculated for your spouse's portion of the budget and for your spouse's percentage of time in each phase of retirement to compute your budget needs.

Percentage of Active Phase:
phase budget x budget x percent of retirement = ...

▶ Percentage of Passive Phase:
phase budget x budget x percent of retirement = ...

▶ Percentage of Dependent Phase:
phase budget x budget x percent of retirement = ...

▶ Now, total these three numbers and you will have an estimate
of the annual income your spouse will need in retirement:

Next, you'll subtract out of these figures the income you expect to have annually to offset the needs. Do you have your most recent statement for Social Security or have you gone to their Web site to get an estimate? If not, you can do so now at *www.ssa.gov/retire2/calculator.htm.*

▶ Jot down the amount you expect to receive from Social
Security here: ....

▶ Jot down your spouse's estimated Social Security benefit here: ....

▶ You also may be one of the lucky few that has a traditional
pension as part of your employee benefit plan. If you do,
check your most recent statement from your employer and
jot down your expected monthly pension benefit here: ....

▶ If your spouse has one too, jot that down here: ....

▶ If you expect to work during retirement, jot down your anticipated
annual earnings here: ....

▶ If your spouse expects to work during retirement, jot down his or
her anticipated annual earnings here: ....

▶ If you expect any other income—it could be ongoing income
from a business, real estate rental property, or any other source
from which you expect to get annual income (do not include
investment earnings here, that is already factored in the Ballpark
E$timate worksheet)—jot it down here: ....

▶ Jot down your spouse's other income here: ....

Calculate Retirement Assets

Now, we'll get to use some of the information you collected for your assets inventory. How much are you saving toward retirement? List that here:

- ▶ Husband's retirement contribution: ....
- ▶ Husband's company match: ....
- ▶ Wife's retirement contribution: ....
- ▶ Wife's company match: ....
- ▶ Husband's personal IRA: ....
- ▶ Wife's personal IRA: ....
- ▶ Other retirement savings: ....
- ▶ Total annual retirement savings: ....
- ▶ What is the current market value of your retirement savings? List that here: ....
- ▶ Market value of husband's retirement account as part of an employer plan [401(k), 403(b), Section 457, SIMPLE IRA, SEP-IRA, or Keogh plan]: ....
- ▶ Market value of wife's retirement account as part of an employer plan [401(k), 403(b), Section 457, SIMPLE IRA, SEP-IRA, or Keogh plan]: ....
- ▶ Market value of husband's personal retirement savings (such as an IRA): ....
- ▶ Market value of wife's personal retirement savings (such as an IRA): ....

Calculate Your Retirement Gap

Now we have collected all the information you need to calculate your retirement gap and figure out how much more you'll need to save for retirement. The complete Ballpark E$timate worksheet is reprinted courtesy of the American Savings Education Council at the back of the book if you want more detail, but a working copy is also placed here. You can also decide to use the interactive version online at *www.asec.org/ballpark*. The interactive version does make it much easier to try out different scenarios for your retirement planning options. Again, if you are married, be sure to do a separate worksheet for each of you.

1. Annual income needed: $ ....
   (This is based on your budget calculations. If you decided not to make up a budget, use 70 percent of your current annual gross income.)

2. Subtract annual income you expect to receive in retirement:

   Social Security: $ ....

   Employer pension: $ ....

   Part-time income: $ ....

   Other: $ ....

   How much income you will receive annually: $ ....

3. Multiply annual need by the age factor to find out how much you will need to make up in savings based on your retirement age: $ ....

   Retire at 55, factor is 21.0
   Retire at 60, factor is 18.9
   Retire at 65, factor is 16.4
   Retire at 70, factor is 13.6

4. Multiply Social Security benefit by early retirement factor: $ ....
   (This will be added to your savings needs. It offsets the reduction in Social Security benefits for early retirement.)

   Retire at 55, factor is 8.8
   Retire at 60, factor is 4.7

5. Multiply current retirement savings by the number of years to
   retirement factor: $ ....
   (This will be subtracted from your needs because it's already saved.)

   Retire in 10 years, factor is 1.3
   Retire in 15 years, factor is 1.6
   Retire in 20 years, factor is 1.8
   Retire in 25 years, factor is 2.1
   Retire in 30 years, factor is 2.4
   Retire in 35 years, factor is 2.8
   Retire in 40 years, factor is 3.3
   Calculate your total additional savings needed for retirement: $ ....

6. Multiply the total needed by the factor for the number of years you have before
   retirement to find out how much you need to save annually.

   Retire in 10 years, factor is .085
   Retire in 15 years, factor is .052
   Retire in 20 years, factor is .036
   Retire in 25 years, factor is .027
   Retire in 30 years, factor is .020
   Retire in 35 years, factor is .016
   Retire in 40 years, factor is .013

   Your additional annual savings needed will be: $ ....
   (Total from number 5 x appropriate factor above.)

   That's it. Great job! You now know your retirement gap numbers. In the next
chapter we'll be looking at strategies for filling that gap. If you have gotten good news
and don't have a gap, then you might want to rework the numbers and see if you can
retire early.

> **For more information on this topic, visit our Web site at www.businesstown.com**

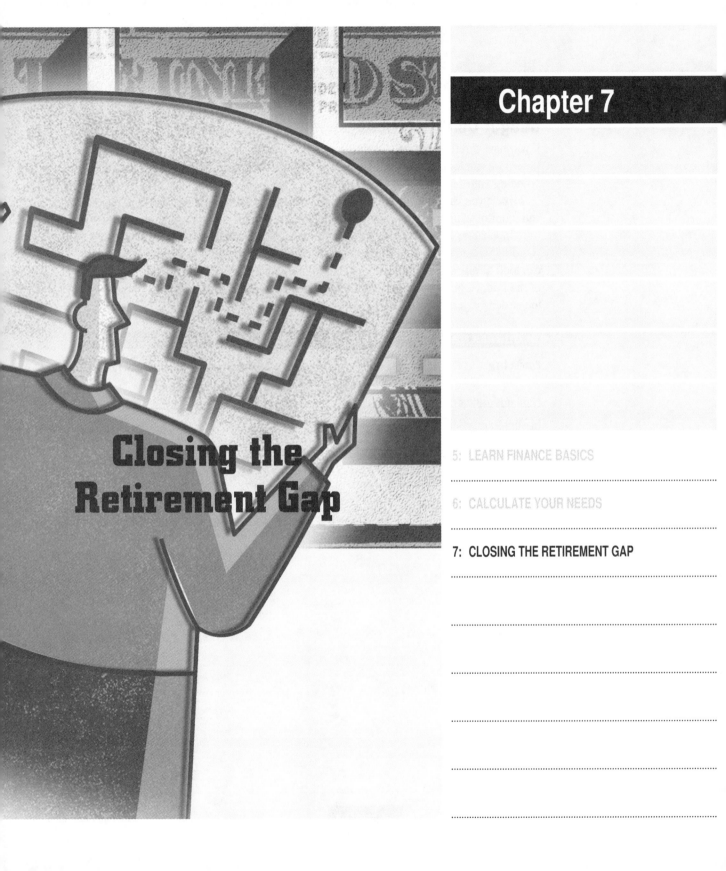

Chapter 7

Closing the Retirement Gap

Budget Considerations

If you have a retirement gap, obviously the best way to fix that is to save more money. Before we can look at how to save more money, we first need to know how you are spending your money today.

Have you calculated a budget for your monthly spending? If so, how closely do you monitor your spending to be sure you are not overspending on a regular basis?

In Chapter 3, we discussed how to develop a detailed budget for retirement. If you don't already have a current budget, you'll need to complete one first before we can look at retirement gap solutions. We're not going to review in detail all the parts of the budget, but a more detailed budget worksheet is included to fill out to make the job easier for you.

▶ CURRENT BUDGET

BUDGET ITEM	AMOUNT SPENT	CATEGORY TOTALS
Food and Shelter		
Current Rent or Mortgage	....	
Homeowner's or Condominium Association Fees	....	
Other Real Estate Costs	....	
Landscaping/Lawn Care	....	
Snow Removal	....	
Home Repairs	....	
Home Maintenance	....	
Household Supplies	....	
Cable/Satellite TV	....	
Internet Service	....	
Phone (regular and cell)	....	
Electricity	....	
Gas or Oil	....	
Sewer/Septic	....	

Budget Item	Amount Spent	Category Totals
Water/Well	....	
Groceries	....	
Dining Out	....	
Alcohol/Tobacco	....	
Toiletries/Cosmetics	....	
Hair Care, Massages, etc.	....	
Total Food and Shelter		....

Health Care

Budget Item	Amount Spent	Category Totals
Out-of-Pocket Costs for Medical Insurance	....	
Out-of-Pocket Doctor's/Clinics/Hospital Expenses	....	
Out-of-Pocket Costs for Prescriptions	....	
Vitamins and Supplements	....	
Other Medical Services	....	
Total Health Care Costs		....

Transportation

Budget Item	Amount Spent	Category Totals
Car Payments	....	
Auto Insurance	....	
Parking	....	
Tolls		
Public Transportation	....	
Gas		
Registration, Taxes, Other Fees	....	
Total Transportation Costs		....

BUDGET ITEM	AMOUNT SPENT	CATEGORY TOTALS
Insurance		
Life	....	
Dental	....	
Vision	....	
Long-term Care	....	
Disability	....	
Homeowner's/Renters	....	
Umbrella	....	
Pet	....	
Legal	....	
Flood	....	
Other	....	
Total Insurance Costs		....
Leisure and Travel		
Vacations/Travel	....	
Equipment	....	
Activities (health club memberships, country club fees, etc.)	....	
Sporting Events	....	
Movies/Theater/Concerts	....	
Parties	....	
Books, Magazines, Tapes, CDs, etc.	....	
Boat or Recreational Vehicle	....	

BUDGET ITEM	AMOUNT SPENT	CATEGORY TOTALS
Pet Ownership/Veterinarian Expenses	....	
Kids' Recreation	....	
Nonbusiness Computers	....	
Other	....	
Total Leisure and Travel Costs		....

Child/Parent Care

School Tuitions	....	
College Savings	....	
Child Care/Babysitting	....	
Support for Aging Parents	....	
Other	....	
Total Child/Parent Care Costs		

Clothing

Purchases	....	
Rentals	....	
Dry Cleaning/Laundry	....	
Repair Costs	....	
Total Clothing Costs		....

Debt/Credit Obligations

Home Equity Loan	....	
Credit Cards	....	

BUDGET ITEM	AMOUNT SPENT	CATEGORY TOTALS
College Loans	....	
401(k) Loan	....	
Stock-Secured Loan	....	
Unsecured Loan	....	
Investment Real Estate	....	
Child Support	....	
Alimony	....	
Other	....	
Total Debt/Credit Obligations		....

Religious and Charitable Donations

Church/Temple Dues	....	
Religious School Tuition	....	
Religious Activities	....	
Charitable Donations	....	
Total Religious and Charitable Donations		....

Professional Services

Lawyer	....	
Attorney	....	
Financial Planner	....	
Accountant	....	
Other	....	
Total Professional Services Costs		....

Budget Item	Amount Spent	Category Totals
Savings and Investments		
Employer Retirement Plans	....	
Non-Employer Retirement Plans	....	
Employee Stock Purchase	....	
Vacations/Major Trip	....	
Other	....	
Total Savings and Investments Costs		....
Taxes		
Social Security Tax	....	
Federal Income Tax	....	
State/Local Income Tax	....	
Property Tax	....	
Other Taxes	....	
Total Taxes		....
Other Items		....
Total Budget		....

I know. Budgeting is not fun, but it is the only way you can get a handle on how you are spending your money now. Once you have that detail, you can uncover ways to shift current spending in order to make room for more retirement savings.

Were you able to fill in all the pieces? Do you think you really know how you are spending all your discretionary cash? If you found it hard to fill in the line items, you may need to step back a moment and figure out how you are actually spending your money. The best way to do that is to keep a log of all spending for about a month. This will give you a good idea of where your cash goes. After doing that, see if you can now fill in this budget sheet more accurately.

Cutting Monthly Spending

Why are being put through this torture? If you have a significant retirement gap, we have to figure how to increase your savings. Now that you know the detail, let's look at what you might be able to cut in your monthly spending.

Let's rank your budget expenses. Put a "1" next to things that cannot change (such as required monthly obligations—mortgage, utilities, etc.). Put a "5" next to line items you think are the least important and could definitely be cut back. Put a "2" next to the items that you are fairly sure you can't change. Following this logic, put a "4" next to the items that you think you might be able to change if you absolutely had to do so. Finally, put a "3" next to the ones that fall in the middle.

Before we get started, jot down the additional amount you need to save each month. Use the annual figure we calculated in Chapter 6 and divide it by twelve.

Jot down your monthly target number here: ....

Now, let's make a list of all the fives and fours. Total all your fives and then total all your fours. Is this more or less than the figure you jotted down above? If it's less than what you need to save for retirement, then you can decide which of these items you want to leave in the budget. If you still need more money, you may need to add some of the threes to get to your goal. Or, if you absolutely can't imagine cutting all these items, you may finally need to accept that you have to go back to the drawing board and revise your retirement dream. But, before you give up, let's try to look at some other ways to get to your goals.

If you have a lot of cuts to make, take it slow. Don't overdo it all in one shot. This could derail your entire retirement plan because you give up in frustration. Plan baby steps to get yourself gradually up to your savings goals.

Budget Cutting Can Be Difficult

I know it is hard to think about making major cuts in your spending. You have to decide how important your retirement dreams are versus how important your current spending is today. No question, it is a difficult choice for everyone to make. But, if you have a goal in mind, it does make the pain of cuts a lot easier to bear. At first, the challenge may seem insurmountable, but as your nest egg grows it will be exciting to watch your success and really begin to think about living your dreams.

Tackling Credit Card Debt

For those of you who have high credit card debt, this definitely should be one of the first things you tackle. Stop using your cards for anything other than a dire emergency. If you don't have the cash on hand, put off the spending. Instead, work toward paying off your cards.

First, let's revisit the liability inventory you developed in Chapter 4. Remember, this is the chart that looked like this:

▶ LIABILITIES INVENTORY

TYPE OF DEBT	AMOUNT OWED	MONTHLY PAYMENT	INTEREST RATE	TERMS/PAYOFF DATE

Total all of your credit card debt and the required monthly payments. Now group your cards by the total amount owed. We are going to develop a payoff plan that is called by financial planners "the snowball effect." Essentially, it looks like a snowball rolling down a hill that gets larger as it goes.

The first question we need to answer is whether you are actually paying more than the required amount of monthly credit card payments or are you simply meeting the minimum monthly payments. If you have only been making minimum payments, you have probably figured out by now that the interest is building up more quickly than you can pay down the debt.

Let's see if you can find some extra cash in your earlier budget crunching to use toward additional credit card payments. Take that extra cash and use it to pay down the card with the smallest balance. Once that card is paid, add the amount you were paying toward the card with the smallest balance to start paying down the card with the next lowest balance. When you get the second card paid off, add the payments you were making to the first and second to increase the amount you are paying toward the card with the third lowest balance.

Let me give you a simple example of how this works. We'll revisit one of our fictitious couples, the Spenders, and their credit card debt. This is just a small portion of their debt. We're not going to include their car loans, mortgage, or student loans:

> Take that extra cash and use it to pay down the card with the smallest balance.

Spender's Credit Card Debt

Type of Debt	Amount Owed	Monthly Payment	Interest Rate	Terms/ Payoff Date
Credit Card	10,000	200	18%	
Credit Card	5,000	100	15%	
Credit Card	2,000	50	14%	
Credit Card	1,000	25	12%	

Right now the Spenders are paying the minimum amount due on each card for a total of $375. In reviewing their spending, the Spenders have decided to make a concerted effort to get rid of these cards. They are going to double the amount they are paying toward credit card debt for a total of $750.

Using the snowball effect plan they will pay $350 to cover the minimum required payments for the cards with the higher balances and pay $400 toward the card with the lowest balance. In three months that card is paid off and they move on to the next lowest balance of $2,000. Now they have $400 plus the $50 minimum payment they can use to pay that card off. They can pay that card off in about five months and start working on the card with the third highest balance of $5,000. Now their snowball is really gathering some steam and they have $450 plus $100 to use toward that card. You get the idea.

Payments will continue to grow and, depending on how large your credit debt is, the growing payment amount will be like the snowball growing larger as you make it down the hill toward debt-free living. Once you get all of your credit card debt paid off you should have a significant payment that you can now use to start saving for retirement.

Getting your debt under control before retirement is critical. Making payments on credit cards for spending prior to retirement will become increasingly difficult as you try to live on a fixed income.

Investment Options

Now that you have some money to save, where should that money go? First, let's look at what your employer offers in retirement savings options. Do they have a 401(k) or 403(b) plan? Does your employer match your savings in that account?

Many employers will match at least some portion of your 401(k) or 403(b) contribution. For example, if you put 6 percent of your salary in a 401(k), it is common for an employer to match 50 percent of that amount or another 3 percent of your savings. The total being saved toward retirement is now 9 percent of your salary. If you are not contributing at least enough to get your full employer match, that should definitely be the first place to put any newly found retirement savings money. By not taking advantage of your full employer match, it's like throwing money out the window.

Individual Retirement Accounts

If you are married, you both should be taking advantage of the employer matching funds. If one of you doesn't have any retirement benefits at work, then the next place to put your newly found

Get Help with Your Debt

If you don't think you can rework the debt obligations yourself, contact a nonprofit credit card counseling service to help you get started. The service may even be able to get your interest rates reduced to help you pay down the debt sooner. In fact, if you have a lot of credit card debt, it would be wise to seek some help in getting interest rates reduced so you can pay down the debt more quickly. National Credit Counseling Services (*www.nccs.org*) and American Consumer Credit Counseling (*www.consumer credit.com*) are two nonprofit services that are members of the International Credit Association & Association of Independent Consumer Credit Counseling Agencies and good choices if you are seeking assistance for paying down your debt.

retirement funds is an Individual Retirement Account (IRA). There are three different types: the traditional tax-deductible IRA, the traditional non–tax deductible IRA, and the Roth IRA. We'll look at the pluses and minuses of each of these plans in Chapter 13.

Whichever of these plans you choose for your newfound retirement savings, you will need to pick investment alternatives for the money. The key will be to find ways to grow your funds faster than the rate of inflation. One of the simplest ways to get started until you have time to learn more about investing is to use an index mutual fund.

Index Mutual Funds

These mutual funds use mathematical modeling to try to match the growth results of a particular index. The most common index that funds match is the Standard & Poor's 500 (S&P 500) of large growth companies. The big advantage of index funds is that their management costs are very low because they don't have to pay for an extensive research staff and don't have significant portfolio trading costs. More of your money goes toward growth and less toward management and administration fees for operating the funds. We'll explore investment options in greater detail in Chapter 16. I just wanted to get you started thinking about the alternatives.

Tax Options

Another major benefit of retirement savings is the ability to avoid paying taxes until retirement. Employer retirement options and the traditional tax-deductible IRA allows you to put money in these investment options before you pay current taxes. These investment options also allow your money to grow tax-deferred until retirement.

Why is this such a big advantage? Let's look at what happens to a $2,000 retirement contribution taken out of your check before taxes versus one that is made after paying taxes. If you are in the 27 percent tax bracket and must pay taxes on $2,000, then $540 of that money would go toward taxes and only $1,460 would end up in your pocket.

> The big advantage of index funds is that their management costs are very low because they don't have to pay for an extensive research staff and don't have significant portfolio trading costs.

By depositing the $2,000 in a retirement account before taxes, you end up being able to save more without having as great an impact on your annual budget. In this example, if the person could only find $1,500 to save for retirement, the tax-deferred retirement options would make it possible to save the full $2,000 before taxes and still have almost the same amount after taxes to spend.

You will need to eventually pay taxes on this money when you start drawing it down at retirement, but if you are certain you will be in a lower tax bracket at retirement, that means you will save even more tax money by having avoided paying taxes up front at a higher rate.

Tax impacts can get very complicated and vary depending on the type of investment options you choose. We'll take an in-depth look at the tax advantages for each type of retirement savings in the next section of the book.

Work Options

If you just don't think you'll be able to make up your retirement gap, you may decide that you will work later in life. Or, you may just decide that you can't imagine stopping work entirely anyway.

After the passage of the Senior Citizens' Freedom to Work Act of 2000 (P.L. 106-182), the penalties for working and collecting Social Security were removed for all retirees who want to work after reaching their normal retirement age. Prior to passage of this law, benefits were reduced if you earned money after you started to collect Social Security. Today only early retirees risk Social Security benefit payment reductions, if they choose to work after they begin collecting benefits.

Tax Impact

The tax impact of deciding to work can still be a stumbling block for retirees. Social Security reports that right now about 20 percent of people who get benefits have to pay taxes on those benefits. As more people decide to work in retirement, that number will rise.

Roth IRA

If current tax savings is not a big priority for you, there is an alternative that will let you draw down the money completely tax-free: the Roth IRA. For this type of IRA, the money is taxed before you put it in. The big advantage of the Roth IRA is that even the capital gains, dividends, and interest can be withdrawn tax-free at retirement, provided the money has been in the account for at least five years.

Social Security benefits are taxed if you are single and your total income is between $25,000 and $34,000. To compute this income you add any money you earn, all your capital gains, dividend and interest income, and other pension income to your Social Security benefits. If this totals between $25,000 and $34,000, 50 percent of your Social Security benefits will be taxed. If your total income is over $34,000, then up to 85 percent of your Social Security benefits will be subject to tax.

If you are married filing a joint tax return, the income level that could result in 50 percent of your Social Security benefits being taxed is between $32,000 and $44,000. The risk of 85 percent of your Social Security benefits being taxed begins if you earn more than $44,000 and you file a joint return.

Now don't misinterpret this. You are not taxed at a 50 percent tax rate, but 50 percent of your Social Security benefits will be axed at whatever your tax rate is in retirement. As you can see, you can earn too much in retirement even if you don't lose benefits for working.

If you do decide to continue working past your normal retirement age, you need to weigh whether to begin collecting Social Security or delaying it as long as possible. When you delay collecting Social Security, your ultimate benefit rises as we mentioned earlier. Once you reach seventy, though, it won't be worth delaying any longer no matter what the tax consequences.

Your Earning Potential

Your best way to make up for that retirement gap may be to find a way to earn more now. If you added a few initials to your name, such as an MBA (business), JD (law), or PhD (doctorate for your specialty), would you be able to earn more at your current job? Rather than going out and partying at night, it might be worth spending a few years getting those additional credentials and dramatically increasing how much you can earn.

Your employer may even be willing to foot the bill for your new learning endeavor if the courses are related to your current job. If not, you may be able to take advantage of the Hope Credit or

> You are not taxed at a 50 percent tax rate.

Lifetime Learning Credits, which are direct tax rebates for all or part of your tuition costs. You also may find some grants or low interest loans to make this a more doable option.

Raising your current income not only helps you make ends meet, but it also raises your ultimate retirement and Social Security benefits, while making you feel better about yourself at the same time. Everyone enjoys being recognized for their efforts and getting a promotion.

Starting Your Own Business

Many people find the best way to supplement income is to start a small business on their own, provided there is no conflict with your employer. You certainly don't want to risk losing your job just to make an effort to earn a little additional money.

Pick something you think you might enjoy doing for some extra cash. You may find that you have a hobby that you could convert to cash with a little extra effort. If it really catches on, you could end up with a business endeavor that may become your full- or part-time work that you can use to supplement your money needs when you get to retirement.

Be creative now. The more thought and effort you put into work options before you actually reach retirement, the better chance you will have at meeting your retirement goals.

Protect Yourself

You probably hate even thinking about sitting down with an insurance salesperson, but it is important to be sure you not only protect the assets you own, but also your life and your ability to work. Loss in any of these areas could derail any carefully developed retirement plan.

Life Insurance

First, look at the insurance you have on your life and the life of your family members. If their income or contribution to the family

Consulting for Your Current Employer

Consulting for your current employer in retirement is becoming a lucrative way many retirees are supplementing their retirement needs. As more baby boomers retire, employers are noticing a "brain drain." There may not be enough skilled workers to replace the number of baby boomers that leave the workforce all at the same time.

You can take advantage of that and find a niche at work that will make your particular knowledge base critical to company operations and help you get some kind of consulting business to make ends meet even after you leave full-time employment. If your employer needs the long-term knowledge you have gathered during your work years, you will probably be able to set a work schedule that can be flexible enough to allow you to fulfill your retirement dreams even if you can't save enough to retire completely.

were lost, would your ability to continue working or your ability to continue living on the same budget be affected? For example, even if your spouse stays home and takes care of the kids, his or her contribution is critical to maintaining your current budget plans. Without that contribution, child-care costs could rise. Life insurance helps to fill the gap, whether it replaces outside income, covers monthly expenses, or covers the costs involved in replacing needed child-care and other in-home expenses.

When does your disability protection kick in?

Disability Insurance

Next, look at the level of disability insurance you have on you and your spouse. If one of you were suddenly disabled, what would happen to your budget? When does your disability protection kick in? Is it in thirty days, ninety days, six months, or some other combination of dates? You may want to take an individual policy to be sure you have the protection you need. Social Security estimates that three out of ten workers who are now in their twenties will need to use their disability insurance at some point in their lives. If you count solely on what Social Security offers, you could end up working at a fast food joint. Social Security will only pay on disability if you can't do any work at all. You can find private disability plans that will cover your particular line of work.

Umbrella Policy

Another type of insurance plan that doesn't cost much, but could save you from catastrophic loss is an umbrella policy. This covers you to some large sum, usually $1 million, for any situation in which you are involved in an accident or other legal entanglement. If you do face a major loss, rather than lose your home and other assets, this policy will cover you.

You probably do have health insurance. Be certain you understand its coverage limits and what type of liability you have if you suffer a major illness or accident. Also, you need to review what type of long-term health coverage you have in case you find you need health care for a longer period of time than what is now covered by your insurance plans.

Taking the time now to look at your protection and the protection for your family members can save a lot of heartache later if the worst happens. Remember, the primary purpose of insurance is to protect you from the catastrophes of life. The insurance company shares the risks with you by offering their coverage options in exchange for a premium payment that you make.

Take Control

All these steps regarding closing your retirement gap require you to take control of your retirement planning and find the solutions that work best for you and your family. The earlier you start working on these solutions, the better chance you will have to truly fix the retirement gap problems and be on the road to living your retirement dreams. In the next section, we'll starting looking at your retirement savings options so you will understand what to do with the new-found money you'll have available after making these changes to close your retirement gap.

> The earlier you start working on these solutions, the better chance you will have to truly fix the retirement gap problems.

For more information on this topic, visit our Web site at www.businesstown.com

PART III

Retirement Plan Types

This part helps you:

- Get the scoop on Social Security.

- Explore 401(k) and 403(b).

- Find out what retirement plans small businesses are offering.

- Look at both traditional and government pensions.

- Figure out what retirement plan to choose if self-employed.

- Explore the different types of IRAs.

- Discuss Medicare and private supplementary insurance.

Chapter 8

Social Security

Social Security Basics

Almost everyone's retirement foundation is Social Security. Even if you never worked, it is likely that you can collect on your spouse's record or, if you were permanently disabled as a child, on your parents' record. There are a few exceptions, which we will cover in detail later. The most common exception is people who work in the public sector and never had to pay into Social Security.

Over 45 million Americans collected more than $400 billion in Social Security benefits in 2001. Today, nine out of ten retired people over the age of sixty-five collect benefits averaging $848 per month. Social Security is the major source of income for most of the elderly. For about two-thirds of the elderly, Social Security benefits make up at least 50 percent of their income.

The Future

Will Social Security be there when you retire? You've certainly seen the stories indicating that Social Security will run out of money before you get to collect your fair share. While it's true that the trust funds will run out of money in the 2030s, it's not unexpected. In the 1980s when Alan Greenspan led a commission to save Social Security, the primary outcomes of those meetings were a reduction in future benefits and an increase in taxes to pay for the future retirement costs of the baby boomers. This increase in taxes is now being used to build up the trust funds. The problem is that not enough is targeted for building the trusts to handle the wave of baby boomers.

While we don't have the ability to see into the future, it is likely that Social Security will be there in some form. The program is far too popular for it to be totally disbanded. Perhaps there will be a reduction in benefits to make up for the coming shortfall when the baby boomers start to retire or there will be an increase in taxes or some combination of the two.

Social Security is primarily a pay-as-you-go system. About 85 percent of the money paid in taxes is spent in the same year toward paying current beneficiaries. Approximately 15 percent goes into the Social Security trust funds for future beneficiaries. U.S. Government Treasury Bonds are purchased with those funds. For a short time,

> Social Security is primarily a pay-as-you-go system.

the U.S. government was using the Social Security surplus to pay down the debt, but thanks to the Bush Administration's ten-year tax cut, the economic costs of September 11, 2001, and a recession, the government is back to deficit spending. Fortunately, the trust funds are still there. While some folks are saying you can't depend on the funds, few financial planners consider government bonds a risky investment.

We'll cover the controversy about the future of Social Security in greater detail later in the chapter. First, let's take a brief look at how all this got started and then review current benefits.

The Beginning

From the onset, Social Security was never intended to be a person's only retirement fund. For the average wage earner, Social Security benefits were designed to cover about 40 percent of a person's current earnings. Financial planners estimate that you need about 70 to 80 percent of your earnings to fund a comfortable retirement.

President Franklin D. Roosevelt orchestrated the start-up of Social Security after the Great Depression that followed the 1929 market crash. Most people lost everything and many of the elderly were living on the streets. He wanted to make sure that this country never again saw this kind of tragedy. Social Security was created as a safety net to guarantee a certain amount of income so people who worked all their lives would not end up in poverty.

After hundreds of pieces of legislation, the program grew into what some people think of today as a monster. Originally, only retired workers collected benefits, but today there are benefits for the family as well as benefits for disabled workers. Before we get into the specifics of the benefits available, let's first look at how you contribute to Social Security and how you become eligible to collect benefits.

> President Franklin D. Roosevelt orchestrated the start-up of Social Security after the Great Depression that followed the 1929 market crash.

Contributions and Eligibility

Unless you work in the public sector for a government entity (whether federal, state, or local) that is exempt from participating in

Social Security Avoiders

Not everyone has to pay into Social Security, but there are very few people who can avoid these taxes. Exceptions include:

- State and local government workers who participate in alternative retirement systems

- Election workers who earn less than $1,000 a year

- Career federal employees hired before 1984 who did not choose Social Security coverage

- College students who work at their academic institutions

- Ministers who choose not to be covered

- Household workers who earn less than $1,100 annually

- Self-employed workers who have net earnings below $400

If you are among the ranks of folks that don't pay into Social Security, it is even more important that you have some safety net for your retirement in place.

Social Security, you are contributing money into the system through payroll taxes. Every worker pays 7.65 percent in Social Security taxes, also known as FICA (Federal Insurance Contributions Act). You may see it on your pay stub as OASDI (Old Age, Survivors, and Disability Insurance) and Medicare. Of that amount, 6.2 percent goes toward Social Security and 1.45 percent is earmarked for Medicare. Your employer matches an equal amount.

If you are self-employed, you are paying the full 15.3 percent of these taxes. You can deduct half of these taxes on your tax return. If for some reason you are not paying Social Security, you are most likely at least being charged for Medicare at the rate of 1.45 percent with your employer matching an equal amount.

In some states, government workers can choose to participate in both Social Security and their state pension program. In these cases, they can collect on both their state pension and Social Security. People who started working for the federal government before 1984 were exempted from Social Security. Their pension system at the time was called the Civil Service Retirement System. Since 1984, any newly hired federal employees must pay into Social Security. We'll cover government pensions in greater detail in Chapter 12.

Earning Credits

Now that you know how you pay into the system, your next question is probably, "How long must I put into the system to be sure to collect Social Security?" The answer is not a simple number of years. Everything you earn is posted to your Social Security record annually. Each year you work, you earn credits toward benefits. You can earn up to four credits a year based on a certain level of earning per credit. In 2002, the earnings credit is $870, so once you earned $3,480 you've earned the maximum number of credits possible that year. The earnings required per credit is adjusted each year based on the national average wage index. By the time you retire you must have a total of forty credits to qualify.

The number of credits you've earned also affects the benefits your survivors will get if you become disabled or die. If you become disabled, the number of credits you need to qualify for disability varies according to your age when you become disabled. Disability before age twenty-four requires only six credits during the three-year period before your disability began. If you become disabled between the ages of twenty-four and thirty, you will need to earn credits for at least half of the period between age twenty-one and the date of your disability. Disability requirements after the age of thirty are shown in this chart from Social Security.

Disability Requirements after Age 30	
Disabled at Age	**Credits Needed**
31 through 42	20
44	22
46	24
48	26
50	28
52	30
54	32
56	34
58	36
60	38
62 or older	40

Survivor Eligibility

If you die before earning forty credits, your survivors may still be able to collect on your record. It all depends on when you were born. If you were born in 1929 or before, one credit is need for each year after 1950 and prior to the year of death. If you were born after 1930, then one credit is needed for each year after age twenty-one and prior to the year of death. In both cases, the maximum number of credits needed is forty.

Dependent children can get survivors' benefits if the deceased worker had six credits in the three years before his or her death, regardless of when the worker was born. Your children could continue to collect benefits until they reach age eighteen (or age nineteen if they are attending school up to grade twelve). A widow or

> If you were born after 1930, then one credit is needed for each year after age twenty-one and prior to the year of death.

widower caring for dependent children who are under age sixteen or disabled may also be able to get benefits.

Your Social Security credits also count toward Medicare, which is an automatic benefit when you reach age sixty-five as long as you've earned forty credits. You may also become eligible for Medicare at an earlier age if you are entitled to disability benefits for twenty-four months or more. If you don't have enough credits for Medicare, you can buy into the system. We'll cover that in more detail in Chapter 14.

Age Factor

Work credits are not the only factor that entitles you to begin collecting. Age is a big factor, too. It used to be a simple answer: age sixty-five, but now it depends on your year of birth. To minimize the impact of the baby boomers, Congress decided to raise the full retirement age in the 1980s. The full retirement age is gradually increasing to age sixty-seven depending on your year of birth. The following is a chart from the Social Security Administration that shows the changes in full retirement age.

> To minimize the impact of the baby boomers, Congress decided to raise the full retirement age in the 1980s.

Full Retirement Age by Birth Year	
Year of Birth	**Full Retirement Age**
1937 or earlier	65
1938	65 and 2 months
1939	65 and 4 months
1940	65 and 6 months
1941	65 and 8 months
1942	65 and 10 months
1943–1954	66
1955	66 and 2 months
1956	66 and 4 months
1957	66 and 6 months
1958	66 and 8 months
1959	66 and 10 months
1960 and later	67

The age you are eligible for early retirement has not yet changed. You can retire as early as sixty-two, but that could be the next thing to change as the baby boomer crunch gets closer. There are also proposals in Congress to increase the full retirement age to seventy.

Benefits

Once you are eligible to collect benefits how much can you get? Of course, that will depend on how much you have earned during your career. The Office of the Chief Actuary for the Social Security Administration compiled these hypothetical benefits in 2001:

Benefits for Retirement Age			
Earnings	**Age 62**	**Age 65**	**Age 70**
Low Wage Earner ($13,711)	$541	$637	$776
Average Wage Earner ($30,470)	$892	$1,051	$1,293
High Wage Earner ($48,752)	$1,163	$1,365	$1,659
Maximum Wage Earner ($80,400)	$1,307	$1,538	$1,879

Low earnings are 45 percent of the national average wage index. Average earnings is equal to (or 100 percent of) that index. High earnings are 160 percent above that index. Maximum earnings is someone who earns the maximum amount taxed on the OASDI contributions and benefits base, which was $80,400 in 2001. The most recent national average wage index available for this chart was $30,469.84 based on 1999 income levels.

You can use this chart to estimate your Social Security benefit based on what you think your average wage will be over a thirty-five-year working history. Unlike private retirement plans, which base the final benefit on your highest three or five earning years or your earnings at retirement, Social Security is based on the thirty-five highest earning years.

Calculating Your Benefits

Social Security uses a complicated four-step process to determine your benefits. We'll explain the formula below, but luckily you don't have to do this yourself. You can use the online calculators at (*www.ssa.gov/planners/calculators.htm*) or call the Social Security

> You can use this chart to estimate your Social Security benefit based on what you think your average wage will be over a thirty-five-year working history.

Administration and ask them to send you an estimated statement of benefits based on your current earnings records.

You may never need to use this formula, but it's important to understand how benefits are calculated, especially when we discuss when to retire and whether or not to work in retirement. Here are the steps:

1. Social Security first determines how many years to use as a base. If you were born after 1928 and will retire after 1990, your base number is calculated using your thirty-five highest years of earnings. If you were born in 1928 or earlier, fewer years are used.

2. In this step, Social Security adjusts your earnings for wage inflation. This is called indexing. This step uses the national average earnings level to adjust your earnings based on inflation. Your age is also considered in this calculation.

3. Your average adjusted monthly earnings amount is then calculated based on the number of years determined in Step 1. If you were born after 1928 and don't have earnings in thirty-five different years, some years will have $0 used to figure this average amount. Women who stayed home to raise a family can be hurt by this step because they tend to have more $0 earning years, which will ultimately reduce their benefits.

4. Social Security multiplies your average adjusted monthly earnings using this formula set by law.

    Take 90 percent of your first $531 of average monthly earnings.

    Then, take 32 percent of the amount between $531 and $3,202.

    Finally, take 15 percent of everything you earn over $3,202 to give you your full retirement benefit amount. (If you start your benefits before you reach full retirement age, this amount will be reduced.) We'll talk about the impact of early retirement below.

As you can see from this formula, a low wage earner will get a much larger share of his or her earnings in Social Security benefits.

> In this step, Social Security adjusts your earnings for wage inflation.

The formula is weighted to ensure a safety net for low wage earners, yet when you look at the chart above and see that a low wage earner gets only $637 per month or $7,644 per year, you may wonder how anyone can live on that amount. Still, that Social Security benefit represents 56 percent of the average wages for the low earner.

Using the chart above of estimated Social Security benefits by age and earnings, you can calculate that average wage earners can expect 41 percent of their current earnings in Social Security benefits if they retire at their full retirement age. High earners can expect 34 percent, and people that earn the maximum amount upon which taxes are collected will get 23 percent or less depending on how high their income goes. Earnings above the maximum, which in 2002 is $84,900, is not taxed for Social Security. Medicare's taxes are still taken out though. There is no maximum for the amount of earnings that can be taxed for Medicare.

Spousal Benefits

As we've previously discussed, you are not the only one who can collect on your work record. Your spouse and children may be eligible for benefits as well. When you retire, your spouse can collect an additional 50 percent of the benefits for which you qualify. For example, if your monthly benefit is $1,000, your spouse would be able to collect $500, provided he or she has reached full retirement age even if he or she never worked.

If your spouse decides to retire and he or she has not yet reached full retirement age, there will be a reduction in benefits for your spouse. The reduction depends on your spouse's age:

> You are not the only one who can collect on your work record.

- If your spouse wants to collect at age sixty-four, the benefit amount would be about 46 percent of the working spouse's full benefit.
- At age sixty-three, the benefit amount would be about 42 percent of the full benefit.
- At age sixty-two, the benefit amount drops to just 37.5 of the full benefit amount.

If your spouse is eligible for benefits on his or her own work record, those benefits are paid first. Your spouse may still get some of your benefits because Social Security will make up the difference if the spouse's benefits total less than 50 percent of your benefits.

For example, let's say a man and his wife retired today at age sixty-five. He qualified for benefits as a maximum wage earner of $1660 in 2002. His wife did not work for many years while raising the children and then only went back part time as a low wage earner, so she qualified for only $660 in benefits. Fifty percent of $1660 is $830. His wife would receive a combination of benefits from her work history and his, totaling the higher amount.

Your spouse's benefits will increase if you die first. After your death, your spouse can collect 100 percent of your benefits. He or she can collect on your work record as early as age sixty, but at a reduced amount. If the worker was disabled, the widow's benefits can start as early as age fifty.

If the survivor begins collecting at age sixty, then he or she is entitled to 71½ percent of the deceased worker's benefit. The survivor of a disabled worker who begins collecting between the ages of fifty and fifty-nine will get 71½ percent of the deceased worker's benefit.

> Your spouse's benefits will increase if you die first.

Children's Benefits

Your children who are under age eighteen (or nineteen if still in high school) can also collect on your work record if you become disabled or die. A disabled child can collect benefits throughout their life, provided that disability started before age twenty-two. An eligible child can be your biological child, an adopted child, or a stepchild. A dependent grandchild may also qualify under certain circumstances.

Children can qualify to collect benefits on your record if they are:

- Unmarried;
- Under age eighteen; or
- Eighteen to nineteen years old and a full-time student (no higher than grade twelve); or
- Eighteen or older and disabled from a disability that started before age twenty-two.

Children can qualify for up to one-half of your full retirement amount if you are still alive and 75 percent after your death, but there is a limit that can be paid to the family as a whole. The total varies depending on the amount of your benefit and the number of family members who also qualify on your record, but is usually equal to about 150 to 180 percent of your retirement benefit.

Once the maximum is reached for a family, the eligible amount is divided equally among entitled dependents. The retired worker's benefit is not reduced, but the amount collected by each of the eligible dependents may be once the maximum is reached.

What If You Can't Work?

If you become disabled and cannot work, Social Security offers disability protection, but it is very difficult to collect. Social Security Disability Insurance (SSDI) is paid only if you cannot do the work you did before becoming disabled and cannot adjust to other work because of your disability. Your disability must be expected to last for at least a year or be expected to result in your death. There are no benefits for short-term disability.

As previously mentioned, you must have worked long enough to qualify for SSDI. If you haven't, Social Security also administers another program called Supplemental Security Income (SSI) for disabled people who haven't worked long enough. To qualify for SSI, you must meet a financial needs test as well as qualify for disability under Social Security's strict rules.

SSI also provides benefits to disabled people over age sixty-five who qualify based on financial need. It provides cash to meet basic needs for food, clothing, and shelter. Most SSI recipients also qualify for Medicaid and food stamps.

The average benefit paid in 2002 for a disabled worker is $815. For a disabled worker with a spouse and one or more children, the average benefit is $1,360. If the disabled worker and his family qualified for Supplemental Security Income (SSI), the payment for an individual is $545 per month in 2001 and $817 for a couple. To qualify for SSI, you must have very limited resources. The total allowed in 2002 is $2,000 for an individual and $3,000 for a couple.

> You must have worked long enough to qualify for SSDI.

As you can see from these numbers, even if you become severely disabled and can meet the strict disability qualification rules, you still may not have enough to live on. As with retirement, Social Security should definitely not be the only source you depend on if you become disabled. Private disability insurance or employer-sponsored disability insurance is a wise choice for protection of you and your family.

> There is a reduction in benefits if you choose to retire early.

Early or Late Retirement

Many people say they would like to retire early, but can they actually do it? The earliest age you can begin collecting Social Security is age sixty-two, but you certainly can retire earlier than that as long as you have the resources to live without a Social Security benefit check.

We have discussed that there is a reduction in benefits if you choose to retire early, but that is not the only thing that could impact what you ultimately collect from Social Security. Let's take another look at that complicated formula Social Security uses to calculate your benefits. Remember, it's based on your highest thirty-five years. If you stop working early and don't have thirty-five years of earnings, some of the years used to calculate your benefit may be $0 earning years. Also, most people's incomes increase as they get older. Your later earning years are likely to be your highest earning years and could have a significant impact on increasing your Social Security benefits.

You may be wondering how much of an impact early retirement will have on your benefits. As with full retirement, the year you were born becomes a key factor in this answer. If you are born before 1937, the calculation is much simpler. Your full retirement age is sixty-five. The reduction in benefits would be:

- 20 percent at age 62
- 13⅓ percent at age 63
- 6⅔ percent at age 64

For folks born after 1937, the amount of your payment is reduced a bit more to offset the later full retirement age, which, as we discussed earlier, is gradually increasing to age sixty-seven. While Congress didn't change the early retirement age, the reduction in benefits could be as high as 30 percent if you are born in 1960 or later.

The chart below from the Social Security Administration will let you calculate your reduction based on the year you were born. The first column shows the year you were born. The second column shows when you can retire at full benefit. The third column shows the number of months you will be retiring early, which equates to the number of months to be used if you retire at age sixty-two. The fourth column is the percent reduction for each month that you retire early. This column can be used to figure your reduction if you want to retire between age sixty-two and your full retirement age. The last column shows the total reduction if you retire at age sixty-two.

Social Security Full Retirement and Reductions* by Age				
Year of Birth	**Full Retirement Age**	**Age 62 Reduction Months**	**Monthly % Reduction**	**Total % Reduction**
1937 or earlier	65	36	.555	20.00
1938	65 and 2 months	38	.548	20.83
1939	65 and 4 months	40	.541	21.67
1940	65 and 6 months	42	.535	22.50
1941	65 and 8 months	44	.530	23.33
1942	65 and 10 months	46	.525	24.17
1943–1954	66	48	.520	25.00
1955	66 and 2 months	50	.516	25.84
1956	66 and 4 months	52	.512	26.66
1957	66 and 6 months	54	.509	27.50
1958	66 and 8 months	56	.505	28.33
1959	66 and 10 months	58	.502	29.17
1960 and later	67	60	.500	30.00

* Percentage monthly and total reductions are approximate due to rounding. The actual reductions are .555 or $5/9$ of 1 percent per month for the first 36 months and .416 or $5/12$ of 1 percent for subsequent months.

This chart may look very confusing. Just to be certain you know how to use it, let's work through an example together. We'll assume you were born in 1950. Looking at the chart you see that your retirement age is sixty-six. The number of months for early

How Long Can You Expect to Collect?

Currently, Social Security's actuaries project the average male aged sixty-five can expect to live until age seventy-eight. Women are expected to live longer, until age eighty-two. Social Security plans its number based on a man living thirteen years after retiring at age sixty-five and a woman living seventeen years. If your family history is one of long life, you'll be one of the lucky few who actually collects more on Social Security than is intended, but you could also be someone who doesn't make it to sixty-five and never gets to collect. For these folks, their survivors do get to collect on their record; so all contributions are not lost. In fact, family members can collect between 150 and 180 percent of your benefits as survivors.

retirement at age sixty-two is forty-eight. The reduction percent per month is .520.

To figure your reduced benefit amount:

$$48 \text{ months x } .520 =$$
$$24.96 \text{ percent—round to 25 percent on the chart}$$

If you want to retire at sixty-three, then you would use thirty-six months to calculate your reduction:

$$36 \text{ months x } .520 = 18.72$$

You may be wondering why this doesn't jump back to the .555 since it falls within the first thirty-six months' calculation above. The answer is that you are retiring later than the earliest age permitted and this more complicated formula allows you to benefit somewhat from retiring one year later.

Actuaries, who are mathematicians that analyze the financial consequences of risk, developed all these complicated figures. Using mathematics, statistics, and financial theory, Social Security's actuaries try to come up with a number that will give the early, on-time, and late retirees equal benefits provided they all live to the same age. Early retirees who live longer than the actuaries expect will actually collect more than the people who retired at full retirement age. But, an early retiree who dies before expected will collect less.

If you decide you want to continue to work after you reach full retirement age, these same calculations can help you get more in benefits. Each year that you delay retirement increases your Social Security benefit until you reach age seventy. At that point your benefits have been increased the most they will ever be and it's time to collect. You gain nothing by putting if off any longer. If you found your retirement gap is too large and you know you won't have the resources, retiring later can help you fill that gap.

As with other Social Security benefit calculations, the year you were born impacts the amount your benefits can increase, but unlike other charts, you will see that you benefit more if you are born later.

Increase for Delayed Retirement

Year of Birth	Yearly Rate of Increase	Monthly Rate of Increase
1930	4.5%	$3/8$ of 1%
1931–1932	5.0%	$5/12$ of 1%
1933–1934	5.5%	$11/24$ of 1%
1935–1936	6.0%	$1/2$ of 1%
1937–1938	6.5%	$13/24$ of 1%
1939–1940	7.0%	$7/12$ of 1%
1941–1942	7.5%	$5/8$ of 1%
1943 or later	8.0%	$2/3$ of 1%

Persons born on January 1 of any year should refer to the rate of increase for the previous year.

Work Rules

If you find that after you retire you need to go back to work, new rules make that decision much easier. Prior to 2000, you could lose benefits if you went back to work after you started collecting Social Security. Now that penalty only impacts early retirees.

When Social Security was enacted in 1935, there was a deliberate decision made to penalize people who went back to work. Congress incorporated the Retirement Earnings Test (RET) because it believed at the time that once someone started collecting Social Security they should be fully retired. The RET took many forms over the years, but its primary purpose was to reduce benefits if a retiree started working again.

People between the ages of sixty-two and the year they reach their normal retirement age can earn $10,680 before RET rules come into play. Under the rules today, the Social Security Administration withholds $1 of benefits for every $2 of earnings in excess of this earnings threshold for younger retirees. In the year that they reach their normal retirement age, retirees are allowed to earn $30,000 and only $1 of every $3 will be withheld. After 2002, these thresholds will be adjusted using a formula based on the national wage index. If this all seems very confusing to you, here is a chart from the Social

Working Again While Collecting

The Senior Citizens Freedom to Work Act of 2000, passed in April 2000, lets seniors work after reaching full retirement age without risking a reduction in benefits. President Clinton said when he signed the bill into law, "Today, one in four Americans between 65 and 69 has at least a part-time job. Eighty percent of the baby boomers say they intend to keep working past age 65." In the most recent data available before the passage of the bill in 2000, 960,000 beneficiaries were affected by the earnings penalty in 1995. In this group, 806,000 were sixty-five or older. They lost a total of $4.1 billion in benefits because of the earnings rules.

Security Administration that helps you estimate the impact of going back to work:

For People Under Age 64		
If Your Monthly Social Security Benefit Is	and You Earn	You Will Receive Yearly Benefits of
$500	$10,680 or less	$6,000
$500	$15,000	$3,840
$700	$10,680 or less	$8,400
$700	$15,000	$6,240
$700	$20,000	$3,740
$900	$10,680 or less	$10,800
$900	$15,000	$8,640
$900	$20,000	$6,140

> Going back to work can also help you increase your benefits, if you had a lot of years of low or no earnings.

The only income at risk of affecting your benefits is earned income. Only wages earned by working for someone else or self-employment income counts toward Social Security's earnings limits for retirees. If you are self-employed, the gross earnings are not considered. Only the net earnings are used in the RET calculations. Nonwork income doesn't count, which includes government or military benefits, investment earnings, interest, pensions, annuities, and capital gains.

Going back to work can also help you increase your benefits, if you had a lot of years of low or no earnings. Each year that you work while collecting benefits, the earnings are added to your work record. Sometimes those additional earnings can mean that your monthly benefit amount will increase. Again, this goes back to the average of thirty-five years of work records. If you earn $15,000 per year working part time in retirement and had some $0 earnings years, the new earnings will replace the low earning years. Social Security automatically recalculates your benefit level if you work after you have started collecting benefits. Even if you lose some benefits because of the RET, you may still end up gaining because you could ultimately increase benefits that can be collected for another twenty or thirty years in retirement.

Social Security Trends and Revisions

Now that we know what the benefits are, I'm sure you are even more curious about whether you will ever be able to collect them. There is no doubt that the Social Security and Medicare trust funds are running out of money. You will find disagreement, however, about how quickly that will happen and what needs to be done to fix the problem.

You know the culprit—the influx of baby boomers into the retirement system. They will be a huge drain on Social Security and Medicare resources, while at the same time the number of people working to help foot the bill will be dropping. Remember, we discussed earlier that 85 percent of current taxes are used to pay benefits. If fewer people are paying taxes to cover those benefits, obviously there is going to be a shortfall.

The Social Security trustees expect that the first year outlays in benefits will exceed income for the program is 2020. They project that over $1.7 trillion will be paid into Social Security and Medicare primarily through taxes and $1.99 trillion will have to be paid out to cover expenses. That year the shortfall will be $238 billion, which will have to be covered by the trust funds, general tax revenues, or a reduction in benefits if there isn't some kind of fix before that time.

After that, the shortfall will increase each year. It is expected to be $3.8 trillion by 2050 and $18.6 trillion by 2075, if no fix is found. These figures include estimates for both Social Security and Medicare. If you consider only Social Security, the situation is somewhat better. The trustees estimate that by using the trust funds to supplement benefit outlays they will be able to pay full benefits until 2038 without a fix.

What will this mean to you? Without a fix, after the trust funds are exhausted in 2038, the trustees estimate that payroll taxes will only be able to cover about 73 percent of Social Security's costs. By 2075 that number drops to 67 percent if there isn't a fix. While there is no doubt that a fix is needed, you can see that the crisis is still years away and there is time to put a fix in place without drastic

Blaming Baby Boomers

Why are baby boomers causing such a huge mess? The number of people receiving benefits will rise steeply between 2010 and 2030. Historically, there have been 3.6 workers paying into Social Security for every retiree. This number has been gradually decreasing and in 2000 there were 3.4 workers for every retiree. By 2075, the trustees expect there to be only 1.9 workers per retiree.

measures. There are a number of possible fixes now under consideration in Congress. These include:

1. Benefit Reductions—Few recommend major benefit reductions. The range for reductions is between 10 and 40 percent. Those recommending higher reductions expect to offset them with personal accounts using the privatization of Social Security.
2. Tax Increases—The most common measures being considered include raising the Social Security tax by one percent or raising the salary level on which taxes are collected.
3. COLA Change—Some suggest a reduction in Cost of Living Adjustments.
4. Stock Investment—Some proposals suggest that investing in stocks as well as bonds could make up a good part of the shortfall.
5. Privatization—This proposal is the most controversial. Basically, the idea is to put some portion of your Social Security tax payment into a personal account. Some plans suggest it should be "carved-out" of current tax payments while others suggest that it should be in addition to current tax payments.

> Privatization has polarized the entire debate about fixing Social Security.

Privatization has polarized the entire debate about fixing Social Security. Proponents say it will give people more control over their retirement future and a better chance to grow their nest eggs. Opponents fear that it will increase the risks that people will not have enough for retirement and destroy the safety net Social Security provides.

One key question to be answered before any of this can be put in place is how will it be financed, since 85 percent of current taxes are used to pay current benefits. Many believe privatization will only worsen the shortfall for the baby boomer population.

Other concerns are raised about the expenses that will be incurred trying to set up millions of small private accounts and administering those accounts. Today Social Security administers its program for a cost of about 2 percent of its income. Privately administered pension system costs range from 10 to 40 percent. Will administration costs eat up any profits made in these small accounts? No one can answer this question until something is on the drawing board.

President George W. Bush's Social Security Commission, which was a sixteen-member panel of privatization supporters, could not come up with a plan to fix Social Security using privatization. Instead they came up with three possible alternatives. Since 2002 is an election year, it is doubtful there will be any serious consideration of a fix to Social Security until the next Congress opens its doors in 2003. As you plan your retirement, watch these changes closely and quickly adjust any retirement plan you put in place as soon as some real details about Social Security's future are known.

Quickly adjust any retirement plan you put in place as soon as some real details about Social Security's future are known.

For more information on this topic, visit our Web site at www.businesstown.com

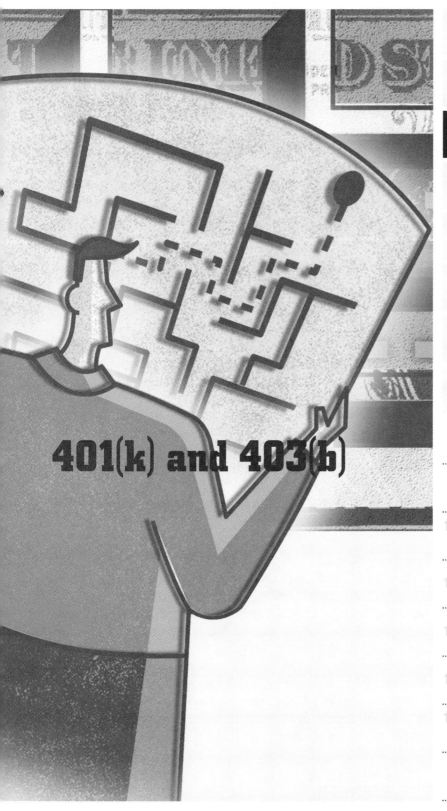

401(k) and 403(b)

What They Are

401(k) or 403(b) may sound like gibberish to you, but if you participate in one of these retirement plans, it is probably the most important thing you are doing to get ready for retirement. In fact, for many people it's the only type of employer-sponsored retirement plan available at their workplace because traditional pension programs are rapidly disappearing from the employee benefits landscape.

At the end of 2000, American workers held over $1.8 trillion in over 42 million 401(k) accounts, according to the Employee Benefit Research Institute (EBRI). While the plans are very popular, many participants do not fully understand how they work and how much responsibility is on their shoulders to be certain they will have enough for retirement.

The names 401(k) and 403(b) actually represent parts of the tax code under which these programs were established. The 401(k) is offered by for-profit companies and the 403(b) is offered by non-profit organizations. In fact, if you work for a nonprofit you may not even realize you are part of a 403(b) because they tend to call them Tax-Sheltered Annuities (TSAs), Tax-Deferred Annuities (TDAs), or savings plans. For those of you who work for the state government, your plan may be similar to the 403(b), but called a Section 457. We'll be taking a closer look at government pensions in Chapter 12.

How They Work

The 401(k) and 403(b) retirement plans are also known as salary reduction plans. How do they work? Your salary is reduced by a percentage or dollar amount that you designate. The amount is deposited tax-deferred in a pension account in your name and it grows tax-free until retirement. Many employers match some portion of your contribution. A typical match is 50 percent of the first 6 percent contributed, but that varies greatly by company.

You may also find that your employer will begin offering a new type of 401(k), dubbed the Roth 401(k), starting in 2005. For these accounts, the money will be deposited after taxes have been taken

> Many participants do not fully understand how they work and how much responsibility is on their shoulders to be certain they will have enough for retirement.

out, but like the Roth IRA, the money will not be taxed at retirement. How these will work is still unknown, but watch for details at your company.

Defined-Contribution versus Defined-Benefit Plans

You may also hear these programs described as defined-contribution plans. They differ greatly from defined-benefit plans, which is the more traditional kind of employer-sponsored retirement plan. Defined-contribution plans specify how much the employee and employer will contribute to the plan, while defined-benefit plans specify the guaranteed benefit the employee can expect at retirement. How much you can expect to receive from a defined-contribution plan is based on how much you and your employer put in and how well you manage those investments. Ultimately, the amount you will be able to draw at retirement is based on the market value of the assets you hold in your account when you retire. You may need to review and adjust the monthly amount taken at retirement if the asset values change dramatically because of market conditions. Without careful management in retirement, you could actually end up running out of money.

For defined-benefit plans, your monthly payout is determined at the time you retire. We'll discuss these formulas in greater detail in Chapter 11. The employer has the responsibility to manage the investments of a defined-benefit plan, putting the onus on the employer to be sure there will be enough to pay you when you reach retirement.

Balancing Risk

In a defined-contribution plan, you have more control over how the money is invested but you also take more risk. If your investment choices are not sound, you may not have enough to receive the benefits you need at retirement. If you've followed the collapse of Enron, you probably heard stories about their employees losing over $850 million in their retirement savings because too much of their 401(k) assets were invested in company stock.

> For defined-benefit plans, your monthly payout is determined at the time you retire.

Many companies make their matching contributions using company stock and limit the ability of their employees to switch to other investments. Enron employees had to wait until the age of fifty to shift Enron stock held in their 401(k) plans. While Congress limited the amount a company could use to fund its defined-benefits plan to 10 percent, a similar rule does not protect 401(k) assets. The Enron fiasco could spur new legislation in Congress to limit the amount of company stock that can be held in defined-contribution plans. There also are likely to be provisions that require companies to allow employees to convert company stock to other investment opportunities. Financial advisors recommend that no more than 15 percent of your retirement assets be held in the stock of the company for which you work.

Your work life and current income is dependent on the company that employs you. You don't need to have your retirement life fully dependent on the success of that company as well. Investing for retirement is all about balancing risk and not putting all your eggs in one basket.

Let's take a look at how much you and your employer can contribute.

> Your work life and current income is dependent on the company that employs you.

Employer and Employee Contributions

The government caps the total amount that you and your employer can contribute on a pre-tax basis. The tax bill passed in May 2001 started the move toward a major increase in these plans to a new maximum of $15,000 by 2006. Prior to that time, the maximum was $10,500. For a 401(k), you and your employer combined can contribute up to 15 percent of your salary with a maximum of $11,000 in 2002. This will increase by $1,000 per year until it reaches a new maximum of $15,000 in 2006. After that year, the maximum will be indexed to inflation. For a 403(b), the caps are the same, but you and your employer can contribute up to 20 percent of your salary.

If you are over fifty, you will also be able to make catch-up contributions. Once you have made your maximum allowable pre-tax contribution, you will be able to add additional money. In 2002, you can put in an additional $1,000. That amount will increase by $1,000 a year until it reaches a maximum of $5,000 additional in 2006. After that point the catch-up contribution amount will be indexed for inflation. Employers can match these contributions, but are not required to do so.

How Employer Matching Works

How does the employer matching work? That varies by company. Some companies only provide the 401(k) as a way for employees to save tax-deferred, but the companies themselves don't contribute at all. The most common practice is to match between 50 cents to a dollar of every dollar you invest up to about 5 or 6 percent of your salary. It's best to contribute at least the amount needed to get the full employer match so that you don't leave any money on the table.

This benefit is one of the best deals in town. The money from both you and your employer is deposited tax-deferred and grows tax-deferred until retirement. If you don't contribute enough to get the full match, it's almost like taking a voluntary salary cut. The money is yours, but you must take the first step. We'll take a closer look at the tax issues later in this chapter.

Additional Contributions

Tax law also allows contributions above those that can be added before taxes. Annual additional money can be contributed to defined-contribution plans after taxes have been taken out of the money. The total amount that can be put into these types of plans is capped at $40,000, which will be indexed to inflation.

We'll now look at how to allocate your contributions to be certain you'll have the best chance to meet your retirement goals.

How to Invest Your Contributions

Broadening employee investment choices is one of key controversies surrounding these plans. As more employees are solely dependent on these salary reduction plans for their retirement nest egg, there is a

How People Build Their Nest Eggs

You *can* build a sizeable nest egg. EBRI found that workers in their sixties with at least thirty years of job tenure at their current employer have an average 401(k) account balance of $198,595. Workers in their forties with more than twenty years of tenure at their current employer have an average 401(k) account balance of about $96,250. EBRI found that 401(k) participants contributed an average of 6.8 percent of their income on a before-tax basis. Only about 21 percent of participants set aside more than 10 percent of their salaries and about 61 percent contributed more than 5 percent.

> If you work for a nonprofit, then your employer-sponsored retirement plan option is called the 403(b).

stronger push for more and better investment options. All salary reduction plans are employee-directed, but the employers designate the investment options.

In a for-profit company, this usually includes company stock, a few mutual funds, a few bond funds, and a cash investment. Many times the choices are made for reasons that do not necessarily have the employees' best interest in mind, but provide the company with the lowest costs of operating the pension plan or for some other business partnership reason. Frequently, the employer match is in the stock of the company. Many financial advisors will recommend that you shift a majority of those funds away from company stock to keep a good asset allocation balance.

If you work for a nonprofit, then your employer-sponsored retirement plan option is called the 403(b). The largest manager of 403(b) assets is TIAA-CREF (*www.tiaa-cref.org*), which manages funds for many colleges, universities, and nonprofit educational institutions. Frequently, nonprofits try to save money on administrative costs and use insurance companies as their 403(b) administrators. Many times this results in high costs for the employees and poor investment choices. If you have more than one 403(b) provider to choose from, be sure you carefully compare costs of the plans. Fees can eat up a good part of your investment gains.

Management fees and investment alternatives are constantly controversial in the 401(k) and 403(b) retirement maze. Tim Younkin, an advocate for these retirement plans, offers an excellent Web site that tracks all the current issues at *www.timyounkin.com*.

Allocating Funds

We've talked about how you contribute to these plans through an automatic reduction in your salary, but do you know how you allocated that money? You made that choice when you signed up for the plans by filling out a form. On this form you allocated a percentage of these funds among various investment alternatives offered by your employer.

Do you remember the instructions you gave your employer? Have you kept an eye on the allocation when you receive periodic reports from the retirement plan administrator? Are you pleased with how your 401(k) or 403(b) is performing? It is important for you to know the answers to these questions.

If you are not sure, stop reading, and take a look at your most recent statement. You should be able to quickly find a summary of how your portfolio is performing, as well as a breakdown of how new deposits are being allocated among investment alternatives. In addition to how your selections are doing, you should also get a list of how the other plan investment alternatives are performing. Compare the alternatives, but don't jump to better performing ones automatically. Look at one-, three-, five-, and ten-year performance levels. Sometimes the hottest fund in the current year will have a much worse long-term record. Also, consider fund types and be sure you have a good balance.

Investment Reallocation

Do you still think you have made the best choices? If not, talk with your plan administrator about shifting your contribution allocation. You can also shift the funds already in the plan into other investment options. This is called investment reallocation. A good practice is to review your portfolio annually and consider possible investment reallocation.

What is the best asset allocation? That all depends on the number of years you have before retirement. If you are in your twenties or thirties, you have a long way to go before needing the funds. At this stage of life you can afford to take more risks because you have more time to recover from a drop in the stock market. If you are in your fifties and sixties, you are much closer to retirement and therefore should be careful about the risks you take.

It is generally believed that for younger employees an allocation of 70 percent to 80 percent in stock or stock funds and 20 percent to 30 percent in bonds or money market funds is a good mix that will build a solid portfolio for the future. As you get closer to retirement—about five to ten years prior to it—that allocation should be gradually shifted to more bonds and money market funds when the market conditions are right for reallocating assets.

Remember the old adage, "Buy low, sell high." As you look to reallocate your portfolio in your employer-sponsored retirement plan,

Allocating Your Retirement Savings

While allocations vary by age, EBRI found on average that 51 percent of total plan balances are invested in equity funds, 19 percent in company stock, 8 percent in balanced funds, and the remainder in bond or money market funds for the year-end 2000. Participants in 401(k) plans where company stock or guaranteed investment contracts (GICs) are not offered tend to have the highest allocations in equity funds. When company stock is offered, participants tend to have substantially lower allocations to all other investment options, especially equity funds. This became painfully obvious when Enron's 401(k) plan losses hit the news. Reports from many companies showed that employees were investing between 30 and 50 percent or more of their retirement savings in their company stock, throwing all the rules of proper asset allocation out the window.

be certain to sell assets at one of their highs and not when that type of asset is generally at a low. That is why you need to give yourself five to ten years to reallocate your portfolio. That way, you are not forced to sell an asset that is in a down phase because you need the money; you can wait instead for its recovery.

Most planners believe that in retirement there should still be some growth stocks in your portfolio, since people are often living twenty years or more in retirement. You don't want to run out of money. A good allocation in retirement actually reverses the allocation percentages for folks in their twenties and thirties: 20 percent to 30 percent in stocks or stock funds and 70 percent to 80 percent in bonds, bond funds, or money market funds. We'll take a much closer look at all this in Chapter 16. Now let's move on to the tax issues impacting your 401(k)s and 403(b)s.

Income-Tax Impacts

The reduction in the amount you have to pay in taxes is one key reason employees should jump at the chance to shelter their money in these retirement plans. Why pay taxes before you have to do so, unless you are certain your tax rate is higher now than it will be in retirement? Can anyone be certain what tax rates will be in the future?

As previously discussed, money deposited in a defined-contribution plan is deposited tax-deferred. For example, if you make a $1,000 contribution and are in a 27 percent tax bracket, it actually costs you $730 out of pocket. Your employer match is added with no tax obligation on your part and grows tax-free until retirement as well. Remember the tax-deferred investing chart in Chapter 5? You can quickly see the benefits of tax-deferred investing if you review that chart.

On-Time Withdrawal

You can see how your money grows much faster when taxes do not eat away at your earnings. Unfortunately, you don't escape taxes completely. At the time you withdraw the funds, you will be taxed at your current income rate. You will most likely be in the same tax

> Can anyone be certain what tax rates will be in the future?

bracket or possibly at a lower tax bracket at the time of retirement, so this should add to the benefits of pre-tax investing as well.

You may qualify for a Saver's Tax Credit up to $1,000 (50 percent of $2,000 contributions) on your 401(k) or 403(b) contributions during tax years 2002 through 2006. To qualify, your adjusted gross household income (AGI) cannot exceed $50,000 if married filing jointly, $37,500 if head of household, or $25,000 if single or married filing separately. The amount of the credit depends on the amount of qualifying contributions and your AGI. This credit is in addition to the deduction or exclusion allowed for the contribution.

Early Withdrawal

If you need the money before retirement, you may have some penalties and interest to pay. Withdrawals before the age of 59½ may incur a 10 percent penalty. In addition to this penalty, you will have to pay taxes at your current tax rate. This can eat up about 30 to 40 percent of the withdrawal. Your company is required by law to take a 20 percent tax withholding from the money you withdraw if the check is made out to you rather than to a trustee in another qualified retirement plan, such as an IRA.

> If you do decide to take out the money, you will have to show that the withdrawal meets certain hardship rules.

Even with these stiff penalties in place, it still is not easy to get your money, which is a good thing because you will be doing serious damage to your retirement goals. If you do decide to take out the money, you will have to show that the withdrawal meets certain hardship rules. Hardship situations can include:

- Payment of medical expenses
- Money to avoid eviction or foreclosure on your principal residence
- Payment of college tuition
- Money to cover funeral expenses for a family member

Some companies may allow hardship withdrawal for other reasons. You will have to document your reasons for needing the money and show that you have no other assets upon which you can draw.

For many companies, penalties don't end when the money is withdrawn. You may be prohibited from contributing to your plan for twelve months after making a hardship withdrawal. Not only do you lose the benefits of tax-deferred growth on your money, you could lose the company matching funds as well. Tapping your 401(k) is one of the most financially destructive things you can do to your retirement plan.

Borrowing from Your 401(k)

Sometimes you may find you need money and regret the amount you have stashed away in your 401(k). You can avoid the stiff penalties of withdrawing the money by borrowing from your 401(k) account. Approximately 80 percent of participants in a 401(k) do have the option of borrowing against their funds, but only 16 percent of them took advantage of that option in 2000. The amount you can borrow and the cost of that loan is set by your company and the custodian of the fund. Typically it is 50 percent of your vested funds.

Most financial advisors recommend that a loan against your retirement assets be taken only as a last resort. The danger of borrowing against these funds is that if you decide to leave the job or are fired, you must repay the loan in full immediately. If you are unable to do so, which would most likely be the case in a situation of lost employment, you will then be subject to the substantial tax penalties just discussed on the funds you could not repay. The money is treated as an early withdrawal from a retirement fund and can cost you a 10 percent penalty plus any taxes due on the money. As was pointed out earlier, this can eat up 30 to 40 percent of your retirement savings. If you do leave a job, all is not lost. There are ways to get access to the money. We'll now take a look at how that works.

Rules for Vesting, Withdrawals, and Portability

We've talked a lot about the benefits of the employer match, but in most cases it does come with strings attached. For one thing, most employers impose what is called a vesting period. You must work

> Most financial advisors recommend that a loan against your retirement assets be taken only as a last resort.

for a company for a certain number of years before the money is entirely yours.

The most common vesting period is five years at the rate of 20 percent per year. During that time, a certain amount vests each year, which means it will go with you if you leave the company prior to retirement. For example, if your money vests at the rate of 20 percent per year and you leave after three years, then 60 percent of the company match will be yours to take with you when you change jobs. The remaining 40 percent reverts back to the company. All the money that you contributed and the earnings on that money are yours as well. Employers can impose a two-year waiting period before vesting its contributions to your 401(k).

If you do decide to look for a new job, don't forget to consider your retirement benefits. When you receive that next job offer, be certain to consider your unvested funds that are building in your 401(k). The new salary may sound great, but as you consider your new job opportunity think about what you may be losing in your retirement account before accepting that offer, especially if you are close to being fully vested in your retirement benefits. Sometimes waiting a year before switching can make a huge difference in how much you can take with you.

Withdrawals and Portability

If you leave the job before retirement, the most common way to get the funds is to roll them over into an individual IRA. That way you can avoid all taxes. If you know where your next job will be and you like the 401(k) options offered by the new company, sometimes you can take the alternative of rolling them into the new 401(k) or 403(b), whichever is appropriate. Whether this is an option will need to be discussed with both your new and old employer.

Distribution options vary by company. Some even require that you leave the funds within the company's plan until retirement. Other companies will insist that you take the funds with you, especially if the amount in your 401(k) is below $5,000. The company has no legal obligation to maintain an account below that amount.

> Distribution options vary by company.

If you do change jobs, you do not have to pay the taxes all at once, as long as you don't just withdraw the money in a lump sum when you leave the company, whether it is for retirement or a new job.

Payout Options

We'll now take a quick look at what happens to your retirement plans when you are ready to retire. We'll be covering these issues in much greater detail in Chapters 20 and 21. You'll find more information there about the tax ramifications of withdrawals and how to best structure your payouts to be sure you'll have enough throughout retirement.

At the time of retirement you have two key options for payout: lump sum or annuity. If you choose the lump sum, you can take it as a cash payment or as an IRA rollover. For tax purposes, the IRA rollover will probably be your best choice or you'll be hit with a tremendous tax bill that year.

The choice can be scary because once you've committed yourself to a decision there is no way to change your mind. Be certain you understand your payout options. If you are unsure, do not hesitate to seek professional help from a tax or estate planner to avoid any costly mistakes and to be certain that the choice you are making will give you the best chance of having enough money to live on throughout your retirement.

We've explored the major provisions of employer-sponsored retirement plans. Now we'll look at what the future may be for these plans. They are, and probably always will be, a moving target.

Plan Trends and Your Rights

The two biggest changes now in the pipeline for defined-contribution plans are rules for providing employees with financial advisors for their plans and an expected review of the amount of stock that can be held in a 401(k). Both of these changes are in response to weaknesses in the current tax laws that established these plans.

As previously mentioned, the Enron Corporation fiasco is likely to lead to new legislation that will better protect employees. Enron,

> Be certain you understand your payout options.

like many corporations, makes its matching contributions using company stock. Employees could not convert this to another investment until they reached the age of fifty, which resulted in huge losses of retirement savings estimated to top $850 million. This problem was compounded by the fact that Enron changed its retirement plan advisor right in the middle of the greatest loss of its stock value, which made it impossible for employees to sell their Enron stock for about a three-week period. Some employees were hit even harder because they had invested all their retirement assets in Enron stock, not only the company matching funds.

Independent Financial Advisors

Learning how to balance 401(k) plans properly is critical for employees. Under new rules from the U.S. Department of Labor, companies will be able to start offering advice and management for 401(k) plans using independent financial advisors. The first company to get approval was SunAmerica in 2001, which hired the investment management unit of American International Group, Ibbotson Associates of Chicago, to provide these services to its employees.

Prior to this ruling, interpretations of the Employee Retirement Security Income Act (ERISA), which created 401(k) accounts, prohibited investment companies who administer employees' retirement accounts from doing any more than coming up with recommendations that investors could either follow or not. The new rules, issued on December 14, 2001, in a Labor Department advisory opinion, would allow mutual fund companies, brokerage firms, and insurers to hire an independent financial advisor to offer investment advice and manage retirement account assets.

For companies to take advantage of this decision, the key to its approval will be the strict independence of the investment advisor, the Labor Department ruled. The advisor would be considered independent as long as the investment company was fully informed about the plan, the investment advice was developed and given exclusively by the advisor, and the advisor acted solely in the interests of the account holders.

Company Stock in Retirement Savings

Employees usually hold an average of 33 percent of their 401(k) in company stock, according to industry analysts. Congress put a 10 percent limit on company stock in traditional defined-benefit pension plans back in 1974, but corporations blocked a similar cap for defined-contribution plans and have already lined up against any plans to change that after the Enron scandal. Congress will most likely review these laws to protect employee plans in the future and require companies to give employees more options to diversify their 401(k) holdings. Provisions that mandate employees hold onto company stock until at least the age of fifty will probably be among the first restrictions to fall.

Another key factor in the Enron debacle was the fact that employees were denied access to their accounts for a number of weeks during the worst of the stock price drop so they couldn't rebalance their plans even if they wanted to do so. Evidence of similar lockouts were shown as well at other companies during severe stock shocks.

> The plan put together by Ibbotson for SunAmerica will include a database of information on investors in 401(k) plans managed by SunAmerica.

The plan put together by Ibbotson for SunAmerica, which received the Labor Department's blessing, will include a database of information on investors in 401(k) plans managed by SunAmerica. This information will be put into the advisor's computerized investment model and allocations between stocks, bonds, and other assets would be proposed based on certain risk parameters. The portfolio allocation would be rebalanced periodically to adjust risk based on market changes or other factors. The new plan would allow workers to opt out and continue making their own investment decisions if they want. Other employers will likely follow suit now that one company has received approval, so keep your eyes and ears open at work.

Know Your Rights

Now that you understand how important these plans are to your future, we'll take a quick look at what your rights are under current law.

With regard to 401(k) and 403(b) plans, there are a number of items your employer must provide:

1. Within ninety days of your eligibility for participating in the plan, your employer must provide you with a Summary Plan Description, which spells out the key provisions of the plan written in a way that you can understand—not developed with a bunch of unintelligible legal language.
2. Annually, your employer must provide you with a Summary Annual Report free of charge that gives you information about the plan's financial status and a summary of the yearly report filed with the federal government. If you want to see the full government report, your employer must provide you with a copy for free.
3. You can submit a written request for an Individual Benefit Statement that includes a description of the benefits earned to date and how much of your benefits are vested. Most companies provide this statement automatically without your needing to request it specifically.

Warning Signs for Employer Plans

The DOL also published a list of warning signs that might indicate a problem with your employer-sponsored plan. Here are the signs:

1. Your 401(k) or individual account statement is consistently late or comes at irregular intervals.
2. Your account balance does not appear to be accurate.
3. Your employer failed to transmit your contribution to the plan on a timely basis.
4. You notice a significant drop in account balance that cannot be explained by normal market ups and downs.
5. Your 401(k) or individual account statement shows your contribution from your paycheck was not made.
6. Investments listed on your statement are not what you authorized.
7. Former employees are having trouble getting their benefits paid on time or in the correct amounts.
8. You notice unusual transactions, such as a loan to the employer, a corporate officer, or one of the plan trustees.
9. You find there are frequent and unexplained changes in investment managers or consultants.
10. Your employer has recently experienced severe financial difficulty.

If any of these things are happening with your plan, there are three government entities that could be called in to investigate: the Department of Labor, the Internal Revenue Service, and the Department of Justice. If you have questions about your plans, you can contact a local DOL office. Check your local phone book or use this interactive tool (*www.dol.gov/dol/location.htm*) to find the DOL office nearest you.

4. You do have the right to ask for a full plan document, which is filled with legal documentation, but your employer is permitted to charge a "reasonable" fee to provide it.
5. Another complicated legal document that you have the right to request is the Pension Trust Document. This document identifies the trustees of the plan who are financially responsible for the investment alternatives chosen. Like the full plan document, the employer has the right to charge you a "reasonable" fee to provide it.

Another key area of concern are the excessive fees imposed on employee plans. After an extensive study by the Department of Labor (DOL) in 1998, it was shown that excessive fees were widespread.

The report concluded that employers were not doing enough to live up to their fiduciary responsibilities to limit employee costs under ERISA rules governing defined contribution retirement plans. To help inform the public about these problems, the Labor Department published an excellent brochure, "Protect Your Pension." Some key questions that DOL recommends you ask include:

1. Do you have all available documentation about the investment choices under your plan and the fees charged to your plan?
2. What types of investment education are available under your plan?
3. If administrative services are paid separately from investment management fees, are they paid for by the plan, your employer, or are they shared?
4. Do any of the investment options under your plan include sales charges, such as loads or commissions?
5. Do any of the investment options under your plan include other fees, such as 12b-1 fees (marketing costs), insurance charges, or surrender fees?

If you want to learn more about participants' rights, you can visit the Department of Labor's Web site at *www.dol.gov/dol/topic/ retirement/participantrights.htm*.

Participation Excuses

With all the good reasons stated in this chapter for participating in employer-sponsored retirement plans, you may be asking why isn't everyone participating? The EBRI found in their study that the primary reason someone chooses not to participate is the lack of funds to do so.

Many lower-income workers say they don't have the extra money to save and that they will count on other resources at retirement. Most of these workers anticipate that they will have to work at least part time in retirement. Non-participating employees say they would participate in their company-sponsored plan if the employer matching contribution were increased or if they had higher salaries.

The EBRI found in their study that the primary reason someone chooses not to participate is the lack of funds to do so.

EBRI found the typical participant in an employer-sponsored plan is middle-aged, college-educated, and has a median household income of $50,000. About 60 percent of these participants had no investments in stocks, bonds, mutual funds, or annuities other than their company-sponsored plans. About 10 percent of these participants have no savings in addition to these plans. These statistics show clearly that without the benefit of these employer-sponsored plans, many more people would enter retirement with little more than their Social Security benefit.

Are you participating? If not, what are your excuses?

For more information on this topic, visit our Web site at www.businesstown.com

Small Business and
Self-Employed Plans

Small Businesses with Retirement Plans

In today's economy, you have a better than 50 percent chance of working for a small business. Small businesses, which we will define as companies with five to 100 employees, comprise more than 99 percent of all employers. If you do you work for a small business, you have less than a 50 percent chance that you are covered by an employer-sponsored retirement plan. That's dramatically lower than people who work for companies with more than 100 employees. Almost 80 percent of the full-time employees of these larger companies have retirement benefits.

The 2001 U.S. Bureau of Labor Statistics' Employee Benefits Survey (SERS) found that only 46 percent of full-time workers in small businesses had retirement coverage. The primary reasons small businesses give for not offering retirement benefits, according to the SERS survey, are that their revenue streams are uncertain, their employees prefer cash or other nonretirement benefits, or that they have a high turnover workforce with a high proportion of part-time and seasonal workers.

Companies that sponsor plans found the benefits to be significant. Eighty-five percent of retirement-plan sponsors report that the plan has an impact on their ability to hire and retain good employees. The same percentage of companies report that having a plan has an impact on employee attitude and performance. Even though small businesses that have plans find very positive responses to the plans, the SERS survey concluded that some nonsponsors may not find these plans as much as a motivator if their employees tend to be younger with less formal education and who change jobs frequently.

In fact, many nonsponsors reported that they do not feel they are at a competitive disadvantage for not offering a plan, but say that motivators for them to start one could include incentives that would increase the affordability of offering a plan:

- Increase in business profits
- Low administrative costs
- Business tax credits for starting a plan

The new tax law also gave small businesses additional incentives for starting and maintaining a retirement plan. A small business can claim a credit for 50 percent of the first $1,000 of administrative and retirement-education expenses for each of the first three plan years for a tax-qualified plan, a SIMPLE IRA, or a SEP-IRA. To qualify, they must have no more than 100 employees with compensation in excess of $5,000 in the preceding year and they must have at least one non-highly compensated employee.

Now that we know in what types of small businesses you are more likely to find retirement plans, we'll take a look at the type of retirement plans small businesses can offer.

Types of Small Business Plans

The 401(k) is still the most popular plan and 58 percent of all small businesses in 2001 offered that type of plan. Size is a key factor though. While 78 percent of small businesses with twenty-one to 100 employees offered 401(k)s, small firms were more likely to offer something else. Simplified Employee Pension (SEP) plans are more likely to be offered by companies with five to twenty employees and by companies with gross revenues below $2 million. Savings Incentive Match Plans for Employees (SIMPLE) are more likely to be offered by companies that have offered a retirement plan for less than ten years. If the small business employer is also a nonprofit, a 403(b) is the most likely type of retirement plan available if they have been around for ten years or more.

Other types of retirement benefits for small businesses can include deferred profit-sharing plans and Keogh plans. Less than one percent of employers are offering a Keogh plan today. Keogh plans are more likely to be an option for self-employed folks who started them many years ago.

You'll find each of these plans has its own maze of rules about whom is eligible and how much must be contributed. The 401(k) rules are essentially the same as for larger companies, so we won't discuss those again here. We'll tackle each of the other plans one at a time.

> The 401(k) is still the most popular plan and 58 percent of all small businesses in 2001 offered that type of plan.

SEP-IRA

The Simplified Employee Pension (SEP) is actually a type of Individual Retirement Account (IRA). The SEP-IRA is the most flexible of small business alternatives and therefore very popular with small businesses that choose to offer plans, especially those with ten employees or less. There is no mandatory contribution that must be made and, in fact, if business is bad, employers can skip a year completely. They can offset a skipped year by putting in the maximum amount when business is good.

The employer makes all contributions to a SEP-IRA. Employees do not contribute to the plan at all, unless the plan was started before 1996 and had a salary-reduction provision. SEP plans that do allow employee contributions are called SAR-SEPs. They were done away with for all newly established employer-sponsored plans in 1996 when the SIMPLE IRA was introduced. We'll talk more about SIMPLE IRAs below.

Employers can contribute up to 15 percent of each employee's salary, but no more than $25,500 per year in a SEP. The key to the plan is equality. Employers must contribute the same percentage of earning for every eligible employee.

The SEP-IRA is also popular with people who are self-employed. Self-employed folks can contribute 13.04 percent of their net income up to the maximum of $25,500. The reason it is lower for self-employed folks is the complicated way the SEP contribution is calculated. First, as a self-employed person, you must figure net earnings on a Schedule C by subtracting business expenses and 50 percent of the self-employment tax. The computation is complicated further because you then subtract your SEP contribution to arrive at your eligible net income figure, which ends up reducing your 15 percent contribution to 13.04 percent.

In addition, employers get a tax benefit by offering a SEP-IRA. Their contributions are fully tax-deductible. Folks who are self-employed can also deduct their SEP-IRA contribution and reduce their Adjusted Gross Income (AGI).

If you work for a company that offers a SEP-IRA, it is set up in your name as an IRA. One big advantage to the employee is that all money put into a SEP-IRA is immediately 100 percent vested.

The money is yours right away, which is different than the 401(k), which usually takes several years to vest. The other big difference is that contributions are excluded from income rather being deducted from it.

SEP-IRAs must be offered to all qualifying employees. To qualify, an employee must be at least twenty-one years old, must have worked three out of five of the immediately preceding tax years, and must have earned at least $400 in the current tax year. An employer can establish less restrictive participation requirements for its employees, but whatever the rules are, they must be consistent across the board. An employer cannot institute more restrictive rules than those stated above.

Eligible employees can also be what are known as "leased employees." Leased employees are actually hired by a leasing organization but perform services for another company. It is possible that a company may have to provide SEP-IRAs for its leased employees. To be eligible for a SEP, the leased employee must meet these three conditions:

1. Provide services under an agreement between the recipient and the leasing organization
2. Perform these services for the recipient or related persons substantially full time for at least one year
3. Perform services under the primary direction and control of the recipient

Employers can exclude employees that are covered by a union agreement, if their retirement benefits are part of a good faith agreement reached between the union and the employer. Nonresident aliens also can be excluded provided they have no U.S. source of earned income from their employer.

If you are in a SEP plan, your options when you change jobs are somewhat limited compared to other employer-sponsored retirement plans. You cannot roll your SEP-IRA assets into your new employer's retirement plan. Your withdrawal options are greater though. An employer cannot require that you keep the assets in your SEP-IRA. Employers are prohibited from setting up withdrawal rules as a

> SEP-IRAs must be offered to all qualifying employees.

condition of accepting SEP-IRA contributions. That doesn't change your possible tax penalties. If you withdraw your money before retirement, you will be subject to a 10 percent penalty, plus all funds withdrawn will be taxed as current income. Generally, withdrawals are subject to the same rules as traditional tax-deferred IRAs.

Contributions for self-employment can be logistically difficult to plan. Frequently, they do not know what their net income will be until the end of the year. This can make it difficult to fund a SEP-IRA until after a self-employed business owner has completed calculating their tax returns. There are tax penalties if too much is invested and some funds need to be withdrawn.

Employers can hold off making their SEP contribution until their taxes are actually filed. This can be a particularly nice benefit if your cash is tight at the end of the year. You don't need to rush to make a contribution to your retirement plan, especially if you know that a major contract payment is coming in at the beginning of the next year. You can even delay adding to a SEP until as late as August 15 of the next year, which is the last day for requesting a tax filing extension.

> SIMPLE IRA was designed by Congress to give small businesses an alternative that would be easier and less costly to administer than the 401(k).

SIMPLE IRA

The newest retirement plan alternative for small businesses is the SIMPLE IRA. It was designed by Congress to give small businesses an alternative that would be easier and less costly to administer than the 401(k). The SIMPLE IRA was born in 1996 but took a while to catch on. Its growth tripled between 1998 and 1999.

The SIMPLE IRA gives small businesses the opportunity to offer a tax-deferred salary reduction plan similar to a 401(k), but without the extensive administrative costs a 401(k) plan can incur. Employees can elect to make contributions up to $7,000 in 2002, which will increase by $1,000 per year until 2005 when it allows a maximum of $10,000. After that year, the maximum will be indexed to inflation.

Employers must match the employee contribution. They have a choice of matching the employee contribution dollar for dollar up to 3 percent of the employee's compensation or match all employees' SIMPLE IRAs with a 2 percent contribution up to a maximum of $3,400 (or 2 percent of the maximum compensation of $170,000).

If you are over fifty, you can make additional catch-up contributions of $500 in 2002. The amount of catch-up contributions allowed will increase by $500 per year until they max out at $2,500 in 2006. Beginning in 2007, the catch-up contributions allowed will be indexed to inflation.

SIMPLE IRAs, like the SEP-IRAs, are set up in each employee's name. Companies can allow employees to designate a financial institution for their SIMPLE IRAs or they can require them to at least initially deposit the SIMPLE IRA money with a specific financial institution. Also as with the SEP-IRAs, the company contributions are 100 percent vested immediately.

SIMPLE IRAs do come with more strings attached than SEP-IRAs. In addition to the requirement for company matching provisions, the rules for transferring SIMPLE IRAs if you change jobs are much stricter. Your SIMPLE IRA account must be open for at least two years before you can transfer the money. If you want to move your money before the two-year period has ended, there is a 25 percent tax penalty whether you withdraw or transfer it to another retirement plan. If you do switch jobs before the two-year period is up, it is best to leave the money in the SIMPLE IRA. The money is in your name. The only reason to take a 25 percent tax penalty hit would be if you thought the financial institution holding the money was at risk of losing it all.

Once the two-year period is up, you do have the choice to roll over the money into another IRA or into your new company's 401(k). Other withdrawal rules for the SIMPLE IRA match those of the traditional tax-deductible IRA. We'll be discussing withdrawal rules in greater detail below.

Employers can set up a SIMPLE IRA plan anytime between January 1 and October 1, provided the employer did not offer a SIMPLE IRA previously. If the employer did have a SIMPLE IRA in the past, to restart it they must establish it on January 1 of that year. Administratively, SIMPLE IRAs are much easier for an employer to set up. Most financial institutions will provide model trust and custodial account documents that can be used for their establishment.

Employers providing a SIMPLE IRA must give employees at least a sixty-day election period immediately preceding January 1 of the calendar year. Employers can provide a ninety-day election period

SIMPLE IRAs Are Catching On

In 2001, the increasing popularity of the SIMPLE IRA was offset by a drop in popularity of 401(k)s and profit-sharing plans, according to SERS. In 1999 and 2000, 401(k)s were used by 67 percent of small businesses, that dropped to 58 percent in 2001, while SIMPLE IRAs increased in popularity from 14 percent in 2000 to 22 percent in 2001. This trend is likely to continue as more companies become aware of its existence and benefits. If your company has no employer-sponsored retirement plans, you may want to send your human resources representative a link to find out more about these plans. Quicken has a good summary you can use: *www.quicken.com/cms/ viewers/article/retirement/ 18288*

if they choose or they can allow election periods for each of the four quarters. Whatever decision is made, there are notification requirements for the companies that offer SIMPLE IRAs.

Any employee earning at least $5,000 during a two-year period and who is expected to earn at least that much during the calendar year for which the contributions are made must be allowed to participate in the SIMPLE IRA. Self-employed individuals with earned income can open a SIMPLE IRA.

In order to participate, an employee must sign a salary reduction agreement during the election period. Your contribution is tax-deferred, just as with a 401(k). Your participation is voluntary, but it is the only way you will get employer-matching dollars. You can choose to elect a percentage of your salary or a specific dollar amount (if the employer makes this option available). If you find you are unable to afford the contribution elected, you can cancel your election at any time during the year.

Employees control how much they want to contribute to the SIMPLE IRA. Employers cannot restrict contributions beyond the maximum contribution restrictions set by federal law, which for 2002 is $7,000.

Employers must deposit your salary reduction contributions to the SIMPLE IRA within thirty days after the end of the month in which you otherwise would have been paid the cash. Employer-matching contributions do not have to be made until the due date of filing their tax returns, which can include filing extensions. If regular deposits of your contributions are not being made into your SIMPLE IRA, it may be a sign of significant problems. We'll discuss your rights and responsibilities in further detail below.

Keoghs

The granddaddy of retirement plans for small businesses and self-employed folks is the Keogh plan, which was established by Congress in 1962. These plans are used primarily by businesses that operate as sole proprietorships or partnerships. Eligibility is limited to people who own their own business and file a Schedule C, have a Subchapter S corporation, are self-employed, are a partner in a

---

Notices about Your SIMPLE IRA

Employers must notify employees of certain key SIMPLE IRA provisions. They include:

1. Employees must be notified of the opportunity to make a change in their salary reduction choice.
2. Employers must notify employees about their choice to make contributions matching employees' dollar for dollar or a set percentage of all employees' salaries.
3. Employers must give employees a summary description of the plan and information about its location. The financial institution selected by the employer usually provides this.

If you get one of these notifications and don't understand it, don't hesitate to contact your plan administrator to have him or her explain the provisions to you.

business that files a Schedule K, or do freelance work. You may also use a Keogh if you are part of a limited liability company (LLC), provided you are actively involved and not just a passive investor. Other types of corporations cannot use a Keogh.

Keoghs offer structures that come closest to traditional pension plans found in major corporations. They are also the most complex type of retirement plan a small business can establish, but they offer the highest level of tax-sheltered investing a small business owner can find. They also provide the small business owner with greater flexibility in establishing criteria for employee participation and eligibility.

A business owner can set up the Keogh as a defined-benefit or defined-contribution plan, while all other small business options must be defined-contribution plans. The other large corporation benefit of Keoghs is that you can make provisions to borrow from a Keogh, which is not allowed with other small business plans.

The Keogh plan comes with its fair share of regulations. There are actually three sets of regulations: one for the self-employed, one for small business owners, and one for employees of a company that has a plan.

Financial institutions do have standardized plans a small business can use to establish its Keogh plan, but to take advantage of the Keogh's full flexibility it's best to seek the help of a lawyer or CPA who is a Keogh specialist to be certain you are setting up the type of plan that best matches your specific situation.

The first thing an employer or self-employed person must do is to name a plan administrator, even if that person is himself or herself. A self-employed person working as a full-time employee at a company that has a defined-benefit pension at work can still establish a Keogh for a side business. The additional income must meet Keogh qualifications to be deposited in the Keogh.

There are four types of Keogh plan structures:

1. A profit-sharing defined-contribution plan
2. A money-purchase defined-contribution plan
3. A paired plan
4. A defined-benefit plan

KEOGH Warning

If your business fails, you can no longer contribute to the Keogh. The money can be rolled over into an IRA, but there could be penalties depending on the type of Keogh you set up. Obviously, this complicated alternative requires professional assistance to establish and has much higher costs to maintain. While Keoghs were popular when first introduced because they finally gave small business owners and self-employed folks a better way to save for retirement, their complexity has now rendered these plans almost extinct except for folks who established them many years ago. The SEP-IRA or SIMPLE IRA is most likely a better choice for you unless you want to take advantage of one of the options to save very aggressively (and navigate the maze of regulations accordingly).

Keogh Complications

While the tax shelter benefits may sound great, Keogh plans are an unpopular option. In 2001, only about 1 percent of small businesses chose this option. The reason for its unpopularity is the huge amount of paperwork required to administer it. In most cases, you will need a Keogh expert to help with the annual paperwork. You could also need an actuary report yearly to justify the annual contribution. Before you take the plunge, be sure you not only understand the initial paperwork, but also have a good understanding of the yearly requirements for managing this retirement savings alternative.

Let's take a quick look at the plan types, but we'll not be discussing these options in detail but rather providing a summary of what is possible. There are numerous ways to structure these plans, but the catch is that if you cannot make the contribution set out in your original documents, you can be penalized in taxes for as much as 100 percent of the amount that should have been contributed.

A person can shelter the highest percentage of their income using a defined-benefit Keogh, which permits contributions of up to $135,000 annually and can be even 100 percent of your income. The maximum contribution allowed in a defined-contribution Keogh is $50,000, which is permitted in the money-purchase defined-contribution plan.

The least complicated structure, and the safest if your business income is uncertain each year, is the profit-sharing defined-contribution plan. You can contribute as much as 15 percent (before adjustments) of your business income or $40,000, whichever is less.

The money-purchase defined-contribution plan may offer you the largest tax shelter opportunities, but it comes with the greatest risk of penalties. You are allowed to shelter as much as 25 percent of your income up to $200,000 ($50,000), but if you are unable to contribute that amount in any one year you will owe up to 100 percent in penalties of the amount you should have contributed and it won't be counted as a contribution. You must select a percentage at the time the plan is set. The percentage can be as low as 3 percent of earnings.

If you are looking for flexibility in a Keogh, the best choice is the paired plan, which combines key provisions of profit-sharing and money-purchase defined-contribution plans. You are locked into making a contribution each year even if your business hasn't made much money, but you can set the percentage low and still contribute up to 25 percent in the good years.

Defined-benefit Keogh plans offer you the greatest chance to shelter the largest portion of your small business income. When you establish this type of plan, you decide on a specific annual benefit you want to receive at age sixty-five, which cannot top 100 percent of your highest three earnings years or a maximum of $135,0000. You fund the plan so that you will be able to receive your desired payout, even if it means you contribute 100 percent of your earnings each year. You will need to work with an actuary to determine how much your annual contribution should be in order to meet your goals. You have to submit the actuary's report each year with your tax return. The defined-benefit plan could be just right for you if you are trying to catch up late in your career.

Deferred Profit-Sharing Plans

Small business employers can supplement any of their retirement plans with a Deferred Profit-Sharing Plan (DPSP). In fact, in 2001, 22 percent of small businesses did offer this type of plan. Employers can contribute up to 18 percent of an employee's compensation.

Employers who offer this type of plan do so primarily to give employees a stake in the business by sharing company profits. This is considered a good way to encourage higher efficiency, increase morale, and ultimately result in higher profits. These plans can also help in employee retention. Vesting provisions keep employees around if they want their money. These vary by company, so if you have a deferred profit-sharing plan at your workplace be sure you understand what you could lose if you decide to change jobs.

DPSPs offer employers a lot of flexibility in how they plan their contributions, so they can better match business conditions each year. Employer contributions are exempt from federal payroll taxes, which helps to offset plan costs. Employers do not have to provide a definite formula for figuring the profits to be shared, but if there isn't a formula, they must make systematic and substantial contributions.

Employers must develop a definite formula for allocating the contribution among the participants and for distributing the accumulated funds to employees, such as after they reach a certain age or after a fixed number of years. If employees forfeit their profit-sharing funds because they leave the company before being vested, the forfeitures can be allocated among the remaining employees or used to reduce future contributions.

> Vesting provisions keep employees around if they want their money.

Income-Tax Impacts

How your income tax will be affected depends on the type of plan. The SEP-IRA or Keogh plans, which are completely funded by your employer, do not have immediate tax impacts for the employee. The employer gets a tax deduction. A self-employed person is also the employer, so they will have a tax deduction for their contributions.

The SIMPLE IRA, a 401(k), SAR-SEP IRA, or a Keogh set up to allow employee contributions all have tax-deferral benefits if you contribute to the plan. Your taxable income is reduced by the amount you contribute to one of these plans. In addition to these contributions, you may qualify for a Saver's Tax Credit up to $1,000 (50 percent of $2,000 contributions) on these contributions during tax years 2002 through 2006. To qualify, your adjusted gross household income cannot exceed $50,000 if married filing jointly, $37,500 if head of household, or $25,000 if single or married filing separately. The amount of the credit depends on the amount of qualifying contributions and your adjusted gross income. This credit is in addition to the deduction or exclusion allowed for the contribution.

When you reach retirement, you will have to pay taxes on the amount you withdraw based on your current tax income bracket. Now let's take a quick look at withdrawal and portability rules. We'll be spending more time on these issues in Chapters 18, 20, and 21.

> The amount of the credit depends on the amount of qualifying contributions and your adjusted gross income.

Withdrawals and Portability

Early withdrawals from a SEP-IRA are similar to a traditional IRA. In most cases, you will incur a 10 percent penalty plus be required to pay taxes at your current tax rate if you withdraw the money before age 59½. Early withdrawal penalties can be avoided under these five circumstances:

1. Unreimbursed medical expenses that exceed 7.5 percent of your adjusted gross income
2. Distributions that do not exceed the cost of your medical insurance
3. Distributions because you become disabled

4. Expenses for higher education

5. Up to $10,000 toward a first-time home purchase

You will have to pay taxes on the distribution as current income even though you avoid the tax penalties. Penalties for withdrawing money from SIMPLE IRA and Keogh plans may be stiffer, which we discussed above.

If you do leave your job before retirement, the best way to get your funds is to roll them over into another employer plan or to set up your own IRA. By doing this you can avoid all taxes until retirement.

When you reach retirement you will have two options: take the money as a lump-sum distribution or as an annuity. If you decide you want the lump sum, you can take it as a cash payment or roll it over into an IRA. You probably want to choose the IRA to avoid having to pay taxes all in one year, but talk with an accountant to be sure that is the best way, taking your personal financial situation into account. If the annuity is an option, then you will be given a number of pay-out options. We'll discuss those further in Chapters 20 and 21.

If you have a SEP-IRA or a SIMPLE IRA, the rules for distribution are generally the same as those for a traditional IRA. You must start withdrawing the money by the time you reach age 70½ or risk penalties. You'll probably want to plan withdrawals based on the joint lifetime of you and your spouse, but there are other options that we'll discuss in Chapters 20 and 21. Keogh plans can have more complicated distribution arrangements. If you have one of those plans, discuss the provisions with your plan administrator.

Which Plan Should You Pick?

If you are an employee, you don't get a choice, but if you are a small business owner or are self-employed, any of the options discussed here are possible. Your head is probably spinning trying to digest the options.

Basically, if you are self-employed and don't want the hassles of establishing a Keogh plan, your best bet is the SEP-IRA. You'll find

Rollover Changes in 2001 Tax Law

The new tax law also added more rollover provisions:

1. Taxable IRA distributions can be rolled over to any tax-qualified plan, a 403(b) annuity, or a Section 457 plan.
2. Surviving spouses who have their own retirement plan can roll over the distributions from a deceased spouse's plan into their own.
3. After-tax employee contributions to a tax-qualified plan can be rolled over into another qualified plan or traditional IRA.

Do everything you can to avoid withdrawing your retirement funds by taking advantage of all the additional choices now available to you. Remember, when you withdraw retirement money, in addition to the tax and penalties you'll have to pay, you not only lose the principal amount but all the years of future growth.

it's easy to set up, does not require annual contributions, and you have the greatest flexibility with how much you can contribute and when you want to make those contributions. You can get the paperwork for establishing a SEP-IRA from the financial institution at which you plan to invest the money.

If you're a small business owner with fewer than 100 employees and want a plan to which both you and your employees can contribute, your best option is the SIMPLE IRA. These require a lot less paperwork than the 401(k), but give you and your employees a lot of the same benefits. You can use it as an incentive for retaining your employees and recruiting new ones.

If you are a sole proprietor, partner in a small business, or a freelancer, you may want to tackle the complications of a Keogh, especially if you need to catch up on your retirement savings to fill a major retirement gap. You'll need a lot of cash to do this, but it does allow you to build your nest egg the fastest.

> If you are a sole proprietor, partner in a small business, or a freelancer, you may want to tackle the complications of a Keogh.

For more information on this topic, visit our Web site at www.businesstown.com

Traditional Pensions

Gradual Extinction

Few people who start work today will find a job that offers a traditional pension, a defined-benefit retirement plan where the employer will guarantee you a set benefit paid monthly when you retire. These types of plans are rapidly disappearing from the workplace.

In 1992, the Employee Benefits Research Institute (EBRI) found that 39.6 percent of households had only a defined-benefit plan. By 1998 that number dropped to 19.9 percent. Instead, households are more likely to have only a defined-contribution plan. In 1992, 37.6 percent of households had only a defined-contribution plan. That number increased to 57.3 percent in 1998. Throughout this time period about 22.8 percent of the households had both types of plans.

Just to review briefly: a defined-benefit plan is one in which the employer has the onus to manage the plan investments and be certain there will be enough to pay you a promised benefit at retirement. Only the employer contributes to this type of plan. The defined-contribution plan, such as a 401(k) or 403(b), is one where both you and the employer likely contribute, and the employee is responsible for managing the assets so there will be enough through retirement. Before we start to discuss why these plans are becoming extinct, let's first talk about how they work.

> The defined-contribution plan, such as a 401(k) or 403(b), is one where both you and the employer likely contribute, and the employee is responsible for managing the assets.

How They Work

Pensions were started in the workplace to provide a reward to employees who were loyal to the company and worked with the company for many years. Their benefits are primarily called "back-loaded." In other words, you have to be with a company a very long time to really see any significant value in the defined benefit.

How does this work? The monthly benefit amount that is promised at retirement is based on your age, earnings, and years of service. Plans can state their benefits as a percentage of your salary and years of service with a company (such as 1 percent of final pay x the number of years of service) or as a specific dollar amount and years of service (such as $25 per month for every year that you worked for a company). Some companies just promise an exact dollar amount at retirement, such as $100 per month.

Rewarding Longevity

To encourage longevity, the benefits are "back-loaded," meaning that older workers accrue benefits that are more valuable as a percentage than do younger workers, according to the EBRI. Let's step through an example to show you how this works. First, here is the formula that is most commonly used:

Pay x Years of Service x Benefit Factor = Pension Payment

- Pay—This varies greatly from company to company. Some will use the highest three to ten years; others will use the most recent three to ten years. In some companies, bonuses and incentive pay are included in the calculation, in others they are not. Read the fine print for your company pension plan to find out exactly how your pay level is determined for your pension formula.
- Years of Service—If you worked steadily for a company with no major breaks in service, this can be a relatively easy number to calculate, but complications arise if you took time off under the Family Medical Leave Act or for other reasons. The critical issue here is how your company offsets years of service if you take a break from work.
- Benefit Factor—This is a factor that will be stated in your pension documents. It usually ranges between 1 (.01) and 2 (.02) percent of your pay. The company will usually set this factor by the percentage of salary they ideally want to pay to a long-term employee who has worked their ideal maximum number of years. For example, if a company wants to reward the forty-year employee with a guarantee of 50 percent of their salary at retirement, the factor would be 1.25 percent (.0125) (40 x .0125 = 50%).

Sometimes there is a fourth component to the formula for early retirement. We'll discuss that further when we get into incentive programs to encourage early retirement.

Now, let's take a look at two employees who worked for a company that averages your highest five years to calculate the pay factor.

> Older workers accrue benefits that are more valuable as a percentage than do younger workers.

The benefit factor is .015, which guarantees the forty-year employee 60 percent of salary. Sally worked twenty-five years for the company and Bob worked forty years for the company. Both ended with the highest five years averaging $50,000. Let's see how their payout will differ:

Sally: $50,000 x 25 x .015 = $18,750
Bob: $50,000 x 40 x .015 = $30,000

A Realistic Look

You can see from this example how longevity pays off, but in today's business environment is that what most companies want to reward? How many people who will start work today want to work for a company their entire work life? How many companies will keep employees that long? The reality of the business environment today is that few young people want to make working for the same company their lifetime goal. Few companies reward loyalty with job security. Layoffs have become very common whenever there is any type of economic slowdown.

With these realities in place, many younger employees prefer a more portable type of retirement program—one that has a cash value they can take with them. Older employees who have put in the time prefer the retirement benefit guarantee. The financial maneuvering by companies to find ways to recruit new folks, while still trying to reward the few they want to keep, have been around for years.

About twenty-five years ago, these maneuverings resulted in some employees being fired just before they qualified for the highest pension benefits and other employees faced the reality of no pensions when their companies were sold or went out of business. Their pension plans were disbanded, leaving them with nothing.

In 1974, Congress tried to get things under control with a new law called the Employee Retirement Income Security Act of 1974 (ERISA). (We'll take a close look at ERISA and how it works below). Other related tax laws have also been passed as loopholes were recognized. This attempt to protect employees has backfired because now many companies are saying that the administrative costs and

Many younger employees prefer a more portable type of retirement program— one that has a cash value they can take with them.

burdens of operating a defined-benefit plan is a "major disincentive to operating this type of retirement plan," according to EBRI.

We'll take a closer look at government protections below. First let's look at how these differences have affected people's defined-benefit pensions.

Cash-Balance Conversions

Instead of putting up with these rising costs, companies are rapidly converting to a new-fangled defined-benefit plan called the cash-balance plan, which falls somewhere between the traditional defined-balance plan and the 401(k).

Cash-balance plans, first introduced in the mid-1980s, were called "revolutionary" by some retirement planning consultants. Some consultants were so excited about the opportunity that they thought these pension plans could become a profit center for the company. The idea caught on rapidly and over 300 large companies converted their plan before the brakes were put on by lawsuits to stop them.

Why did they catch on so quickly? Employers convert the current value of their traditional benefit plan to cash in each employee's name and continue to contribute to the plan on a cash basis, similar to a 401(k). The big difference is that rather than guarantee the employees a defined benefit they are guaranteed a cash value, which is usually rolled over at retirement. The employer takes the investment risk rather than the employee, as with a 401(k). Usually, the employer will guarantee a rate of return, which is not the case with a 401(k). The reason the cash-balance plan can become a profit center is that if the company is able to achieve better investment results, it gets to keep the profit. In some cases, companies use other complicated conversion rules that help them build those profits, while cutting back on employee retirement benefits.

Taking the Matter to Court

Older employees quickly realized they were being taken advantage of by these conversions and filed lawsuits. One of the most public fights occurred between IBM and its employees. IBM announced its plans to convert to a cash-balance plan in May 1999 with the conversion set to take place on July 1, 1999. Employees quickly organized against it and within two weeks they had a Web site on Yahoo!, which had 1.7 million page views by September 20, 1999. IBM quickly backtracked and doubled the number of employees who would be allowed to stay in the traditional pension plan, permitting anyone who was forty years old and had at least ten years of service to opt to stay in the old plan.

Not all companies backtracked like IBM. Employees of Georgia Pacific were the first to make it to the appellate court level over the company's conversion to a cash-balance plan. It was a major victory for employees that helped them to win rights when companies were considering conversion. The big question still to be decided is what is a fair method for companies to use when valuing an employee's defined-benefit retirement plan and converting it to cash.

The waters are still very muddy for what will be allowed by the courts. Most attorneys are recommending that their company clients halt conversion plans until the IRS and the Pension and Welfare Benefits Administration (PWBA) rule on their legality and provide regulations for how these conversions should be done. The Pension Benefits Guarantee Corporation (PBGC) is also investigating the issue and when it puts in its two cents, it could further complicate problems for companies that insure their plans through the PBGC.

The GAO's summary of the problem is excellent. Companies that chose to go forward did so because of the "need to remain competitive and the potential impact on workers. Key reasons for adopting a cash balance plan included lowering total pension costs, increasing the portability of pension benefits, and the ease of communicating the value of plan benefits. Key reasons firms gave for not adopting a cash balance plan included possible adverse effects on workers who are older, longer-tenured, and less mobile; uncertainty about possible changes in regulation of cash balance plans; the impact of adverse employee and public reaction to cash balance plan conversions; and increased costs."

The GAO's study did help encourage some immediate legislative action. The GAO told Congress that employees were not receiving adequate information about the proposed conversions to cash-balance plans. In the 2001 tax law, Congress required employers to give employees clearer notice about the significant benefit reductions that may be a part of the conversion. Employers can avoid the notice requirement provided employees are given the option to choose either the new cash-balance plan or the old traditional defined-benefit plan. Congress amended ERISA rules to include the notification requirements and added stiff penalties if a company is found not to be in compliance. Failure to properly notify employees can result in penalties as high as $500,000, and based on $100 per day per employee not notified.

The Age Problem

Why do these plans sometimes look like age discrimination? Younger workers tend to benefit from the cash-balance plans because of the portability of the funds once they are vested. They also have a much longer time for their contributions and those of their employers to grow. Older workers tend to lose because traditional pension plans are based on the last three to five years of salary. Since those are usually the higher earning years, almost half of a person's ultimate benefit amount is earned in the last five years on the job.

As employers design these plans, the trick will be to make them fair to a company's workers, whether young or old. One way to handle the age problem is to increase the amount initially set aside in older workers' accounts or to allow older workers the option of remaining in the traditional plan. The key question is at what age do you cut off access to the old plan? IBM initially cut off access at age fifty, but then had to lower that to age forty.

> Older workers tend to lose because traditional pension plans are based on the last three to five years of salary.

Allowing Employees to Decide

Some alternatives being recommended to employers who want to go forward now include allowing employees to run the numbers and then decide, based on their individual circumstances, which plan they prefer. Towers Perrin, a global management consulting firm, is recommending to its clients that they do exactly that, but it comes with responsibility. Towers Perrin believes companies must include

Choose Wisely

Whatever option you choose will be in place for the rest of your life, so choose wisely. Your company will probably offer you retirement counseling for both you and your spouse. Take advantage of these sessions. If you are still baffled by your options when you come out of these sessions, don't hesitate to contact a financial planner who can look at your pension benefits as well as other retirement assets and help you make the choices that are best for you and your family. We'll be looking at integrating your retirement resources in greater detail in Chapter 15.

an educational process so that employees can make the right choice for themselves and their families.

Age is not always the deciding factor. Employees who plan to be with their company for a short time would definitely be better off with a cash-balance plan, but employees that plan to stay with a company until retirement would probably be better off with the traditional defined-benefit plan. Towers Perrin found that the results of such a conversion plan were not too surprising. Most younger employees chose the cash-balance plan, which is much more portable, while older workers decided to stay with the traditional plan.

Whatever you do decide, if cash-balance conversion is a possibility at your company, your next major decision will probably be how you want to receive your pension when you retire.

Payout Options

If you have accepted the conversion, the most likely option will be a lump sum and, as we discussed with the 401(k), your best option will be to roll over that money into an IRA or annuity. If you still have a traditional defined-benefit plan at the time of payout, you'll have numerous options to choose from.

If you are single, the safest option to guarantee you a benefit for life will be the lifetime annuity. If you are married, you will probably want to ensure that your spouse receives some pension benefits. In these cases, you would probably take a benefit based on your life and the life of your spouse, so whoever lives the longest will continue to receive benefits. The joint life option will also probably be the lowest payment option, especially if your spouse is considerably younger than you are. If you are married, you must either choose a benefit that protects both you and your spouse or your spouse must sign away his or her rights to your pension. Typically, there are also options for payments on some type of installment plan, such as equal payments for five, ten, or fifteen years.

You may also want to consider retiring early. Some companies do allow for this and, in fact, offer incentives to make it more attractive.

Early-Retirement Incentives

Incentives for early retirement were all the rage in the late 1980s and early 1990s when this country was deep in a recession and there were numerous corporate restructurings. A human resources consultancy group, Watson Wyatt Worldwide, found that 61 percent of Fortune 100 companies offered early retirement incentives to its employees between 1989 and 1998, with most of the offers being accepted in the early 1990s by fifty- and sixty-year-olds.

Many companies have some provision for early retirement, which supposedly adjusts your benefit based on actuarial computations to estimate a payout that would be equal to someone who waited until full retirement age. So a person who wants to retire at sixty rather than sixty-five would take a reduction in the monthly amount to retire early, which would essentially offset the fact that they started to collect retirement benefits before it was time to do so. If the retiree lived longer than the actuaries expected, he or she would do better than the employee that waited until sixty-five. If the retiree died earlier, he or she would collect less.

When a company wants to encourage early retirement, they sweeten the pot and make it more attractive by offering less of a reduction in benefits or include other incentives, such as a lump-sum cash payout plus benefits. In the 1990s, after employees accepted the early retirement package, some had regrets because they thought their deal actually was not as good as expected. They filed suit against their employers on issues of age discrimination. To avoid a lawsuit, Congress passed legislation in 1990 that required employers to provide clear information about the early retirement options, that employers give employees at least forty-five days to consider retiring early once the plan is announced, and that employers give employees seven days to change their mind once they have accepted the incentive.

We looked at the formula commonly used by companies to calculate your retirement benefits above. If you are retiring early, they will essentially use the same formula but add on a factor for early retirement, which reduces the monthly benefit or lump-sum cash payout.

Early Retirement Incentives on the Rebound

Early-retirement incentives disappeared as an attractive option until late in 2000, when they started popping up again. As the country moved deeper into a recession, major corporations saw early retirement incentives as a better option than laying people off. *BusinessWeek* reported in February 2001 that a partial list of companies offering early-retirement incentives included Chrysler, Unisys, Whirlpool, Xerox, and Union Pacific. However, if your company reopens its early retirement window or distributes information about new incentives to retire early, don't rush to join the party. Carefully weigh your options and be sure you understand the pluses and minuses of continuing to work or retiring early.

Government Protections

We've mentioned ERISA several times now. It's the primary federal law that sets the minimum standards for pension plans in private industry. This law specifies participation rules, vesting rules, and pension rights for your spouse after your death. ERISA does not require companies to establish pensions, but if established they must meet certain minimum standards.

The key champion for the employees is the person or persons with fiduciary responsibility. Their primary responsibility is to run the plan solely in the interest of the participants and beneficiaries with the exclusive goal of providing benefits and to pay plan expenses. They must diversify plan investments to minimize the risk of large losses. They also must avoid conflicts of interest or engaging in transactions that benefit parties related to the plan, such as other

ERISA Rules

- Requires plans to provide employees with information about the plan features and funding on a regular basis and automatically upon becoming eligible to participate in the plan.

- Sets minimum standards for how long a person may be required to work before eligibility to participate and accumulate benefits, as well as to have a nonforfeitable right to those benefits.

- Establishes detailed funding rules that require employers to provide adequate funding for their retirement plans.

- Requires accountability of plan fiduciaries, which includes anyone who exercises discretionary authority or control over a plan's management or assets, including anyone who provides investment advice to the plan. Fiduciaries who do not follow the principles of conduct may be held responsible for restoring losses to the plan.

- Gives participants the right to sue for benefits and breaches of fiduciary duty.

- Guarantees payment of certain benefits if a defined-benefit plan is terminated, through a federally chartered corporation, known as the Pension Benefit Guarantee Corporation (PBGC). Most companies that offer a defined-benefit plan must carry insurance, which pays for these PBGC benefits.

fiduciaries, services providers, or plan sponsors. In the case of defined-benefit plans, Congress mandated that no more than 10 percent of the assets could be held in company stock. If a court finds that a fiduciary did not follow these rules, it can hold the fiduciary liable to restore any losses to the plan and can even go so far as to remove the fiduciary from his or her duties.

All of these rules are under the jurisdiction of the Department of Labor, which enforces them under Title I of ERISA. Some plans are not under the protections of Title I, however. These include:

- Federal, state, or local government employee plans, including plans of certain international organizations. We'll cover those in greater detail in Chapter 12.
- Certain church or church association plans.
- Plans maintained solely to comply with state workers compensation, unemployment compensation, or disability insurance laws.
- Plans maintained outside the United States primarily for nonresident aliens.

The Department of Labor is not the only agency that has responsibility for regulating retirement plans. The Department of the Treasury ensures that all retirement plans are in compliance with the Internal Revenue Code. Companies definitely want to write off "tax-qualified" pension plans so they can take advantage of the special tax benefits that employers offering such plans enjoy.

Another major player is the Pension Benefit Guarantee Corporation (PBGC), which is a nonprofit corporation created by the federal government to guarantee the payment of pension benefits under defined-benefit plans that are terminated with insufficient money to pay benefits. In order to offer these protections, the PBGC charges employers a fee per enrolled employee.

Security for Your Pension

The Pension Benefit Guarantee Corporation's responsibilities have dropped off dramatically as the numbers of defined-benefit plans in the private sector have dwindled. In 1985, there were 114,000 defined-benefit plans in existence. In 2001, that number dropped to 38,000 private-sector defined-benefit plans. The reduction in the number of plans has primarily been among plans with 100 or fewer participants, according to PBGC.

PBGC reports an increase in the number of workers and retirees covered by PBGC pension insurance, rising to 43 million in 2001 versus 38 million in 1985. Once the issues are clarified for cash-balance plans this number could shift again, but for now cash-balance plans are considered a type of defined-benefit plan.

Employee Rights

So now that we know who is responsible for regulating your pension plan, let's turn to the rights employees have under ERISA. ERISA sets rules about how employers must determine eligibility, benefit accrual, and vesting.

Generally, a year of service is defined as 1,000 hours of service during a twelve-month period. Sometimes the methods for calculating service are different, depending upon whether the issue involves participation, vesting, or benefit accrual. Check your summary plan description to find out how service is calculated for your plan.

Employer plans are designed to cover certain positions. You must be allowed to participate in the plan once you have reached twenty-one and have completed at least one year of service, provided your position is covered by the particular pension plan in question. It is not uncommon for a company to have different plans for different positions, especially if some employees are members of a union and others are not.

Older workers are protected from age discrimination by ERISA. An employer cannot exclude them from participating in a retirement plan just because they are near the age of retirement. Employers can require that you complete two years of service before becoming eligible, if you become 100 percent vested (meaning benefits are not forfeited when you leave) when you become a participant in the plan. Tax-exempt educational institutions can require that you are at least twenty-six years old (instead of twenty-one) if you become vested after you complete one year of service.

Vesting Schedules

Whether you are vested or not relates to the amount of time you must work for a company before you earn a nonforfeitable right to your benefits. When you are 100 percent vested, your accrued benefits are yours, even if you leave the company. ERISA provides two types of vesting schedules: the seven-year "graded" vesting schedule and the five-year "cliff" vesting schedule. A company must allow you to vest your pension according to one of the following schedules.

> Older workers are protected from age discrimination by ERISA.

7-Year "Graded" Vesting Schedule

Years of Vesting Service Completed	Percentage of Accrued Benefit That Is Vested
Less than 3	0%
At least 3 but less than 4	20%
At least 4 but less than 5	40%
At least 5 but less than 6	60%
At least 6 but less than 7	80%
At least 7	100%

5-Year "Cliff" Vesting Schedule

Years of Vesting Service Completed	Percentage of Accrued Benefit That Is Vested
Less than 3	0%
At least 5	100%

These schedules are a minimum for vesting. A company may provide a more generous vesting schedule if they so choose. Check your summary plan description to find out what your vesting schedule is at your current employer.

There is also a third vesting schedule if you work under a multiemployer plan. This involves a situation where several unrelated employers contribute to a retirement plan under one or more collective bargaining agreements, in other words, usually related to a union plan. If you are in a multiemployer plan, you could have a slower vesting schedule that takes ten years to be fully vested. Before ten years has expired, you could have zero percent vested in your name under these plans.

> If you are in a multi-employer plan, you could have a slower vesting schedule that takes ten years to be fully vested.

Accrued Benefits

Now that you know how long it can take to vest your benefits, let's look more closely at how you accrue them. Basically, accrued benefits are the amount of money or benefit that has been allocated or accumulated under your name. ERISA does not set benefit levels, but the levels set by the company must be shown to accrue on a reasonable and consistent basis. A part-time employee with at least 1,000 hours of work per year must be credited with a pro-rata portion of the benefit he or she would have accrued if employed full time.

Just because you start working for a company that has a defined-benefit plan, it doesn't guarantee you that it will still be available when you retire. ERISA does not prohibit an employer from amending the plan to reduce benefits in the future. If there is going to be a significant reduction in the rate of future benefit accruals after the employer decided to amend its retirement plan, you must receive notice at least fifteen days before the effective date of the plan amendment.

> ERISA does protect you for short breaks in service, especially if they are shorter than five consecutive years.

If you decide to take a few years off, for example, to raise a family, it could affect your pension benefits if they are not yet fully vested. ERISA does protect you for short breaks in service, especially if they are shorter than five consecutive years. If you are thinking of taking an extended leave of absence from your job, be certain to check the rules affecting your pension to be sure you don't inadvertently or unnecessarily lose the pension benefits you've worked so hard to accrue.

You can work past your normal retirement age and continue to accrue benefits, regardless of age, but a company can limit the total number of years of service that will be taken into account for accruing benefits. If you decide to go back to work after you have already started collecting benefits, ERISA requires that a company permit you to continue to accrue additional benefits provided you have not exceeded the total number of years of service allowed under the plan.

Pension Plan Distributions

When you are finally ready to retire, ERISA has specific rules regarding when you may or must begin getting your pension benefits after you leave a job. The most common requirement is that you must have the option to begin receiving benefits within sixty days after the end of the year in which you reach age sixty-five, provided you began participation in the plan at least ten years earlier. However, you can receive benefits earlier than age sixty-five. You can't be forced to take out your benefits prior to the normal retirement age, provided your vested benefits are greater than $3,500. If you have accrued less than $3,500 in benefits, you can be required to take your benefit when it first becomes distributable, such as when you quit your job. You should find all the rules related to your pension plan distributions in the summary plan description.

ERISA also protects how your benefits must be paid. You must be able to take out the benefits in some form of a lifetime annuity—whether you receive them monthly, quarterly, or yearly—for the rest of your life. If you are married, your employer must offer some form of a qualified joint and survivor annuity, which covers both you and your spouse. This annuity would be paid in equal periodic payments, continuing for the rest of your life and the life of your spouse if he or she outlives you.

The periodic payment for a surviving spouse must be at least 50 percent but cannot be more than 100 percent. If you choose a plan that cuts the payment to 50 percent for the surviving spouse, the initial periodic payments will be higher, but it could leave your spouse in serious financial difficulty so be certain you understand the consequences of your choice. If you choose a different plan than a joint and survivor annuity, your spouse must sign a statement agreeing to waive his or her benefit rights.

Plan Termination

Remember, pension plans are not guaranteed even if you decide to work for a company that currently offers them. A plan can be terminated or become insolvent. ERISA does offer you some protection if this happens. If a tax-qualified plan is terminated, any of your accrued benefits become 100 percent vested immediately to the extent the plan is funded. If the company does not have enough to pay the promised benefits, all is not lost. Your plan most likely is insured by the PBGC, and the PBGC will cover your benefits up to the limits set by law. PBGC will make an attempt to recover additional amounts from the employer before paying them.

Research Your Pension Insurance

If you want to find out more about the insurance protection for your pension plan, write to the Pension Benefit Guarantee Corporation, Administrative Review and Technical Assistance Department, 1200 K Street, N.W., Washington, D.C. 20005; telephone (202) 326-4000. You may also want to visit their Web site at *www.pbgc.gov*. This is also the contact point if you worked for a company that had a pension and is now out of business. You can find out from them what pensions you are now entitled to collect at retirement.

When a plan terminates, the money in the plan is used to purchase annuity contracts from an insurance company to pay pension benefits in the future. The U.S. Department of Labor will work with the pension plan fiduciaries to be certain that a sound insurance company is selected to assure the future benefits will be there for plan participants and beneficiaries. If your company merges with another company and the plans are merged, you will be entitled to receive at least a benefit equal to the one you would have received before the merger.

With all this talk about plans being terminated and merged, you may be wondering what protections are in place to be sure your benefits are being accurately computed. There have been questions raised by employee groups if they believed there was a problem with the calculation of accrued benefits. Periodically, a group of employees will hire outside counsel to be certain they are receiving their fair share.

The Department of Labor put together this list of the ten most common causes of error in pension calculation:

> There have been questions raised by employee groups if they believed there was a problem with the calculation of accrued benefits.

1. All relevant compensation, such as commissions, overtime, and bonuses (if these were to be included in your plan), was not included in calculating your benefits.
2. The calculation was not based on all your years of service with the company, or all work within different divisions.
3. The plan administrator used an incorrect benefit formula, such as the wrong interest rate.
4. The plan used incorrect Social Security data in calculating your benefits.
5. Basic information, such as your birth date or Social Security number, was incorrect.
6. Your company merged with another company or went out of business, and there is confusion about which pension benefits you qualify for.
7. Assets in your account were improperly valued.
8. Your employer failed to make required contributions on your behalf.
9. Basic mistakes were made in the mathematical calculations.
10. You failed to update your personnel office with changes (marriage, divorce, death of spouse) that may affect your benefits.

Your Next Steps

By now, hopefully you're thoroughly convinced that even if you have a traditional pension plan, you still must be a watchdog for your benefits. If you haven't read your summary plan description, pull it out and do so now. Be certain you understand how your plan works and what to do if you suspect some promised benefits might be taken from you.

Review any annual statements you may receive and be sure you are aware of your accrued benefits and what percentage of them is vested. Start a pension file today and begin keeping all paperwork you receive about your pension benefits in this file, so they are easily accessible if you receive notice of a change.

If you want to learn more about your pension rights and protection, the Department of Labor has an 800 number you can call for more information: (800) 998-7542. You can also find a wealth of information on the Department of Labor's Web site (*www.dol.gov/dol/topic/retirement/participantrights.htm*). If you do have a pension plan, take the time to visit the site and learn all that you can. You will be in a much stronger position if your company does decide to significantly change what you think it has promised you toward your retirement future.

> Review any annual statements you may receive and be sure you are aware of your accrued benefits and what percentage of them is vested.

For more information on this topic, visit our Web site at www.businesstown.com

Government
Pensions

Public Sector versus Private Sector

Public-sector workers face a much different retirement environment than private-sector workers. Whereas in the private sector it is more common to have a defined-contribution plan, public-sector workers are much more likely to be covered by a defined-benefit plan or a combination of the two. Public-sector plans are influenced most strongly by political realities, while private-sector plans are impacted by business needs.

State and local plans dominate the public-sector retirement market. Approximately $2.7 trillion is held as part of state and local government retirement assets. The federal plans, including both civilian and military assets, total $696 billion.

There are two primary retirement programs for federal employees: the Civil Service Retirement System (CSRS) and the Federal Employees Retirement System (FERS). State and local employees face a much more convoluted system of retirement benefits, with each state and many jurisdictions making up its own set of retirement rules. There are commonalities and we'll be looking at the key issues facing state and local workers as well.

Civilian Federal Employees

Civilian federal employees first earned the right to retirement benefits in 1920, when legislation created the Civil Service Retirement System to provide retirement, disability, and survivor benefits for most civilian federal employees. Prior to that time, civilian employees had no retirement benefits and many simply worked until they died because they had no other means of support.

This chapter will focus on the specifics of the benefits for standard federal civilian employees. There are special benefit provisions for law enforcement, firefighters, air traffic controllers, congressional employees, and foreign service employees. If you fit into one of these categories, your benefits will be different and you should check with your agency for your benefit information.

Both the employee and the government contribute to the retirement fund to finance benefits today. Employees under CSRS receive

Federal Retirement Gets Started

When the federal employees retirement system started in 1920, there were more than 4,000 retirees that took advantage of the new law, some were even in their eighties and nineties. The first federal civilian employee to retire was Mr. Edwin B. Simonds who was eighty-nine years old and who had worked for the government for thirty-seven years. Today, civil service pays retirement benefits to over two million people and starts benefits for about 10,000 new retirees each month. Approximately $3.5 billion is paid out monthly in federal retirement benefits to former employees.

retirement benefits based on their length of service and the average salary over the highest three years of pay.

Replacing CSRS with FERS

Federal retirement benefits were changed dramatically in 1987, when the Federal Employees Retirement System (FERS) replaced the CSRS. FERS-covered employees receive reduced guaranteed benefits under the defined-benefit part of the new plan, but have a defined-contribution component called Thrift Savings Plan (TSP). Another key difference is that FERS employees must pay into Social Security, which is a third component of their plan. Most CSRS employees do not pay into Social Security and will receive no Social Security benefits.

Any employees hired after 1983 are automatically covered by FERS. Other CSRS employees were given the option to convert to FERS, but most choose to remain in CSRS. There are still many employees under CSRS rules and more than two million retirees are receiving CSRS retirement and survivor benefits each month.

FERS employees pay a smaller contribution into the defined-benefit part of the plan than CSRS employees, but they also receive less in return. The defined-benefit part of the plan is called Basic Plan Benefits, which is based on an employee's highest three consecutive years of basic pay. Length of service is also part of the benefit calculation. Some employees with enough years of service may qualify for retirement before Social Security kicks in. These employees receive a "Special Retirement Supplement" until they can get Social Security at age sixty-two.

How the TSP Works

The defined-contribution component of FERS, the Thrift Savings Plan (TSP), is similar to a 401(k) plan and offers the same type of savings and tax benefits that are found in many private corporate plans. Contribution limits are set for employees. FERS employees can contribute up to 12 percent of their salaries. The government contributes an automatic 1 percent of salary and matches the first 3 percent of contribution dollar for dollar and fifty cents on the dollar for the next 2 percent of an employee's contribution, for a

> FERS employees pay a smaller contribution into the defined-benefit part of the plan than CSRS employees.

total government contribution of 5 percent of the employee's salary. If an employee chooses not to participate in the TSP, then he or she will receive only a 1 percent government match.

FERS employees that are highly paid (which in 2001 included anyone earning more than $95,455) risk the possibility of losing some of their government match if they contribute too much to their TSP. The maximum employee contribution allowed in 2002 is $11,000 (which at a savings rate of 12 percent means employees earning more than $91,677 should be careful about the amount they contribute). Once an employee contributes his or her maximum, their contribution stops as does the government's match.

Tax Credit for Lower-Income Workers

Employees may qualify for a Saver's Tax Credit up to $1,000 (50 percent of $2,000 contributions) on their TSP contributions during tax years 2002 through 2006. To qualify, the adjusted gross household income (AGI) cannot exceed $50,000 if married filing jointly, $37,500 if head of household, or $25,000 if single or married filing separately. The amount of the credit depends on the amount of qualifying contributions and their AGI. This credit is in addition to the deduction or exclusion allowed for the contribution.

CSRS employees also have the option of participating in the TSP, but they receive no matching funds. CSRS employees can contribute up to 7 percent.

Allocation Changes

Employees must decide if they want to change their TSP contributions during open season, which occurs between November 15 and January 31 each year. In 2002, federal military employees will also have the option to contribute to the TSP for the first time. We'll look at retirement coverage for military employees in greater detail later. Employees can change their contribution allocation or transfer among funds twenty-four hours a day, seven days per week using an automated telephone system.

Holdings in the TSP are growing rapidly and are expected to top the $100 billion mark soon. Roger Mehle, Executive Director of

> The amount of the credit depends on the amount of qualifying contributions and their AGI.

the TSP's investment board, testified before the President's Commission to Strengthen Social Security saying that the participation rates for the TSP among federal employees is 86.6 percent. A majority of those are FERS employees. Approximately 1.3 million FERS employees contribute and about 206,000 FERS employees don't get the 1 percent government match. Nearly 630,000 CSRS employees also invest using the TSP.

Understanding Investment Choices

Initially, employees were given the choice of three investment options as part of their TSP: (G) Fund, which invests in short-term nonmarketable U.S. Treasury securities; (F) FUND, which invests in fixed-income securities based on the Lehman Brothers Aggregate Index; and (C) Fund, which invests in equities based on the S&P 500 stock index. In 2001, two additional funds were added: (S) Fund, which invests in small capitalization stocks based on the Wilshire 4500 index; and the (I) Fund, which invests in international stocks based on the Morgan Stanley EAFE (Europe, Australia, Far East) index.

One huge advantage for employees of the TSP is its low administrative fees—between .05 and .07. TSP contributions do pay the full costs of administrative fees, but they are reduced by account forfeitures. People who leave the government before their 1 percent government contributions are vested forfeit those contributions, but they do not lose their own contributions. Mehle estimates their forfeitures save investors about .02 percent. Even without that savings, an operating cost of .07 to .09 is still very low, especially when you compare these fees to private index mutual funds.

Vesting in the TSP affects only FERS employees and only the government's automatic 1 percent contribution is at risk if they leave before vesting. Employees are vested after completing three years of federal civilian service. Congressional employees and some non-career positions become vested after just two years of service. If an employee dies before completing the service requirements, all government TSP contributions become 100 percent vested immediately.

How Federal Employees Invest Their Money

Annual reports have not yet been released for 2001 so there is no information yet on how well accepted the new funds were, but based on information available in December 2000, $56.6 billion was invested in the (C) Fund, $32.5 billion was invested in the (G) fund, and $4.3 billion was invested in the (F) fund. Given the volatility of the stock market, it will be surprising if many people took advantage of the more aggressive fund options in 2001, but if people do begin to believe a stock market recovery is possible there may be more interest in 2002.

Borrowing Money

Federal employees can borrow from the TSP, but it should be a decision of last resort just like with the 401(k). There are two types of loans allowed with the TSP. One is a general-purpose loan and the second is a loan for the purchase of a primary residence. General-purpose loans must be repaid in one to four years, whereas residential loans allow for repayment in as much as fifteen years.

The minimum loan amount is $1,000 and the maximum is $50,000. Employees can only borrow on money that they contributed. They cannot borrow on funds contributed by the government. Employees can expect a wait of six to eight weeks for a check. Loan money is disbursed once a month.

Loans are repaid through payroll allotments. If for some reason an employee cannot repay their loan, such as due to separation from service, the loan will become a taxable distribution and, as is the case with a 401(k), the employee could be subject to a 10 percent penalty for early withdrawal as well as having to pay taxes at their current tax rate. If the employee is still working for the government and is not able to pay the loan, not only must the penalty and taxes be paid, but the employee will also not be able to apply for another loan for twelve months. This situation can sometimes occur accidentally if the employee changes jobs or takes a leave without pay or if an error is made in the paycheck.

> There are two types of loans allowed with the TSP.

Other Early Withdrawals

Early withdrawals from a TSP can only be made for two reasons while the employee is still working for the federal government: when an employee reaches 59½ or for hardship reasons. If an employee decides to withdraw money, it cannot be repaid and his or her retirement savings are permanently depleted.

An employee who withdraws money after age 59½ must withdraw at least $1,000 or their entire account balance if less than $1,000 from their TSP. By taking this withdrawal, the employee will lose the right to take a partial withdrawal after he or she leaves government employment.

Financial Hardship Withdrawals

Employees who apply for a financial hardship withdrawal must complete an extensive application and provide documentation about the financial hardship. There is a Financial Hardship In-Service Withdrawal Package that includes a worksheet that allows employees to determine if they qualify for the withdrawal. An employee who takes a hardship withdrawal will not be able to contribute to his or her TSP for six months. Government matching contributions will also be cut off, but the 1 percent annual automatic government contribution will continue. After getting a hardship withdrawal, an employee cannot apply for another withdrawal for six months.

Spousal Consent

Spouses who are married to a FERS participant must consent to any in-service withdrawal. Spouses of CSRS employees must be notified of the withdrawal even if the couple is separated. After the application is completed, it can take as long as four weeks to get the money. Checks are disbursed once a month. Money is paid to the employee unless he or she requests a transfer of the money to an IRA or another eligible retirement plan.

Money withdrawn after age 59½ is taxed as ordinary income at the employee's current tax rate. Before age 59½, withdrawals are subject to a 10 percent early-withdrawal tax penalty plus the taxes due as ordinary income.

When an Employee Leaves Federal Service

An employee who leaves federal service for thirty-one or more days can withdraw money from their TSP. There is a special booklet for these circumstances called, not surprisingly, "Withdrawing Your TSP Account After Leaving Federal Service." As with a 401(k), you can roll over the money into an IRA or another qualified retirement account.

When you leave federal service, you can get your money in one of three ways: as a single payment, as a series of monthly payments, or by purchasing a life annuity. If an employee's TSP is less than

Leaving Federal Employment

When leaving employment in the federal government and planning to reinvest the money in an IRA or other retirement plan, it makes more sense to have the money rolled over into that plan rather than receiving the money directly. Even though no taxes are due in the case of a rollover, if the employee is going to receive the money first, 20 percent of the money must be withheld for taxes.

Money withdrawn after leaving federal employment, but before age fifty-five is subject to a 10 percent penalty plus current taxes. After you turn fifty-five there is no longer a penalty for withdrawal even though a person who is still employed is liable for an early-withdrawal penalty until age 59½.

$3,500, the federal government will automatically send it as a single payment unless other instructions are received.

Spousal Protections

Employees who have more than $3,500 in their TSP will have to consider their spouse when making their withdrawal choice. Spouses of FERS employees, even if they are separated, will have the right to a joint and survivor annuity with 50 percent survivor benefit, level payments, and no cash refund feature unless the spouse sends a waiver of his or her right to that annuity. Spouses of CSRS employees must be notified of any withdrawal election.

Here is an excellent chart from the Federal Office of Personnel Management that summarizes Spouse's Rights regarding the TSP.

Spouse's Rights Regarding the TSP			
Retirement System	**Activity**	**Requirement**	**Exceptions**
FERS	Loan	Spouse must give written consent to the loan.	Whereabouts unknown or exceptional circumstances.
In-Service	Withdrawal	Spouse must give written consent to the withdrawal.	Whereabouts unknown or exceptional circumstances.
Post-Employment	Withdrawal*	Spouse is entitled to a joint life annuity with 50% survivor benefit, level payments, and no cash refund feature unless he or she waives this right.	Whereabouts unknown or exceptional circumstances.
CSRS	Loan	TSP must notify spouse of the participant's loan application.	Whereabouts unknown.
In-Service	Withdrawal	TSP must notify spouse of participant's request.	Whereabouts unknown.
Post-Employment	Withdrawal*	TSP must notify spouse of the participant's election before withdrawal.	Whereabouts unknown.

* Spouses' rights apply only to accounts of more than $3,500.

When Employees Must Withdraw from the TSP

Employees can leave money in the TSP if they leave federal service, but are not yet ready to collect it. They must begin withdrawing from the TSP by April 1 of the year following their 70½ birthday. If they are already 70½ when they leave their federal job, they must begin taking out money the year after they separate from government employment. The IRS sets "required minimum distributions" for TSP withdrawals, which are the same as for IRAs. We'll discuss minimum distributions in Chapter 21.

If an employee dies before the TSP is completely withdrawn, the money goes to their designated beneficiary.

Purchasing an Annuity

If an employee decides to purchase an annuity with his or her TSP funds, they are purchased from Metropolitan Life Insurance Company. There are three types of annuities available.

1. Single life—Paid during the employee's lifetime.
2. Joint life with spouse—Paid to employee while both parties of the couple are alive. After one dies the payment is made to the surviving spouse.
3. Joint life with someone other than a spouse—As with the spouse, the payment is made to the retiree while he or she is alive. When one of the beneficiaries dies, the payments continue to the survivor for life.

Payment for joint life annuities can be either 100 percent or 50 percent, which means after death the person who survives will either get 100 percent of the payment or 50 percent of the payment, depending on the choice made at the time the annuity was started. The initial annuity payment is higher if the 50 percent option is chosen. Other options are also available. If you are a federal employee and close to retirement, you should contact your agency personnel office for more details about annuity options.

What Happens If You Don't Designate a Beneficiary?

If you fail to file a beneficiary designation form, the money is not lost. TSP distribution is done according to law in this order:

1. To widow or widower
2. If none, to child or children equally, and descendants of deceased children by representation
3. If none, to parents equally or to the surviving parent
4. If none, to the appointed executor or administrator of the estate
5. If none, to the next of kin who is entitled to the estate, according to the laws of the state in which you reside at the time of your death

Ready to Retire

Rules for employees ready to retire are different depending upon whether they are in the FERS or CSRS system. FERS employees' minimum age is gradually increased from fifty-five to fifty-seven. The minimum age for CSRS employees depends upon on their age and number of years of service.

FERS Retirement

FERS employees can choose to retire immediately upon separating from service, defer their retirement, or retire early. Eligibility for any of these options depends on age and number of years of service. The first thing a person must check is whether they meet the minimum age requirements.

> The first thing a person must check is whether they meet the minimum age requirements.

FERS Minimum Retirement Age Requirements

If you were born . . . . Your MRA is
Before 1948 55
In 1948 . . . . 55 and 2 months
In 1949 . . . . 55 and 4 months
In 1950 . . . . 55 and 6 months
In 1951 . . . . 55 and 8 months
In 1952 . . . . 55 and 10 months
In 1953 through 1964 56
In 1965 . . . . 56 and 2 months
In 1966 . . . . 56 and 4 months
In 1967 . . . . 56 and 6 months
In 1968 . . . . 56 and 8 months
In 1969 . . . . 56 and 10 months
In 1970 and after 57

If a person wants to retire within thirty days of the date he or she stops working, then the following sets of age and service requirements must be met.

FERS Service Requirements—Immediate Payout	
Age	**Years of Service**
62	5
60	20
Minimum Retirement Age (MRA)	30
MRA	10

If a person has reached the minimum retirement age having worked at least ten years but less than thirty years, then his or her benefits will be reduced by 5 percent a year for each year before age sixty-two. For example, someone whose MRA is fifty-six and who has worked ten years will have six years of reductions at 5 percent for a total reduction of 30 percent. The only exception to this rule is that if the person has reached sixty with at least twenty years of service there will be no reduction in benefits.

Early retirement has a different set of rules for FERS employees. First, the employee must either have left employment involuntarily or voluntarily as part of a reorganization or reduction in force. They will be eligible for early retirement under these circumstances if they are at least age fifty with twenty years of service or any age with more than twenty-five years of service.

The third group of retirees are those who deferred retirement, in other words delayed retirement rather than withdrawing their funds when they separated from the federal workforce. In order to qualify for deferred retirement, they must have completed at least five years of civilian service.

The ages at which this group of FERS employees is eligible to receive benefits is shown in this chart:

> In order to qualify for deferred retirement, they must have completed at least five years of civilian service.

FERS Service Requirement—Deferred Payout	
Age	**Years of Service**
62	5
60	20
MRA	30
MRA	10

The reduction for employees who retire at the MRA with at least ten years but less than thirty is the same as noted above. The retirement benefit will be reduced by 5 percent a year for each year the retiree is under sixty-two unless they have twenty years of service and are at least sixty-two.

CSRS Retirement

CSRS retirement eligibility is a bit different. Here is a chart from the Office of Personnel Management.

Eligibility for CSRS Retirement

You may retire under the Civil Service Retirement System (CSRS) at the following ages, and receive an immediate annuity, if you have at least the amount of federal service shown in the table below:

Type of Retirement	Minimum Age	Minimum Service (Years)	Special Requirements
Optional	62	5	None
	60	20	None
	55	30	None
Special Optional	50	20	You must retire under special provisions for air traffic controllers or law enforcement and firefighter personnel. Air traffic controllers can also retire at any age with 25 years of service as an air traffic controller.
Early Optional	Any Age	25	Your agency must be undergoing a major reorganization, reduction-in-force, or transfer of function determined by the Office of Personnel Management. Annuity is reduced if under 55.
	50	20	
Discontinued Service	Any Age	25	Your separation is involuntary and not a removal for misconduct delinquency.
	50	20	
Disability	Any Age	5	You must be disabled for useful and efficient service in your current position and any other vacant position at the same grade or pay level within your commuting area and current agency for which you are qualified. Must be prior to retirement, or within one year of separation, except in cases of mental incompetence.

Retirement Preparations

How one goes about retiring from the federal government can be almost as complicated as reading about the plans. The key thing to remember as a retiree is not to resign before applying for retirement.

In fact, a retiree should never formally resign. The completed and signed retirement application is equivalent to a letter of resignation. Planning for federal retirement should begin five years before a person expects to leave the job. The reason federal employees must start so early is that in order to have life and health insurance coverage in retirement, these must be in place five years before retirement. The five-year participation requirement can be waived in exceptional circumstances at the discretion of the personnel office.

Another critical item to check five years out is the official employee personnel folder to be sure all military and civilian service records are there. If any are missing, the employee has time to make sure the errors are corrected. As you have seen above, years of service are critical to the amount of the final retirement benefit.

Calculating Benefits

Calculating benefits can be a very complicated task. In fact, the Office of Personnel Management staff have an extensive manual on how to do it, which you can access online at *www.opm.gov/asd/htm/ HOD.htm*. Unless you really have a strong desire to learn the nitty-gritty details about how to calculate benefits, you are much better off using the retirement calculator at *www.seniors.gov/fedcalc.html*.

Federal employees have the most comprehensive calculator available on the Internet, which computes not only their retirement benefits under CSRS or FERS, but also incorporates the current and future TSP savings and Social Security benefits. It will even calculate normal and early retirement, as well as disability benefits.

The calculator can be used by almost all federal employees including special occupations such as law enforcement, firefighters, air traffic controllers, and congressional retirees. The only major group of federal employees excluded from this calculator is foreign service employees. While the Ballpark E\$timate calculation we did to find your retirement gap is useful, especially if your spouse is not a federal employee, this calculator will give you even more accurate estimates if you are a federal employee.

WARNING! Your Family Could Lose Benefits

A retiree who dies after separating from employment but before filing the retirement application can really hurt their survivor benefits. If no retirement application has been filed, the retiree's family will get no life insurance, no survivor benefits, and no survivor health insurance coverage. Not only will your family have to deal with the shock of your death, they will also face a major reduction in the money you planned as part of your retirement funding. When getting ready to retire, take things slowly and be sure to jump through all the hoops correctly to protect your family.

Survivor Benefits

Survivor benefits can get complicated; we'll just take a quick look at the key points. A surviving spouse can collect benefits for life unless he or she remarries before fifty-five. If a marriage lasted longer than thirty years, a surviving spouse can collect benefits even if he or she remarried before age fifty-five. A federal employee who does not provide for his or her spouse when applying for benefits will deny any benefits to his or her spouse after death.

Children under the age of eighteen who are unmarried and dependent upon the employee are eligible for benefits. These benefits can continue until the age of twenty-two if the child is in school. Children who were disabled before they turned eighteen can receive survivor benefits as long as the disabling condition continues and the child is not capable of self-support. Benefits do end even for a disabled child if he or she marries.

Divorce can add a major complication to the payment of your benefits if your ex-spouse has a court order awarding his or her benefits. Under CSRS, the maximum benefit payable after the death of a retiree is 55 percent of the annual benefit. Under FERS, the maximum is 50 percent. If the court awarded an ex-spouse 35 percent, the surviving spouse could only receive 20 percent under CSRS or 15 percent under FERS. If the ex-spouse was awarded the entire benefit, then a retiree can ask that a contingency award be put in place if the former spouse dies or becomes ineligible for the survivor benefit, primarily because of remarriage.

As you can see, federal benefits get very complicated. If you are a federal employee or retiree and want to learn more about the retirement programs, go to *www.opm.gov/retire*.

Federal Retirement and Social Security

Two provisions can affect federal retirement benefits and their relationship to Social Security. The Government Pension Offset can lower a spouse's benefit and the Windfall Elimination Provision can lower a federal retiree's benefits.

The Government Pension Offset can reduce a spouse's Social Security benefit if a federal employee has a government pension

> Divorce can add a major complication to the payment of your benefits if your ex-spouse has a court order awarding his or her benefits.

from work not covered by Social Security. A spouse's Social Security benefit can be reduced by two-thirds of any federal pension based on employment not covered by Social Security. Employees exempt from this Offset include those automatically covered by FERS and those who transferred to FERS before January 1, 1988, or during the belated transfer period that ended on June 10, 1988. If an employee chose FERS after June 10, 1988, he or she must have five years of federal employment covered by Social Security to be exempt from the Offset.

The Windfall Elimination Provision can lower federal retirees' Social Security benefits if the worker reached age sixty-two or became disabled after 1985 and qualifies for a federal pension after 1985. Retirees are not impacted by the Windfall Elimination provision if one of these three conditions exists:

1. Eligible to retire before January 1, 1986
2. First employed by federal government after December 31, 1983
3. Have thirty or more years of substantial earnings under Social Security

Employees can determine the impact of the Windfall Elimination Provision or the Government Pension Offset by contacting the Social Security Administration.

FEDWeek publishes excellent planning guides for federal employees that are updated annually. These guides do a good job of translating the sometimes difficult to understand information on CSRS and FERS. You can order the guides online at *www.fedweek.com/Publications/default.asp* or write or call them at FEDweek, 11551 Nuckols Road, Suite L, Glen Allen, VA 23059, (804) 288-5321.

Federal Military Employees

Folks who serve now or previously served in the military have very different benefits. In fact, if they have at least twenty years of service, regardless of age, they can retire and collect benefits. Some people can begin collecting benefits in their late thirties or early forties if

FEDWeek publishes excellent planning guides for federal employees that are updated annually.

they started their military career early in life. The catch—there are no retirement benefits if you serve less than twenty years.

Recommendations have been made to replace the military retirement system with a civilian plan that vests participants at age fifty-five or older, but any change along these lines likely would require the revamping of the compensation of personnel systems of the U.S. Armed Forces. At least at this point, there is no strong support for such a move and the Department of Defense believes it would "hurt retention and erode the quality and motivation of U.S. military forces."

Retirees who entered active duty prior to September 8, 1980 receive benefits determined by multiplying a service factor (2.5 percent up to a maximum of 75 percent of base pay) by active duty base pay at the time of retirement. Retirement benefits for anyone who joined the military after that day will be figured on a different base pay. The base pay for them will be calculated using the average of the highest thirty-six months of active duty base pay. These later retirees will also see their initial cost-of-living adjustment reduced by 1 percent. The military has an excellent Web site to find out more details about the retirement program: *www.dfas.mil/money/retired*.

In October 2000, legislation was passed to allow military employees to contribute to the TSP. Military employees were allowed to enroll for the first time during their open season—October 9, 2001 to January 31, 2002. TSP participation is optional, as it is for the CSRS participants. The maximum contribution for 2002 is 7 percent of pay.

State and Local Retirement Plans

There were over 2,200 state and local retirement systems nationwide at the end of 1999 according to the U.S. Census Bureau. The task of developing benefit information on all these programs would be mind-boggling, so we won't even try that here. You will find a summary of key commonalities using the report, "State and Local Retirement Plans: Innovation and Renovation," prepared by the Employee Benefits Research Institute. If you are a state or local employee, contact your employing agency for more information about your plan. Plan sponsors can include state, county, and municipal governments; school districts; and other special-purpose authorities.

Defined-Benefit Plans More Common for Public Employees

Ninety percent of full-time public-sector employees were covered under a defined-benefit plan and 14 percent have a defined-contribution plan in 1998, according to the U.S. Department of Labor's Bureau of Labor Statistics. Some full-time public-sector employees have both a defined-benefit and defined-contribution plan. Part-time employees are less likely to have retirement benefits. Fifty-nine percent had a defined-benefit plan and 5 percent participated in a defined-contribution plan. More public-sector employees are adding defined-contribution plans, so there will probably be an increase in the number of employees participating in these plans.

In most states where defined-contribution plans are being added, they are added as a supplement. There are a few notable exceptions. Michigan attempted to replace its defined-benefits plan with a defined-contribution plan for state employees and public school employees retiring after March 31, 1997. Public school employees fought the change and the required change was repealed for them. In 2001, a bill was introduced to give state employees a choice between the defined-benefit and defined-contribution plans. Florida created an optional defined-benefit plan and will allow its current and new employees a one-time option to choose between the two types of plans. Washington state's mandatory plan, approved in 2000, includes both a defined-benefit and defined-contribution component. The state funds the defined-benefit portion and the employee funds the defined-contribution portion.

Public-Sector Funding

Funding of most public-sector plans is very secure. In fact, according to EBRI's research study, 46 percent of these plans were 100 percent funded in 1998. Another 30 percent of the public-sector plans had funding levels between 75 percent and 99.9 percent. Assets held in public-sector plans make up 30 percent of the entire retirement market. These numbers may have dropped since 1998, since many of these funds do invest in stock and the market took a considerable nosedive since that time. Once complete information is available from the Federal Reserve and other sources regarding end-of-year numbers for 2001, the public-sector employees will have a better idea of how their retirement funds rode out the stock market storm.

Public-Sector Retirement Benefits

Contributions to public-sector plans vary dramatically. In 2001, Workplace Economics reported that employee contributions ranged from 1.25 percent to 9.75 percent of salary, if contributions were required at all. State contributions ranged from 0 to 19.38 percent. Contributions from employees are required in forty-four out of the fifty states.

Public Funds File Suit Against Enron

Public-sector retirement assets were affected by the fall of Enron, as were many mutual funds and other investment portfolios. The states of Georgia, Ohio, and Washington have filed suit and asked to be named lead plaintiff in a class action lawsuit against Enron Corporation. These three states alone estimate a $330 million loss as a result of alleged fraud. The state of Georgia sent its Teachers Retirement System members a memo stating that the Enron loss represented only .02 of 1 percent of the current assets totaling $39.5 billion.

Vesting in public-sector plans is usually based on a "cliff vesting" schedule, as illustrated earlier, whereby employees must wait five to ten years to be fully vested in their plans, depending on the plan's vesting rules. Workplace Economics reported that for statewide plans twelve states required ten years of service before an employee is fully vested, two states required eight years of service, and twenty-seven states required five years of service.

Minimum retirement age varies widely across plans as well. Bureau of Labor statistics found that 41 percent of the public-sector plans had no age requirement, but did require various levels of service ranging from twenty to thirty-five years. Plans that did include an age requirement varied from age fifty-five to sixty-five with various service requirements ranging from five to thirty years of service.

Formulas for defined benefits varied, but 75 percent of the retirement plans were calculated by multiplying the total number of years in service times the average final compensation (based on a set number of years or months) times a factor for benefit accrual (which averaged 1.9 percent in 1998 according to the U.S. Department of Labor).

While most private plans do not have provisions for cost-of-living increases, 55 percent of state plans do offer some form of cost-of-living adjustment for employees, according to the U.S. Department of Labor (DOL). Workplace Economics reported in 2001 that almost all general-coverage state systems provide some form of cost-of-living adjustment, but it is automatic in only thirty-seven states.

Public-sector defined-benefit retirement plans are not portable, so many public-sector employees are allowed to purchase service credit if they change jobs and enter another public-sector retirement system. The DOL reported in 2000 that 72 percent of full-time state and local employees were able to purchase credits for prior government service based on a 1998 survey. DOL found that forty-seven out of fifty statewide retirement systems did allow at least some participants to purchase out-of-state teaching service credit.

Section 457s

Most public-sector defined-contribution plans fall under Section 457 of the U.S. tax codes and so, like 401(k)s and 403(b)s, they are known as Section 457s. Prior to 2001, these funds could only be rolled over into another Section 457. Under the new 2001 tax law, these funds are now more portable and can be rolled over into other types of qualified retirement plans and into IRAs.

There is also another unique tax-code entity in the public sector called 401(a)s. Many states are creating these for their matching contributions, so employees can contribute the maximum amount they are allowed to deposit in a Section 457. In 2002, public sector employees could contribute a maximum of $11,000, which is increased by $1,000 per year until it tops out at $15,000 in 2006. After that year, the maximum contribution amount will be indexed to inflation. Catch-up contributions are also allowed for people after they reach the age of fifty. In 2002, people fifty and older will be able to put in an additional $1,000. The catch-up contributions allowed increases by $1,000 per year until 2006 when it tops out at $5,000. After that date, the maximum catch-up contribution will be indexed to inflation.

State employees who participate in their Section 457s may also qualify for a Saver's Tax Credit up to $1,000 (50 percent of $2,000 contributions) during tax years 2002 through 2006. To qualify, their adjusted gross household income (AGI) cannot exceed $50,000 if married filing jointly, $37,500 if head of household, or $25,000 if single or married filing separately. The amount of the credit depends on the amount of qualifying contributions and their AGI. This credit is in addition to the deduction or exclusion allowed for the contribution.

> Catch-up contributions are also allowed for people after they reach the age of fifty.

Future Trends

The future for public-sector retirement plans is probably more stable than private-sector plans. This is primarily due to the political forces of change or attempts to block changes that rule over modifications to these types of retirement programs. According to a 1999 study done by the Congress's General Accounting Office (GAO), there are a number of changes being considered. The GAO found that states that were considering change, favored switching to a defined-contribution plan because of possible cost reductions and increased portability. Opponents of a switch to defined-contributions primarily fight for further study. Some states have found a lack of interest and support for any change.

Certainly, you have figured out by now that the public-sector retirement world is very complex. If you are a public-sector employee at the state or local level, you have little protection under federal laws because state plans are primarily exempt from ERISA. The forces that keep most public-sector employees secure in their benefits are public opinion and the political savvy of public-sector lobbyists.

For more information on this topic, visit our Web site at www.businesstown.com

Traditional and
Roth IRAs

Types of IRAs

The backbone to everyone's personal retirement saving is the Individual Retirement Account (IRA). First introduced in 1974, it's taken on many faces since then. In fact, the IRA became so popular so quickly, it didn't take long for Congress to take back some privileges. By the 1980s, Congress was already tightening deposit rules and tax incentives.

There are still some remnants of the original IRA in existence, but only for low- and middle-income wage earners or folks who don't have a retirement plan at work. Today, the IRA has many alternatives. Which one you should use depends on your personal financial situation as well as your eligibility for each type.

Our first order of business is to define the types of IRAs. The tax-deductible traditional IRA represents what's left of the original IRA introduced in 1974. It's primarily for workers who don't have a retirement plan at work, single workers with adjusted gross incomes (AGI) of less than $44,000, or a married couple filing jointly with AGI of less than $64,000. Workers earning more than that with a pension plan at work have a choice of two options. The best alternative is the Roth IRA, provided their AGI is less than $110,000 if single, or $160,000 if married.

All is not lost for workers who don't qualify for either of these two; they can use the non-tax-deductible traditional IRA. There are no income limits to qualify for the non-tax-deductible IRA.

To contribute to any of the IRA types, you must have earned income that at least totals the amount to be contributed or be the spouse of someone who does. Earned income can be derived from wages, salaries, tips, bonuses, professional fees, and any other service you provide and report as income to the Internal Revenue Service (IRS). Spouses who don't have earned income can use the Spousal IRA. There is also another type of IRA, called the Education IRA, that we won't be discussing here because it's primarily for college savings. We've already discussed the SEP-IRA and SIMPLE IRA in Chapter 10 so they too won't be covered again here.

The IRA retirement landscape is a moving target and will continue to be one through at least 2008, thanks to the 2001 tax law. The good news is that as you prepare for retirement, the changes will

> The IRA became so popular so quickly, it didn't take long for Congress to take back some privileges.

give you the opportunity to invest even more in your IRA accounts. In fact, if you are fifty or older, you have even more incentive to use the IRA for savings. Since contribution levels are the same for all types of IRAs, we'll be discussing those first here. The following chart, which shows the changing contribution landscape, will help you plan for each year.

Allowable IRA Contributions by Tax Year		
Tax Year	Allowable Contribution	Additional Contributions for those 50+
2002–2004	$3,000	$500
2005	$4,000	$500
2006–2007	$4,000	$1,000
2008	$5,000	$1,000
After 2008	Adjusted for inflation in $500 increments	

Now, we'll move on to the nitty-gritty. We'll take a closer look at the eligibility and contribution rules for each of the IRA types.

Plan Basics

The tax-deductible IRA is primarily for folks who have no retirement plan at work or have earnings below eligible limits. There are some exceptions though, depending on your earnings.

For a single person with an employer-sponsored retirement plan, the most he or she can earn is an AGI of $44,000 in 2002, but even at that level will not be able to deduct the full contribution. Just to make things difficult, Congress added a complicated phaseout rule for AGI earnings between $34,000 and $44,000, which is adjusted for inflation periodically. If you are married and filing jointly, the phaseout rules impact your AGI earnings between $54,000 and $64,000, provided both of you are participating in employer-sponsored retirement plans. The IRS provides a worksheet to help you calculate how much you can contribute to a tax-deductible IRA and write it off as a deduction on your 1040 if you are in the phaseout rules earning level.

The IRS provides a worksheet to help you calculate how much you can contribute to a tax-deductible IRA and write it off as a deduction on your 1040 if you are in the phaseout rules earning level.

Another key exception is for married couples when only one member of the couple has an employer-sponsored plan. In these situations, the person not covered by a plan at work can make the full contribution to a tax-deductible IRA and deduct it on their joint tax return as long as the couples' AGI is below $150,000. If the couple earns more than that, the person not covered by an employer-sponsored plan can make a partial contribution subject to the phaseout rules for $150,000 to $160,000.

If you are married filing separately, almost no IRA deduction is allowed. The deduction phaseout rule begins at $0 and no deduction is allowed if you earn over $10,000.

Roth IRA

If you don't qualify for a tax-deductible IRA, your next best option is the Roth IRA. The Roth IRA might even make sense for you if you don't need the tax deduction.

The greatest advantage of the Roth IRA is that at retirement all your money is withdrawn from the Roth IRA completely tax-free as long as you are at least 59½. So you might lose the deduction up front, but on the back-end you don't have to pay taxes even on the earnings as long as the money is in the Roth for at least five years. Another big advantage is that you don't have to start taking out your money at any age, while the other types of IRAs require you to start taking out money at age 70½. The folks who inherit anything left over from your retirement funds will also appreciate the Roth IRA, because they don't have to pay taxes on your contributions, only on the earnings.

Roth eligibility is not affected by your participation in an employee-sponsored retirement plan, but there are maximum earning limits. In fact, its benefits are so good, Congress made it difficult to figure out whether you can contribute if your earnings are near the contribution limits of $110,000 for singles or $160,000 for married couples.

> Roth eligibility is not affected by your participation in an employee-sponsored retirement plan.

TRADITIONAL AND ROTH IRAS

The first thing you must figure out to determine if you are eligible is your modified adjusted gross income (MAGI). Here are the IRS rules for calculating your MAGI for Roth purposes:

1. Subtract any income resulting from the conversion of an IRA (other than a Roth IRA) to a Roth IRA (conversion income). Conversions will be discussed in greater detail below.

2. Add the following deductions and exclusions:

   Traditional IRA deduction
   Student loan interest deduction
   Foreign earned income exclusion
   Foreign housing exclusion or deduction
   Exclusion of qualified bond interest shown on Form 8815
   Exclusion of employer-paid adoption expenses shown on Form 8839

Effect of Modified AGI on Roth IRA Contribution

This table shows whether your contribution to a Roth IRA is affected by the amount of your modified adjusted gross income (MAGI).

If you have taxable compensation and your filing status is:	And your modified AGI is:	Then:
Married Filing Jointly	Less than $150,000	You can contribute up to $2,000 for 2001 ($3,000 for 2002 or $3,500 for 2002 if age 50 or older).
	At least $150,000 but less than $160,000	The amount you can contribute is reduced based on the phaseout rules.
	$160,000 or more	You cannot contribute to a Roth IRA.
Married Filing Separately and you lived with your spouse at any time during the year	Zero (-0-)	You can contribute up to $2,000 for 2001 ($3,000 for 2002 or $3,500 for 2002 if 50 or older).
	More than zero (-0-) but less than $10,000	The amount you can contribute is reduced according to the phaseout rules.
	$10,000 or more	You cannot contribute to a Roth IRA.
Single, Head of Household, Qualifying Widow(er), or **Married Filing Separately** and you did not live with your spouse at any time during the year	Less than $95,000	You can contribute up to $2,000 for 2001 ($3,000 for 2002 or $3,500 for 2002 if age 50 or older).
	At least $95,000 but less than $110,000	The amount you can contribute is reduced according to the phaseout rules.
	$110,000 or more	You cannot contribute to a Roth IRA.

Record-Keeping Is Crucial

Even though the tax advantages are not as great for the tax-deductible IRA, it still allows you to grow your money tax-deferred. You will pay taxes on the earnings, but not on your contributions. Record-keeping for this type of IRA is critical in order to avoid paying unnecessary taxes. If you can't prove how much you contributed, then you will have to pay taxes on all your withdrawals in retirement. Unless the financial institution through which your IRA is invested keeps track of your contributions for you, the easiest way to keep a paper trail is to file your annual year-end statements for your IRAs.

For tax years beginning after December 31, 2001, you will also have to add any deduction for qualified tuition and related expenses. Once you have computed your MAGI, you can then use the chart from the Internal Revenue Service on page 213 to figure out whether you can contribute to a Roth IRA. Unfortunately, Congress had succeeded in making this very convoluted.

Now that we've got that nasty business out of the way, let's look at what you can do if you don't qualify for a Roth IRA. You'll basically be in this boat if your income exceeds $110,000 as a single person or $160,000 as a married couple. Anyone who is still married but filing separately can't contribute to a Roth IRA if they are earning more than $10,000.

Non-Tax-Deductible IRA

No matter how much you are earning you can contribute to a non-tax-deductible IRA. You can also contribute even if you have an employer-sponsored retirement plan. In other words, if you can't qualify for a tax-deductible IRA or a Roth IRA, you will qualify for a non-tax-deductible IRA.

Spousal IRAs

A spouse who has no earned income can still take advantage of one of these IRA types provided his or her spouse earns enough to cover his or her contribution. This type of IRA is called the Spousal IRA. Any of the IRA types mentioned above can be used for this IRA, but the eligibility rules for each do apply to the choice of IRA for the Spousal account.

Contribution Options

You can contribute to an IRA at any time during the year for which the contribution is intended as well as into the next year until you actually file your taxes (typically, April 15). To get the most out of the growth of your money, the best time to make a deposit is January 1 (or as soon after that date as you can) of the tax year for which it is intended. Many people make monthly or quarterly deposits because they find it fits better in their budget. Others wait until the last possible minute when they file their taxes.

Unwinding

There's no good reason to wait to invest unless you just don't have the funds. If for some reason you find out you need the money later in the year, you can withdraw the money, which is also known as "unwinding" the contribution, as long as you do so before your tax filing date.

The one thing you definitely don't want to do is contribute too much in any one tax year. With the allowable contribution into an IRA becoming such a moving target since the 2001 tax law, be sure you are depositing the right amount for the right tax year. If you make a mistake and don't correct it by "unwinding" the payment, you could be socked with a 6 percent excise tax on the excess amount and any gains. If you do withdraw an IRA contribution for any reason, be sure you take out any gains made on that money as well to avoid a penalty.

Rollovers

Another way to contribute to your IRAs is to roll over another type of retirement savings into your IRA, such as the balance of your 401(k) after you leave a job. There used to be some limitations on rolling over funds from a 403(b) and Section 457 plan, but after passage of the new tax law in 2001, those funds can be rolled over into your IRA as well.

If your spouse dies, you can also roll over any of his or her retirement savings from his or her tax-qualified retirement plans into your IRA. The new tax law also made it possible for you to roll over after-tax employee contributions to your tax-qualified plan at work into an IRA, but if you do so, be sure to keep track of the money on which you already paid taxes. You certainly don't want to pay the taxes twice.

When rolling over funds into an IRA, the best way to do it is to roll the funds from one type of retirement plan into another

> When rolling over funds into an IRA, roll the funds from one type of retirement plan into another without personally touching the funds.

without personally touching the funds. That way you avoid any tax consequences. If for some reason you don't want to do a direct rollover, you can have the money sent to you. Once the money is withdrawn from your tax-qualified retirement plan, you have sixty days to redeposit it into another tax-qualified retirement vehicle, such as an IRA. If you miss the deadline, you could be subject to penalty and taxes, which we'll discuss in greater detail below under withdrawal options. The IRS can waive the penalties if failure to comply was caused by casualty, disaster, or events beyond your reasonable control.

How to Invest

Once you've picked the type of IRA for which you qualify, your next step will be to decide where to open the account. You can start an IRA at a bank, insurance company, mutual fund, or brokerage company. The primary force driving this decision will be the types of investments you want to make and the type of assistance you would like from the company holding the funds. Another key factor you should watch closely is the administrative and investing costs your account will be charged.

Insurance company alternatives may give you what appears to be the safest investment opportunity by offering to guarantee your basis plus a small gain, but they will also charge you the highest fees to provide that security. Discount brokers may offer you the lowest investment costs, but they will provide the least amount of advice as you build your portfolio. You also won't get much advice when you directly purchase funds from a mutual fund company, but well-balanced funds can be less risky and require less research time than purchasing stocks directly.

If you do want to seek advice for how to invest your money, your best bet would be to work with either a bank or full-service broker. Another alternative would be to hire a fee-based financial planner to provide investment assistance. The advantage to choosing a fee-based financial planner is that they do not make their money through commissions from product sales and are least likely to be

> Discount brokers may offer you the lowest investment costs, but they will provide the least amount of advice as you build your portfolio.

influenced by money to be made and therefore can give more objective advice. If you do work with a planner, you will still need to open an account with a bank, broker, mutual fund, or insurance company to actually invest the money.

Withdrawal Options and Income-Tax Impacts

Once your money is securely in place, the next time you'll want to think about those funds is when it comes time to withdraw them. You can start making withdrawals once you reach age 59½ without having to pay penalties, but you will have to pay taxes on withdrawals for all IRAs except the Roth IRA. Early withdrawals could cost you. There is a 10 percent penalty on funds withdrawn before age 59½ plus you must pay taxes on the money withdrawn as though it were current income.

You can avoid penalties before age 59½ if you are withdrawing funds for one of these reasons:

1. You have become disabled.
2. You're buying your first home and want to withdraw $10,000 or less. In this case, you can also avoid taxes on the withdrawal as current income.
3. You must pay off significant medical expenses.
4. You lost your job and must pay for medical insurance.
5. You want to go back to school and use the money for qualified higher education expenses.
6. You have reached the age of fifty-five and have retired or were terminated from your job.

If you have a Roth IRA and the money has been deposited for at least five years, you can withdraw your own contributions without any tax or penalty. In most cases, you will have to pay taxes on earnings for early withdrawal if the money has been on deposit for five years. You can withdraw IRA money completely tax-free that has been on deposit for more than five years even if you are not 59½, if

Special Rules for Early IRA Withdrawal

If you really need the money, but aren't yet age 59½, there is one other way to avoid the penalty for the traditional IRA. You can take what is called an annuity. You must take this annuity as annual payments for five years or until you turn 59½, whichever is longer. The amount you can take is in an annuity based on the number of years the IRS thinks you still have to live. It's a rather complicated formula, but you can find out more about it on the IRS Web site at *www.irs. ustreas.gov/prod/forms_pubs/ pubs/p93903.htm.* Once you set up a payment period, you will not be able to change your distributions or you will be penalized. After the payment period ends, you can change your distributions. If you do plan to annuitize your IRA, it's best to do that with the advice of a tax specialist.

you are using the money to buy a first home or if you become disabled. Remember, that money was put into the Roth IRA after you already had paid taxes on it.

With all IRAs, except the Roth IRA, there comes a time when you must take out your money. Once you reach age 70½, you must start withdrawing from your IRA by April 1 of the next year. If you don't start taking out your money, you could face a 50 percent excise tax on the money you did not withdraw as required. This rule is called the "minimum required distribution." We'll explore how this works in much greater detail in Chapter 21.

Another fact of retirement life you will face if you don't have a Roth IRA is paying taxes on your withdrawals from the IRA as though they were current income. There are two exceptions: Roth IRA withdrawals in retirement are completely tax-free and only the earnings part of your withdrawals from a non-tax-deductible IRA is taxed.

Converting to a Roth IRA

You may be thinking that since the Roth is such a great deal at retirement, it might make sense to convert to a Roth IRA right away and avoid taxes on any future gains. Rollovers from a traditional IRA to a Roth IRA are allowed as long as your adjusted gross income (AGI) is $100,000 or below. If you want to convert your IRAs, you will have to pay taxes immediately on all your funds in a traditional IRA that you roll over, except contributions which may already have been taxed in the non-deductible type.

If you must use your IRA funds to pay the taxes, it will negate most of your tax savings, so don't do it. You'll lose all the future growth on that money you withdrew to pay the taxes. You don't have to convert all your traditional IRAs in one year, to help make the tax bite easier. If you are sure your taxes will be lower in retirement than they are now, it definitely doesn't make sense to convert and pay the higher tax rate.

If you must use your IRA funds to pay the taxes, it will negate most of your tax savings.

Which IRA Is Best for You?

If you have gotten to this point and realized you qualify for more than one type of IRA, you may be wondering which one is best for you. The decision will depend on lots of variables, such as your current tax situation, whether you need a tax deduction, and whether that tax deduction would make it possible for you to contribute more to your IRA.

Basically, if you are sure you will be in a lower tax bracket when you get to retirement, the best rule is to avoid paying taxes now. So, for example, if you are currently in a 27 percent tax bracket and expect to be in a 15 percent tax bracket in retirement, your best bet would be to avoid taxes and use the tax-deductible IRA. This way you defer the taxes until your tax rate will be lower.

Tax rates are more of a moving target than IRAs under the new tax law. There has been a new 10 percent tax rate added for the first $7,000 of income for singles and $14,000 of income for married couples. Other tax rates are also dropping as well. Here's a chart to show you what is happening to various tax brackets over the next few years (that is, of course, if Congress doesn't act to stop or delay the reduction now that the government has moved back to deficit spending).

Tax rates are more of a moving target than IRAs under the new tax law.

Future Tax Rates

	2002–2003	2004–2005	2006 and after
28% Rate Reduced to:	27%	26%	25%
31% Rate Reduced to:	30%	29%	28%
36% Rate Reduced to:	35%	34%	33%
39.6% Rate Reduced to:	38.6%	37.6%	35%

A married couple filing jointly may also be able to count on a lower tax rate beginning in 2005 because the new law provides marriage tax penalty relief. If you are retiring after 2005 this could mean you'll be paying lower taxes.

Unfortunately, no one can be sure of their tax obligation because Congress could change its mind several more times before we ever get to retirement.

Unfortunately, no one can be sure of their tax obligation because Congress could change its mind several more times before we ever get to retirement. It's somewhat of a crapshoot to try to plan your life around what your future tax bill might be.

Here is a chart that compares a fully funded tax-deductible IRA versus a partially funded Roth IRA. To simplify the calculation for demonstration purposes, we've chosen $4,000 as the fully funded amount and 26 percent, which is the tax rate when the $4,000 contribution will take effect. Remember, contribution limits are changing each year between now and when you retire. The Roth IRA figures are developed assuming that the amount you will need to pay in taxes will reduce the amount you can deposit into your Roth.

Annual Contributions: Roth vs. Tax-Deductible IRA*			
	10 years	20 years	30 years
Roth @ 15%–$3400	$53,195	$168,038	$415,976
Roth @ 26%–$2960	$46,311	$146,292	$362,144
Tax Deductible–$4,000	$62,582	$197,692	$489,384

*Assume 8% growth rate, Roth funding reduced by needed tax payment

If you do have the resources to fully fund your Roth IRA, even though you don't have the tax deduction benefits, then it is a no-brainer. You should definitely select the Roth. Tax rates are always an uncertainty and the tax-free growth plus greater flexibility at the time of withdrawal makes the Roth the best choice.

As you can see from the chart, if you are taxed at a 26 percent tax rate and reduce your contributions by the amount lost to taxes, there is a significant difference at retirement. As long as your tax rate at retirement will be 15 percent, you should definitely use the tax-deductible IRA to build the larger nest egg.

For example, let's look at the first year of retirement after thirty years of contributing to the IRA. If you are taking out 5 percent your first year, the withdrawal for the Roth at 15 percent is $20,799 and the Roth at 27 percent is $18,107. Both of these amounts are withdrawn tax-free. The withdrawal from the tax-deductible IRA would be $24,469. At first glance that might look better, but you must pay taxes on the money. At a 15 percent tax rate, that would be $20,799 and at a 25 percent tax rate it would be $18,352. You can see in this scenario you do a bit better with the tax-deductible IRA at a 25 percent tax bracket.

There is only one reason to choose a non-tax-deductible traditional IRA: You don't qualify for the Roth IRA or deductible IRA. Don't despair, it still makes sense to defer taxes on the growth of your money that you are putting aside for your retirement nest egg.

Closing Your Gap

IRAs are a great tool to help you close your retirement gap. If you are married, both you and your spouse should open individual IRAs. If you can only afford to fund one of them, then fund the IRA for the person who has the lowest level of retirement benefits at work.

Roth Conversion Calculator

This comparison of Roth IRA versus a traditional IRA is based on some very simple assumptions. You may want to take a closer look at your specific set of circumstances to find out whether a conversion to a Roth makes sense for you. There is an excellent online calculator that compares the Roth to the traditional IRA at: *www.datachimp.com/ articles/rothira/rothcalc.htm*.

For more information on this topic, visit our Web site at www.businesstown.com

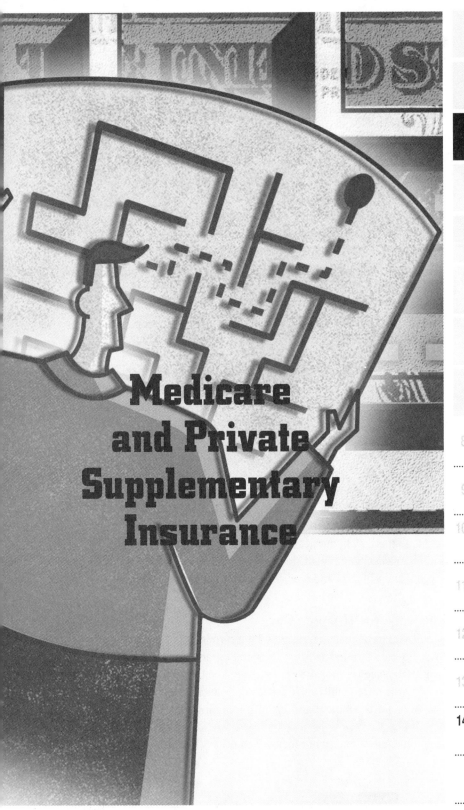

Medicare and Private Supplementary Insurance

Plan Basics

Unexpected medical costs in retirement can be the biggest budget buster you will face. While everyone who qualifies for Social Security also qualifies for Medicare, and if you don't you can buy into it, there are still many gaps in the coverage Medicare provides.

Let's start with the basics. You may think it sounds like a Chinese menu. You get some coverage under Part A and some under Part B. Part A, which everyone who is eligible gets automatically, covers hospitals, nursing homes, home health care after being released from a hospital, and hospice care. Part B covers all other medical expenses, if they are covered at all. There is no premium for Part A coverage. Part B's premium in 2002 was $54, and that is adjusted yearly based on costs. We'll now take a closer look at what is and is not covered.

Part A will cover a semiprivate room in a hospital or skilled nursing facility plus meals, general nursing, and basic hospital services and supplies. It will not cover private duty nursing, television, or telephone. The extra costs of a private room will not be covered unless it is medically necessary.

You can only get coverage for a skilled nursing facility after a three-day hospital stay. Part A will also cover home health services after a hospital stay if recommended by the doctor; otherwise, these services may be covered by Part B. These services include part-time skilled nursing care, physical therapy, occupational therapy, speech-language therapy, home health aide services, medical social services, durable medical equipment (including wheelchairs, hospital beds, oxygen, and walkers) and medical supplies, and other services.

Coverage for Hospice Care

If you have been diagnosed with a terminal illness, Part A will cover hospice care in the home, hospital, or at a specialized hospice facility. Hospice is a holistic approach for the care of terminally ill people, which frequently includes legal, financial, and emotional assistance for the patient and his or her family in addition to medical care. If hospice care is approved by Medicare, it will cover drugs for symptom control and pain relief, which otherwise are not covered.

Is Medicare in Trouble?

Over 39 million folks are covered by Medicare, which makes it the largest public health program in the United States. While you hear horror stories about Social Security being in trouble, Medicare is actually in worse shape. It's expected to run short of funds in 2016 if a fix is not put in place and will be insolvent in 2029, according to the 2001 Annual Report of the Trustees of the Social Security and Medicare Trust Funds.

Part A Costs

While there is no premium cost for Part A, you will not have 100 percent coverage of your costs. Medicare participants have to pay both a deductible and co-insurance for each stay in a hospital.

Medicare deductibles and co-insurance are not set by the year, but rather by the benefit period, which is how Medicare tracks your use of hospitals and skilled nursing facilities. A benefit period begins when you enter a hospital or skilled nursing facility. It ends when you haven't received hospital or skilled nursing care for sixty days. As long as you are out of the hospital or skilled nursing care facility for sixty days, a new benefit period begins. There is no limit to the number of new benefit periods you can have.

Each time a Medicare recipient starts a new benefit period, a new inpatient deductible of $812 is required. Co-insurance is also affected by the benefit periods. In 2002, co-insurance for an inpatient hospital stay was $203 a day for the sixty-first to ninetieth day of each benefit period. After ninety days, Medicare has another unique concept called Lifetime Reserve days. Medicare recipients get a total of sixty reserve days for their lifetime. Once a patient is in the hospital for more than ninety days in a benefit period, co-insurance jumps to $406 a day until the lifetime reserve days are used up. Once those days are used up, the Medicare recipient is then 100 percent responsible.

Co-insurance in a skilled nursing care facility is less. A patient can pay up to $101.50 a day for day twenty-one to day 100 in these facilities. After 100 days, you are responsible for all costs in a benefit period. Some folks get around this by going home with a relative for care for at least sixty days. Then, if another inpatient stay is needed, they can go back into the hospital for at least three days, the clock is restarted, and a new benefit period is available for another 100 days.

It doesn't require a lot of imagination to see how quickly a major illness can eat up your resources on a fixed income. This is one place where Medigap insurance steps in. We'll look at that in greater detail below.

The good news is that if you go home after an inpatient stay and still need some home health care services approved by Medicare,

Sticker Shock for Major Illnesses

Just to give you an idea of how much you must plan to spend if you need to stay in a hospital 100 days as a Medicare patient, here are the out-of-pocket costs:

Day 1 to Day 60 = $812 Deductible

Day 61 to Day 90 = $6,090 Co-insurance

Day 91 to Day 100 = $ 4,060 Co-insurance

Out-of-Pocket Cost = $10,962

You can see how quickly a major illness can dramatically increase your out-of-pocket costs and bust your budget. You may also need to take a huge chunk out of your retirement savings that was set aside for future years.

there is no cost to you for those services. There is a 20 percent co-payment for Medicare-approved durable medical equipment. You will also have coverage for outpatient prescription drugs after a hospital stay with a co-payment of $5.

Part B Coverage

Now that we've got Part A and inpatient care taken care of, let's take a look at what might be covered under Part B. Part B is optional, but most people do take it since the premium is just $54 per month. The deductible for Part B is a lot less than Part A–$100. Co-payments of 20 percent are also required for all Medicare-approved services and equipment. There is no prescription drug coverage under Part A. Outpatient mental health care requires a 50 percent co-payment.

Part B covers doctors' appointments, outpatient medical and surgical services and supplies, diagnostic tests, ambulatory surgery center facility fees for approved procedures, and durable medical equipment (such as wheelchairs, hospital beds, oxygen, and walkers). Also, there is coverage for second surgical opinions, outpatient mental health care, and outpatient physical and occupational therapy, including speech-language therapy.

If you need home health care and have not had a recent hospital stay, then Part B will cover the cost of part-time skilled nursing care, physical therapy, occupational therapy, speech-language therapy, home health aide services, medical social services, durable medical equipment (such as wheelchairs, hospital beds, oxygen, and walkers), and medical supplies provided they are approved by Medicare. There is also coverage for ambulance services (when other transportation would endanger your health), artificial eyes and limbs; braces for arm, leg, back, or neck; limited chiropractic services; and emergency care.

Medicare Coverage

I'm sure you've seen a long list of things that are covered and not covered in your employer health care policy. Medicare works the

> There is no prescription drug coverage under Part A.

same way. I'm not going to list everything here, but you do get a booklet when you qualify for Medicare that lists all the specifics.

Medicare also pays for some preventive services. These include:

- Bone Mass Measurements—The frequency of this testing varies with your health status.
- Colorectal Cancer Screening—Fecal Occult Blood Test once every twelve months.
- Flexible Sigmoidoscopy, which is done for colon cancer screening and other types of bowel disorders—Once every forty-eight months.
- Colonoscopy—Once every twenty-four months if you are at high risk for colon cancer. If you are not at high risk for colon cancer, once every ten years, but not within forty-eight months of a screening flexible sigmoidoscopy.
- Diabetes Services and Supplies—Coverage for glucose monitors, test strips, and lancets, as well as diabetes self-management training.
- Glaucoma Screening—Once every twelve months. Must be done or supervised by an eye doctor who is legally allowed to do this service in your state.
- Mammogram Screening—Once every twelve months. Medicare also covers new digital technologies for mammogram screening.
- Pap Test and Pelvic Examination (includes a clinical breast exam)—Once every twenty-four months. Once every twelve months if you are at high risk for cervical or vaginal cancer.
- Prostate Cancer Screening—Digital rectal examination once every twelve months and a Prostate Specific Antigen (PSA) test once every twelve months.
- Shots (vaccinations)—Flu shot once a year in the fall or winter.

There is one other thing you must watch out for when you go to a doctor called "assignment." Assignment means that a doctor agrees to accept Medicare's fee plus your 20 percent co-payment as full payment, even if his or her normal fees are higher than this combined amount. If the doctor or supplier does not accept assignment,

There is one other thing you must watch out for when you go to a doctor called "assignment."

you may have to pay the entire charge at the time of service. You could be stuck with charges higher than the 20 percent co-payment even if Medicare reimburses some of the coverage later.

Another term you may be used to seeing in relation to medical insurance is "exclusions from coverage." Medicare's exclusions from coverage include: routine or yearly physical exams, outpatient prescription drugs, acupuncture, dental care, cosmetic surgery, custodial care, hearing aids and exams, orthopedic shoes, routine foot care, routine eye care, and most shots.

Now that we've got those details out of the way, let's take a look at the rules for enrolling.

Enrollment Window

If you retired early and are already collecting Social Security, Medicare coverage starts automatically; you don't have to do anything. Your Medicare card will show up in the mail. If it doesn't, that's when you have to make a few calls. Otherwise, you can sign up for it as part of your Social Security application.

If you are not collecting Social Security at the age of sixty-five, you should sign up for Medicare about three months before your sixty-fifth birthday. Unlike Social Security, where you could get higher benefits by delaying retirement, you could actually miss out on coverage if you don't apply for Medicare on time. Your initial application for Medicare must be made within a seven-month window beginning three months before your sixty-fifth birthday. If you miss this window, you will have to wait until the next general enrollment period, which is January 1 to March 31 each year.

Paying More for Part B

In addition to possibly missing several months of coverage the first year, you could also end up paying more for Medicare Part B if you apply late. When you apply for Medicare, Part B is automatic. If you don't want to pay for it, you will have to cancel it. But, if you do decide not to take it, you will have to pay an additional premium to get it later. In fact, there is a 10 percent penalty added for each year you didn't pay for Part B. For example, if you decide to delay taking

> If you are not collecting Social Security at the age of sixty-five, you should sign up for Medicare about three months before your sixty-fifth birthday.

Part B coverage for two years and then decide you want it, your penalty would be 10 percent per year of delay or $10.80 ($5.40 per year). Your premium would be $64.80 rather than $54.

Delaying Medicare Benefits

Sometimes you can have a good reason to delay paying, such as continued coverage from your workplace. If you are still working at the age of sixty-five for a company with twenty or more employees (100 or more if you are disabled), you can keep your company health plan until you retire. You can switch to Medicare if your company plan is not a good one and you think Medicare's coverage will be better. If you do delay starting Medicare benefits, you must apply for Medicare within eight months of leaving your job or you will face the same penalties we discussed above when you try to get coverage.

The rules are different if you work for a small company with less than twenty employees. You cannot delay Medicare in this situation. You must sign up for Medicare within the seven-month window mentioned above, starting three months before your sixty-fifth birthday. Private insurers for small companies will only pay what Medicare does not normally cover. By not signing up for Medicare, you risk not having full coverage plus you will end up with Part B penalties because you didn't sign up in time.

Medicare Credit Poor?

Most people pay into Medicare even if they are not paying into Social Security. The Medicare taxes are 1.45 percent of your salary, which is matched dollar for dollar by your employer. To gain eligibility for Medicare you earn a quarter of coverage every three months up to four quarters per year. You must earn forty quarters of coverage (ten years) to be eligible for coverage.

All is not lost if you haven't earned enough credits. You can still buy into Medicare at age sixty-five. The costs can be steep though. If you are just a bit short and have thirty to thirty-nine credits, Medicare Part A will be $175 per month plus you'll still have to pay the Part B premium at $54 per month for a total of $229 per month.

> Private insurers for small companies will only pay what Medicare does not normally cover.

It gets more expensive if you have less than thirty credits. In that case, you will have to pay a Part A premium of $319 per month plus $54 per month for Part B totaling $373.

Medicare Alternative

Everything I've talked about thus far has described the traditional fee-for-service Medicare plan. Medicare also offers Health Maintenance Organization (HMO) plans as well. This became possible after Congress passed legislation allowing Medicare+Choice with the intention of giving Medicare recipients more options for their health care. Congress hoped to add Medicare Managed Care plans (similar to HMOs) and Medicare Private Fee-for-Service plans.

So far, the experiment has not been very successful in most states. You may find you have no Medicare+Choice in your state at all or, if you do have it, it's not really a much better option. But, if you are lucky, you may be able to find coverage that exceeds the coverage of the original, fee-for-service Medicare plan.

When Medicare+Choice first started, it included prescription coverage, which is not available under the current traditional plan, as well as other extended benefits that minimized out-of-pocket expenses. Plans differ greatly state by state; there is no exact statement of benefits.

If you do have a Medicare+Choice option available, it will most likely be a managed care plan, similar to the HMO offered by your employer. You must use a doctor in the HMO to have coverage. In very few states you may find a fee-for-service plan, but right now there are only two organizations offering the option so it is rare.

The most common reason people choose to use Medicare+Choice plans is because they believe they will be able to save out-of-pocket costs. Initially this was true. When Medicare+Choice first became available, there were no fees to participate and more benefits were available. Unfortunately, this is no longer true today. In many states, these extra benefits are being cut back and, in some places, additional fees are being added, bringing the out-of-pocket costs much closer to those expected under the traditional Medicare fee-for-service plan.

Just to give you an idea, here's a sample of a Medicare+Choice plan from the state of Georgia.

Medicare+Choice Plans and Other Medicare Managed Care Plans (e.g., HMO)						
Medicare Health Plan(s)	Monthly Premium (in addition to the $54 Part B premium)	Doctor Choice (can you go to any doctor?)	Outpatient Prescription Drugs	Routine Physical Exams	Vision Services	Dental Services
Blue Cross Blue Shield Health Care GA BlueChoice Platinum (H1168-004)	$55	Usually must see a doctor or specialist who belongs to your plan	✓	✓	✓	
Blue Cross Blue Shield Health Care GA BlueChoice Platinum-Basic (H1168-005)	$20	Usually must see a doctor or specialist who belongs to your plan		✓	✓	
Kaiser Permanente Senior Advantage Kaiser Permanente Senior Advantage (H1170-002)	$40	Usually must see a doctor or specialist who belongs to to your plan	✓	✓	✓	

As you can see, for an additional $40 to $55, two of the plans offer prescription drug coverage plus one routine physical and some vision coverage. The third plan for $20 more per month offers only a routine physical and some vision coverage. Here are some additional details about these choices:

A quick summary of highlights for the Blue Cross plan showed that one big advantage of its HMO is that there are set fees for co-payments of $10 for a doctor visit and $25 for a visit with a specialist, provided Medicare approves the specialist. A 20 percent co-payment under the traditional plan could be more costly over the year. Another big savings is on hospital deductible and co-payments.

Blue Cross patients' deductible was considerably lower than traditional Medicare deductible—only $250. Plus the per day costs were less as well: $50 each day for day(s) one to ten and $0 each day for day(s) eleven to ninety for a Medicare-covered stay in a network hospital with unlimited days each benefit period.

Kaiser structured their plan differently with no co-payments as long as you saw doctors in their network. Inpatient stays required a $400 deductible but after that all costs were covered for a Medicare-approved stay with an unlimited number of days in a benefit period.

As you can see, both of these plans would offer costs savings to a person with a hospital stay, plus patients would probably incur lower costs provided they used doctors in the networks of their Medicare+Choice plan.

Medicare+Choice coverage and costs change yearly, so whatever you find in Medicare's Personal Plan Finder will probably not be the same when you are ready to retire. You still may want to check out what is available in your state, or if different, the state you plan to retire to in order to estimate your medical care budget for retirement.

A major consideration if you do plan to travel in retirement will be coverage of medical expenses outside of your network. While traditional Medicare covers you anywhere in the United States, you could find that traveling can be difficult on some Medicare+Choice plans because the cost of care would be so much higher out-of-network on the plan you chose.

A big problem for people who choose Medicare+Choice is what to do when your coverage choice pulls out of your state. The number of people affected by those changes is shown in this chart.

Medicare+Choice Losses

Year	Affected Enrollees
1999	407,000
2000	327,000
2001	934,000

In most cases, a change in coverage means a change in doctor. For seniors, this can be especially traumatic if they are dealing with some chronic disease.

Providers who pull out say they are doing so because "payment increases in high enrollment areas are not keeping up with the continuing escalation of health care costs," according to the conclusions of a report released by the Centers for Medicare and Medicaid Services (CMS).

The federal government is trying to fix this problem. One initiative is to reduce the administrative burden for Medicare+Choice. CMS plans to redesign Medicare+Choice administratively so there will be more of a focus on providing care and less on paperwork.

The fixes primarily affect the relationship between the federal government and the organizations that want to offer a Medicare+Choice program. Only time will tell if they do so successfully and are able to negotiate something that truly offers a choice to Medicare recipients.

Medigap

Another option for filling the medical coverage gaps of the traditional Medicare plan is Medigap insurance. Unfortunately, it's more expensive as well. If you are lucky, you may have some kind of Medicare supplement offered by your former workplace as part of your retirement package. Otherwise, you will have to find insurance on your own. Medicaid will take over if you run out of funds after Medicare but only after you have drained almost all of your assets.

Medigap is a type of private insurance that will cover medical expenses not covered by Medicare. The coverage is supplemental and you must have both Medicare Part A and Part B to purchase a Medigap plan. Medigap plans must include the following:

- Hospital co-insurance
- Full coverage for 365 additional hospital days (after Medicare hospital reserve days are exhausted)
- Twenty percent co-payment for physician and other Part B services
- Three pints of blood

After these key coverages, things get pretty confusing. There are numerous options offered under ten different formulas labeled A

> Medicaid will take over if you run out of funds after Medicare but only after you have drained almost all of your assets.

to J. Each formula includes a different set of benefits. The more benefits you want, the greater the premium will be. Options can include full coverage of the hospital deductible, skilled nursing care facility co-insurance, coverage of Part B deductible, coverage when traveling outside the United States (without it, you only have coverage for the first two months of a trip under Medicare), doctor's fees that exceed Medicare-approved charges, and prescription drug coverage.

There are some things for which coverage just isn't available. These include: custodial care (such as feeding, bathing, and grooming) either at home or in a nursing home, long-term skilled care in a nursing home, unlimited prescription drugs, vision care, dental care, and private nurse.

Cost Variances

These varying laws have the greatest impact on costs. Costs can vary by age, where you live, and the insurance company from which you purchase the plan. When you start pricing coverage, be sure you are comparing the same plan options. Not only do insurance companies have ten options to price, they have three different ways of pricing them based on your age: Community Rating, Issue-Age Rating, and Attained-Age Rating.

- Community Rated premiums are based on the cost of providing coverage in your area. They are not based on your age. Increases in premiums are based on inflation.
- Issue-Age Rated premiums are based on the age at which you first buy the plan. The premiums do not increase as you get older. Inflation is the only reason for your premiums to go up. The younger you are when you first buy this insurance, the cheaper your premiums will be.
- Attained-Age Rated premiums change each year based on your age. These plans may look the cheapest to you if you are buying them at age sixty-five, but the premium is not locked-in like the Issue-Age Rated or Community Rated premiums. Insurance companies can raise premiums based on age and on inflation. Usually by age seventy or seventy-five, the Attained-Age Rated premiums will be higher than the other two options.

> When you start pricing coverage, be sure you are comparing the same plan options.

Optional Riders	Medigap Coverage Options									
	A	B	C	D	E	F*	G	H	I	J*
Basic Benefits	✓	✓	✓	✓	✓	✓	✓	✓	✓	✓
Part A: Inpatient Hospital Deductible	✓	✓	✓	✓	✓	✓	✓	✓	✓	
Part A: Skilled-Nursing Facility Co-insurance			✓	✓	✓	✓	✓	✓	✓	✓
Part B: Deductible			✓			✓				✓
Foreign Travel Emergency			✓	✓	✓	✓	✓	✓	✓	✓
At-Home Recovery				✓			✓		✓	✓
Part B: Excess Charges						100%	80%		100%	100%
Preventive Care					✓					✓
Prescription Drugs								Basic Coverage	Basic Coverage	Extended Coverage

*Plans F and J also have a high-deductible option with substantially lower premiums. You pay $1,580 out-of-pocket per year before they pay anything.

Some states do offer different options than the standard ones above: Massachusetts, Minnesota, and Wisconsin. If you live in one of these states or plan to retire there, you can find their standardized plans here at *www.medicare.gov/MGCompare/Search/ StandardizedPlans/StandardPlans.asp*.

Medigap can be even more confusing to figure out than Medicare. Not only do you have to worry about federal laws, but each of the fifty states get to put their two cents in as well because it falls under their individual medical rules. Health care, no matter what age you are, is regulated on a state level.

Shop around and ask for lots of quotes before you pick a plan, but when comparing costs be sure you are comparing the same type plan as well as the same type of rating. Women can sometimes find better discounts, as can nonsmokers. Some companies will offer married couples a discount.

Medical Underwriting

Once you find just the right plan, the next biggest hurdle is to get past underwriting. Insurance companies review your medical history and health status using a process called medical underwriting. It is during this process that the insurance company decides whether to accept or reject your application. When applying for insurance you will need to fill out an extensive application, which you should fill out very carefully.

Even if you are approved, medical underwriting can impose a waiting period for pre-existing conditions, if permitted by your state. The insurance company will also set your Medigap premium based on your medical condition.

Medicare SELECT

One way to keep your Medigap costs down is to purchase a Medicare SELECT plan. These plans usually require you to use specific hospitals and, possibly, specific doctors to get full coverage. If you had a Preferred Provider Option (PPO) at your workplace, this compares to that type of option. If Medicare SELECT options are available in your state, be sure to review the list of preferred providers to be certain your doctors are on the list. If not, you may be forced to switch doctors to get full coverage. You can find Medigap policies for your area in the Medicare Personal Plan Finder mentioned earlier.

Long-Term Care Insurance

As you get older there is a much greater chance that you will need help with the basics of daily living, including eating, dressing, washing, using the restroom, and transferring from place to place. You could even need twenty-four-hour care in a nursing home or other

Nursing Home in Your Future?

Studies have shown that 50 percent of people over the age of sixty-five will spend some time in a nursing home. Nursing home costs average $30,000 a year and can be as high as $100,000 a year in some areas. For seniors, the average nursing home stay is nineteen months. Alternatives to nursing homes are assisted living facilities, if you don't need twenty-four-hour nursing care. Assisted living facilities are a bit cheaper than nursing homes and part of your costs that meet Medicare requirements can be covered.

facility for a time-period that is much longer than that covered by Medicare or Medigap. Long-term care insurance fills this gap in retirement.

If you're not a millionaire, you can quickly see that if you need long-term care your resources will likely be depleted rapidly. You can buy some insurance against that, but the cost is expensive. Long-term care insurance premiums bought over the age of sixty-five can range from $2,000 to $10,000 annually. Your options are great though with over 100 insurance companies selling long-term care policies today.

The best way to keep your premiums low is to buy long-term care coverage before age sixty-five. In fact, most financial advisors will recommend that you buy long-term care insurance between the ages of fifty-five and sixty, but for this to work you must get a policy with premiums that are guaranteed to stay level for life. If you don't, your coverage could become too expensive to carry, just when you probably will need to use it.

Know What You Are Buying

Long-term care policies are filled with hard-to-understand legal mumbo jumbo and sales people are usually very aggressive with their tactics. In fact, many times they will overstate the coverage that is actually being offered. Sales training in many parts of the long-term care industry is designed to scare seniors into making a quick buying decision.

Unfortunately, most people don't find out their coverage is not adequate until they actually need it. Be sure you carefully research the plans you are considering and the options being offered. If you are finding all this very confusing, it can't hurt to ask an attorney or financial planner familiar with these types of contracts before you make a decision. You could find the small cost of that consultation will save you thousands of dollars later in life.

Coverage limitations vary greatly among policies. Some policies will severely limit what they will cover and where you can receive care. Others require that you get to the point where you need "continuous one-on-one assistance" before their coverage kicks in. The

Sales training in many parts of the long-term care industry is designed to scare seniors into making a quick buying decision.

Health Insurance Portability and Accountability Act

Financial advisors used to recommend to people that they give away assets so that they could qualify for Medicaid when they ran out of funds. This practice is no longer possible and, in fact, is illegal. In 1996, the Health Insurance Portability and Accountability Act was passed, which made it a crime to deliberately spend down assets so you could go on Medicaid. Initially, Medicare recipients were penalized with jail time, but that didn't go over well politically. Today only attorneys and estate planners can get penalized with jail terms.

better policies will help you long before that time so you can stay at home with assistance.

Know the Insurance Company

In addition to comparing coverage, it is also important to check out the insurance company selling the policy. You certainly don't want to pay premiums for years just to find out that the company has gone out of business when you actually need the coverage. There are two insurance ratings services that can help you check out the financial stability of the companies whose policies you are considering: A.M. Best (*www3.ambest.com/ratings/Advanced.asp*) and Standard and Poor's (*www.standardandpoors.com/RatingsActions/ RatingsLists/Insurance/InsuranceStrengthRatings.html*). If you don't have online access, you can find this information at a local public library.

Coverage Options

We'll now briefly take a look at the coverage options you'll need to consider. First, you must decide how long you want your coverage to last. Your options can vary from one to six years. The next big consideration is how long the elimination period should last, which will determine how soon your benefits will begin.

You will also be able to select how much coverage you want to receive each month. Monthly amounts usually range from $1,000 to $6,000. In addition, there are lifetime caps on the total amount of money you can receive. These can vary from as low as $36,000 up to $450,000. You also get to select what percentage of home health care costs you want covered, which can vary from 50 percent to 100 percent. Your monthly premium will vary greatly by the options you choose. Obviously, the more coverage you select, the higher the premium will be.

One other thing you should watch is the renewal requirements at the end of a year. You definitely want a policy that renews automatically as well as guarantees your premium amount.

Some employers are offering their employees a long-term care group policy, which you may even be able to pay for using pre-tax dollars. If your company does this, compare the plan offered with other non-group plans. Frequently, the cost of company-based plans is considerably lower than individual policies. But, be sure the rates won't go up dramatically if you leave the company. If your rate must be renegotiated when you leave the company, you will probably be better off locking in a rate on an individual plan.

Future Trends

When we started talking about Medicare, I mentioned that Medicare was actually in worse financial shape than Social Security. We'll take a closer look at some of the fixes being considered for the program.

First, let's review some financial basics. Part A is financed through payroll taxes and a trust fund in which surpluses are deposited, as is the case with Social Security. Part B is financed using general tax revenues and premiums collected from seniors participating in the plan. Participant costs for Part A services (deductibles and co-payments) are determined by the amount available through payroll taxes. To avoid running out of funds, the participant costs are raised each year to cover the rising costs of medical care. If more money is needed, payroll taxes can be raised.

When Congress established Part B, it decided the premium paid by recipients plus general tax revenues would be enough to cover its costs. By law, the costs are shared on the basis of 25 percent paid by beneficiaries and 75 percent paid by the government. There is no cap on how much can be spent from general revenues for Part B. With this structure, Medicare Part B could become a very large drain on general revenues. Today, 40 percent of Medicare spending is for Part B benefits and that is expected to rise dramatically as the baby boomers move into retirement.

Breaux-Frist

Fixes being considered include privatizing Medicare or combining Parts A and B into one insurance plan with a different type of cost-sharing. First, we'll take a look at the privatization of Medicare. A bill was first introduced by two senators in 1999: Senators John

> To avoid running out of funds, the participant costs are raised each year to cover the rising costs of medical care. If more money is needed, payroll taxes can be raised.

Breaux (D-La.) and Bill Frist (R-Tenn.). They introduced a stripped-down version of it in 2000 and then reintroduced both options in 2001.

The goal of both plans is said to "ensure more competition, add universal prescription drug coverage, include protections for low-income, rural Americans, create new measures to keep the program solvent and provide a competitive system outside of the federal Health Care Financing Administration (HCFA)." Breaux-Frist I is more comprehensive and is based on the recommendations of the National Bipartisan Commission on the Future of Medicare, which Senator Breaux chaired. Senator Frist served on the commission as the Senate's only physician.

In the original bill, Breaux-Frist I, the plan gives HCFA the tools to modernize the current, federal fee-for-service Medicare plan so it can compete with private plans based on premiums, costs, and quality of benefits. Breaux-Frist II is narrower but guarantees that seniors, including those in rural areas, have access to prescription drug benefits, but the change is done more slowly and the reforms are incremental. You can find out more information about the National Bipartisan Commission on the Future of Medicare at *http://medicare.commission.gov/medicare.*

> Breaux-Frist II is narrower but guarantees that seniors, including those in rural areas, have access to prescription drug benefits.

Opposition to Privatization

The senator leading the charge against the privatization movement is senator Jay Rockefeller of West Virginia, who also serves on the commission. He believes the Breaux-Frist plans are an "untested, risky reform scheme that would be a dangerous and confusing leap from the security of today's system. . . which threatens to void the Medicare contract."

The Breaux-Frist comprehensive plan "would essentially give Medicare recipients a set amount of money to spend on private health plans. But in privatizing Medicare, the proposal abandons the promise of quality, affordable medical care for every senior," Rockefeller believes. "Seniors who are unable to access a private plan that meets their needs would be forced to enroll in what's left of traditional fee-for-service Medicare. Medicare could very well become two distinct programs—a luxury plan for wealthy Americans or those in competitive markets and a cut-rate plan for Americans of modest means or those in rural communities."

You probably haven't seen much about Medicare privatization. The Kaiser Family Foundation did a study that showed seniors are very confused about what this program might do. The Medicare Commission held only one meeting outside of Washington before developing the plan. Hopefully, there will be more public debate before Congress seriously considers the plan. The opponents of the plan believe it does little to address the real crisis—the impact of the baby boomers moving into retirement and the rising costs that will be incurred to pay for their medical care.

Combining A and B

Many members of Congress are pushing for a more measured approach that would first concentrate on getting costs under control. One thing being carefully eyed is putting Parts A and B of Medicare together. Few insurance plans today separate hospital and other medical coverage. While that was common when Medicare started, it is rare today.

Combining the programs has some major pitfalls. A key one is program financing. As previously mentioned, Part A is paid by payroll taxes with a trust fund that gets any surplus in those taxes. Medicare recipients and the government share Part B costs. Plans presented to combine these two parts come with major shifts in cost-sharing. While the shifts being considered could dramatically cut costs for people with a major illness who end up with huge hospital bills, they also likely would increase the costs for folks who don't experience a major illness in any one year.

So far, the design for combining Parts A and B has not gotten major support because it will likely result in less costs being paid for most seniors. Instead, Congress is looking at ways to rethink the relationship between Parts A and B to get a better handle on costs. A big first step would be to link the information from Parts A and B.

> Combining the programs has some major pitfalls.

Sharing Information

Currently, Parts A and B are managed by different contractors, so beneficiary payments must be compared through a system at the

Health Care Financing Administration (HCFA). While private insurance companies have almost instant data to work with in order to find problems developing with claims and services, HFCA is hampered by its outdated systems, according to the U.S. General Accounting Office (GAO).

Not only does this outdated system limit HCFA's ability to respond quickly to problems, but it can also raise program costs. The Office of the Inspector General for Medicare has found that some claims are paid twice, once under Part A and once under Part B, because of information system difficulties. The Inspector General's 1999 audit found potential improper payments to Part B providers and suppliers totaling $47.6 million.

Congress believes that Medicare could benefit by looking at ways in which private insurers have gotten a handle on costs, especially through preferred-provider networks. Insurance beneficiaries face lower out-of-pocket costs by staying within the network. Not only do people benefit by paying less, the private insurers can negotiate lower payment rates and save money. This is not so easy for Medicare to do because Medicare cannot go out and negotiate individual contracts for providers without a major change in the way the law is written. As a national program it must establish a set of rules that everyone uses in order to ensure a level playing field.

Disease Management Program

Improved sharing of information between Parts A and B could also help Medicare establish a disease management program. Private insurers use these programs to provide patient education, patient monitoring, and specialized services. Their goal is to improve the quality of care and reduce costs by identifying patients with high-risk conditions. When a patient with a high-risk condition is identified, contact is made with his or her health care provider to coordinate practice guidelines, patient non-compliance related to prescribed medications, tests ordered, and physician visits. These programs are designed to encourage patients to follow health-promoting behaviors and support a strong patient-doctor relationship.

While disease management programs have been very successful in the private sector, there is a big question about how they could be

> Medicare cannot go out and negotiate individual contracts for providers without a major change in the way the law is written.

implicated for Medicare recipients. Let's use annual preventive mammograms as an example. Medicare could collect information about testing using payment information and send out a notice to recipients when it's time for their next annual test. Some folks in Washington fear this could cause major complaints from recipients because they may protest the government telling them how they should monitor their own health care.

> Changes in Medicare not only impact Medicare recipients, they also affect doctors, hospitals, and other health care providers and equipment suppliers.

Medicare, a Moving Target?

You've now gotten an idea of how difficult it will be to make any major changes in Medicare. Each time an idea is suggested there will always be a major force opposing the idea. Changes in Medicare not only impact Medicare recipients, they also affect doctors, hospitals, and other health care providers and equipment suppliers. Any time even a mention is made about Medicare reform the lobbyists fill the halls of Congress to promote whatever side of the medical business they represent.

Just as with Social Security, Medicare will be a moving target and is quite dependent on shifting political winds. As you plan your retirement, watch for any changes closely and adjust your plans accordingly.

> For more information on this topic, visit our Web site at www.businesstown.com

PART IV

Putting It All Together

This part helps you:

- Discuss the key components to building a successful retirement portfolio.

- Explore stocks, bonds, and cash investment alternatives as well as the types of risks you take when investing.

- Learn how to monitor your investments.

- Figure out strategies for moving your retirement money without a tax bite when you change jobs.

- Review your asset allocation.

- Discuss how to minimize the impact of surprises.

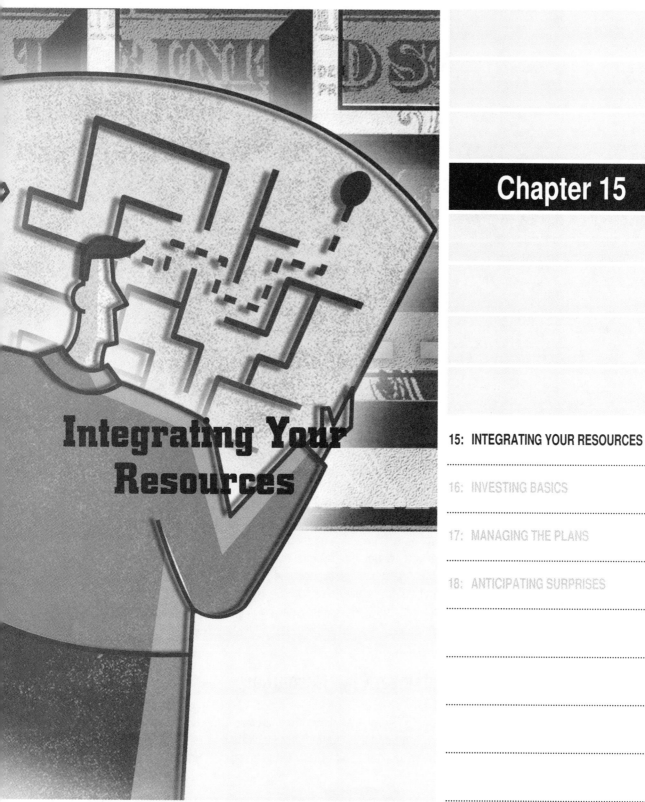

Chapter 15

Integrating Your Resources

Build Your Portfolio

You may be making the mistake most people do by thinking that your portfolio consists purely of the assets you hold in your retirement accounts. Your financial life is much more complicated than that, so when you start thinking about your portfolio, bring together all the resources you have.

We're not only looking at your stock and bond investments, but also the other ways you build your assets including the family home, any vacation property, rental property, stock options you may have at work, insurance policies that have a cash value, collectibles, business assets, and possibly inheritance or some lucky windfall. All these pieces could become part of your retirement portfolio and can help you reach your goals.

The only reason to leave something out of your retirement portfolio is that you are certain you will not have it when it comes time to retire. But, one word of caution, don't overstate your assets just to make your numbers look better. The only person you are fooling is yourself. You'll be the one stuck with the consequences of not having enough at retirement.

When you're calculating your portfolio value, it is important to evaluate all holdings, both inside and outside your retirement plan, to be certain you are not too dependent on one asset. This is true for any kind of equity holding, even if it's outside your own company. To truly judge your level of diversification, it's very important to integrate both your and your spouse's portfolios, but equally important that you are building retirement funds individually. In fact, if you have two different employer-sponsored plans, take advantage of the greater variety of investment alternatives. Your plan may have a better aggressive stock fund, while your spouse's plan has an excellent low-cost bond fund. You can plan your asset mix to use the best of both plans.

Employer Plan Resources

First, let's start with employer plans. We've already talked about the tax-deferred savings plans, but there are other benefits that may also help you build a portfolio. These include profit-sharing plans, stock ownership plans, and other savings plans.

> The only reason to leave something out of your retirement portfolio is that you are certain you will not have it when it comes time to retire.

Most of these plans depend on the future success of your company. Enron clearly showed people how they must diversify their holdings and be sure that not all their eggs are in one basket. If your employer does match your contributions with company stock, it can be even more critical that you make your contributions into your 401(k) plan by buying something other than company stock and shifting stock holdings if your portfolio becomes too heavily loaded with company stock. Before we get started with the integration, let's quickly review what each of these non-401(k) plans are and how much the government allows you or your company to put into the plans, if there are government limits.

Profit-Sharing Plans

Some companies actually decide they want to share their profits with you. When they do, they can set up a tax-qualified defined-contribution plan into which the employer makes all contributions. These types of plans are completely discretionary, but to qualify for the tax break, the funds must be equitably distributed among employees. Deposits into a profit-sharing plan can range from 0 to 25 percent of compensation up to $200,000, but the maximum dollar amount that can be put into all your qualified retirement plans in any one year is $40,000.

Owning Company Stock

Employees have four possible ways to own company stock. Many companies match your 401(k) contributions with stock and allow you to buy stock as part of your contribution for the year. But that's not the only way to get an interest in your company. There are also Employee Stock Ownership Plans, Employee Stock Purchase Plans, and Employee Stock Options.

The Employee Stock Ownership Plan (ESOP) is the most restrictive for employees, but offers the biggest tax incentive for employers because of the tax deductions that are allowed as well as the additional working capital for the company. With an ESOP, you receive a certain number of shares each year based on your compensation. It's considered another benefit. You don't have to pay anything into the plan. Vesting rules are similar to the 401(k), but even

> The Employee Stock Ownership Plan (ESOP) is the most restrictive for employees, but offers the biggest tax incentive for employers.

Are Stock Options Really an Incentive?

Options are frequently used as a way for companies to provide non-cash incentives so they can offer lower salaries with the promise of a future payback, provided the company does well. They were all the rage during the technology stock boom, but have fallen out of favor as so many people ended up with options that were "under water." In other words, their grant price was higher than the market price and they never got to take advantage of their options. If options are offered as a benefit to lure you away from a higher-paying job, think twice about taking it.

if you are fully vested you can't touch the stock until the age of fifty-five with at least ten years of service.

You also don't get possession of the stock in an ESOP until you actually leave the company. When you leave the company, there may be provisions to roll over the shares; if not, the taxation and distribution of shares can be very complicated. If your ESOP has been built over many years with the company, it's best to seek advice from a financial planner or tax specialist to be sure you minimize any tax hit.

Employee Stock Purchase Plans (ESPP) are more flexible, but they also require you to pay for the stock. The advantage is that you are offered the stock at a discount to the price at which it is being sold on the market. Discounts usually range from 5 to 15 percent of the market price. You don't get this discount tax-free. When you sell the shares, the discount is treated as income. You will also need to pay capital gains on any gain over the market value at the time of purchase. Employees do control their ESPP stock as soon as they purchase the shares, but if you do want to sell them be sure you check with a tax advisor to be certain you understand the tax consequences of the sale.

Employee Stock Options may or may not be worth anything to you. Basically, what these plans do is give you the right to buy the stock at some point in the future at a set price, which is known as the "grant" price. The grant price is usually the market price at the time the options are granted to the employee. Employees can buy the stock at the time of the grant, but most will wait until some later date with the hope that the stock price will increase and they will then be able to buy the stock at the older, cheaper price and sell it at the current market price. This transaction is called "exercising" options.

What Type of Option Do You Have?

If you are one of the lucky few that can make a huge profit on his or her options, do so with great caution. The tax hit could be tremendous and you must be sure you understand the tax implications before you exercise your options. First, you need to check what type of option you have. There are two types: the nonqualified option (NSO) and the incentive stock option (ISO).

If you have an NSO, then you will be taxed immediately as current income on the difference or "spread" between your grant price and the market price. For example, if your option grant price was $5 and you exercised the option when the stock price was $40, then your spread would be $35. The company gets to deduct the amount of your spread. You are taxed whether you sell the shares immediately or you hold them. This is how a lot of folks got in trouble when they exercised their options worth hundreds of thousands of dollars and didn't set aside money for taxes right away. After the technology stock bubble burst, many owed more in taxes than their shares were actually worth.

Employees with ISOs are in much better shape tax-wise. The employee does not have to pay taxes when exercising the option, but the company gets no tax deduction. In order to avoid paying taxes on the spread completely, the employee must hold the shares for at least two years after the option "grant" and one year after they exercise their options. After this waiting period is over, the employee only pays capital gains based on the difference between the exercise and sale price. If the employee doesn't wait for at least this three-year period, the taxes on the ISO will be the same as the NSO. Employees with an ISO still are not completely home free. The spread between the purchase and grant price are subject to the Alternative Minimum Tax.

The upshot of all this is that exercising options is tricky tax business. Before taking the first step, consult your tax advisor to be sure you are doing things exactly right and that you set aside enough money to pay the taxes due. Even with these warnings, the value of exercised options could be a nice boost to your retirement nest egg, provided you avoid a major tax bite.

If you want to learn more about the various employee ownership plans, the National Center for Employee Ownership provides an excellent collection of articles at *www.nceo.org/options/option_articles.html.*

> If the employee doesn't wait for at least this three-year period, the taxes on the ISO will be the same as the NSO.

Thrift Saving Plans

Thrift savings plans are not common in the for-profit world. You are more likely to find them if you are a government employee or are in the non-profit sector. We talked about these types of plans in Chapter 9, which included the non-profit sector, and Chapter 12, which covered government retirement plans. In the private sector, these plans allow employees to put after-tax dollars into a tax-deferred savings plan, which is similar to a non-tax-deductible IRA. In 2006, a newfangled variety, called the Roth 401(k), will probably take over in the private sector, which will allow employees to save tax-free. Keep your eyes open for any mention of new tax-free savings options.

Government Plan Resources

For a majority of people, the only type of payments they will receive from the government as retirees is Social Security. As you integrate your resources, don't forget to include Social Security. If you are uncertain how much you can depend upon, you can calculate the promised benefit conservatively by reducing your monthly benefit. Even with no fix for Social Security in place, the worst-case estimate puts benefits at 67 percent of current promises.

If you do work for the federal, state, or local government, be certain you are including all possible payouts at retirement. You most likely will have a guaranteed payout as part of a defined-benefit plan and could have some money from a defined-contribution plan. If you are unsure of how much to include in your plan, contact your retirement plan administrator at work.

> If you do work for the federal, state, or local government, be certain you are including all possible payouts at retirement.

Variable Life and Annuities

Unless you have put the maximum amount in all your other retirement savings possibilities or are trying to shield money from a lawsuit, there is no reason to have a variable universal life (VUL) or variable annuity as part of your retirement savings plans. Annuities might make sense when you actually start retirement.

Many people are stuck with these policies because of a smooth-talking salesperson whose primary interest was to make a big commission. You may be stuck with an annuity as part of your employer-sponsored plan, especially if you work for a non-profit company and have a 403(b) administered by an insurance company.

Variable Universal Life Annuity

Just so you don't get caught by the next fast-talking salesman, we'll review the basics of VULs and annuities. A VUL is a policy that combines life insurance and investment, which can also be thought of as a hybrid between a term life and whole life insurance policy. The death benefit on a VUL can be a fixed amount or it can vary based on the success of your investments.

In addition to paying premiums on the death benefit, you will also be contributing to a tax-deferred savings account. But, you'll save a lot of money by just buying a term insurance policy and investing the difference, because the fees on the life insurance policy will be much higher than any other investment vehicle. Not only are the fees and commissions high, but insurance company policies have also notoriously low returns as compared with other investment choices.

Fees hidden in a VUL include the annual mortality and expense charge, the premium load (premium expense charge plus premium tax charge), sales load (if any), monthly administrative charge, and monthly cost of insurance. There also could be policy surrender charges if you decide to withdraw funds early. On top of these charges, you could also be faced with a tax penalty similar to the ones imposed on IRAs if you take out your money before age 59½.

There is no question that the fees will eat up a lot of your investment returns. Some people that really need life insurance may find a VUL easier to get than a term policy. If you do face difficulty getting a term policy, you may want to consider a VUL, but be sure to shop carefully for a low-fee policy.

Variable Annuities

Variable annuities offer a lot less insurance, but must offer some in order to qualify as a tax-deferred vehicle. Most financial advisors will tell you that you have to hold a variable annuity for at least fifteen to twenty years before its tax-deferral advantages will make this a favorable choice over using a low-cost mutual fund. As with VULs, the biggest disadvantage of variable annuities is their hidden costs. In addition to commissions for that fast-talking salesman, there are also fees on the investment accounts to cover insurance costs and surrender charges. Morningstar.com reports that the average annual expenses for a variable annuity is 2.08 percent, whereas mutual funds average 1.34 for their annual expenses.

If you are still interested in purchasing a variable annuity, you must shop carefully to ensure you are minimizing your costs. Low-cost

> As with VULs, the biggest disadvantage of variable annuities is their hidden costs.

Fixed versus Variable Annuity

Don't confuse this discussion with the one about annuities that are taken at the time you are ready to retire. At that time, you may be given the option of a variable annuity as well as a fixed annuity. Obviously, the fixed annuity is safer if you want a guaranteed income. A variable annuity may give you a better chance to grow your funds, but if the investment account does poorly, you could end up with less money annually than you planned in your retirement budget.

annuity products are available through Vanguard, Fidelity, and TIAA-CREF, for example. In fact, TIAA-CREF offers excellent information about personal annuities at their Web site at *www.tiaa-cref.com/ pas/index.html.*

Home Equity and Other Real Estate

We talked about your home and how its value may play into your retirement savings in Chapter 4. Now that you've gotten further along in your planning, you should have a good idea of what you might want to do with that asset. You could develop your plan considering each of the options: staying in the home, selling the home and using the assets to buy a smaller home and investing the rest, or borrowing on the assets of your home to help fill your retirement gap.

You may also have other real estate investments, such as rental property or vacation property. You need to consider how you want to integrate these into your retirement savings plan. They could serve as cash assets if you think you will sell them when you retire or they could be income-producing assets, if you plan to continue renting them. Possibly, you could be considering making your vacation home your retirement residence and planning to sell or rent your current home for additional cash.

Collectibles

Are you someone who has a passion for buying art or other collectibles? If so, do you know the value of your collectibles? Calculating the value of your collectibles to include them in retirement planning must be done realistically. While their appraised value may be high, you've got to consider how much you could actually sell these collectibles for on the open market. Just like other investments, collectibles can go up and down in value depending on how popular that particular collectible is when it comes time to sell it.

But beware; collectibles are also a market where lots of scam artists like to ply their trade. If you are collecting items with the idea of selling them in the future to make up a retirement shortfall, be certain you've researched the market and understand the true value of what you are buying.

Your Business Assets

If you or your spouse is a small business owner, one of the trickiest things to figure out will be how much of this asset will be useable in retirement. No doubt you've sunk lots of your hard earned money into building the business, as well as a good deal of sweat and tears.

As you try to evaluate the business on a cash basis, you need to ask yourself a number of questions. If you decided to sell the business, what assets are marketable to a third party? So many times a small family business is dependent on the founder's continued involvement to keep the customer base he or she so carefully built. No one can be sure if these customers will continue working with a new owner, unless you and the new owner plan a very smooth transition.

Another option for small family businesses is that one or more of the family members are interested in carrying on its operation. If that's in your plans, then it's important to be certain a transition is in place that all members of the family support or a battle for control can disrupt what is otherwise a well-run business.

As you plan for retirement, you may also need to consider whether all that hard work and cash sunk into the business is helping you build an asset for retirement or if it is just draining the funds that you would otherwise invest toward your retirement goals. Sometimes you have to make a hard decision that the business just isn't growing the way you had dreamed, and it might be best to sell it and find another income source so you can build your nest egg.

If your business is a major part of the capital you expect to have at the time of retirement, be certain you do a realistic estimate of its value. Trying to overstate its worth will only come back to haunt you when you don't have enough to live on in retirement. You also need to consider the taxes that will eat up any profits you may be counting on after the sale of your business.

Another consideration is that you may plan for your business to be an ongoing income source when you turn it over to your children or other relatives. If that is part of the plan, you'll probably also need to expect to spend some time helping with the business to be certain this income source is maintained.

As you complete the asset allocation worksheets below, carefully track the percentage of your assets tied to this business. Do you

Keeping or Selling Your Business Can Be a Hard Choice to Make

Deciding what to do about your business requires some tough choices, especially if you've spent most of your working career trying to build a business. Now is the time to look at the hard facts. What is your return on the money invested in the business? Do you expect that your business will continue to grow or is it showing signs of decreasing sales? Do you have any saleable assets or is most of your business value in the goodwill you have built? If you wanted to get out of the business tomorrow, how much cash could you get for it? To help you get a handle on how to determine your business' value, you may want to read *Small Business Valuation Book* by Lawrence Tuller.

think you have enough diversification of your assets? Or, is too much of your retirement nest egg dependent on this one asset? If so, you might want to start an aggressive move toward sheltering some of your profits in one of the small business retirement plans discussed in Chapter 10.

Inheritance and Other Windfalls

The last component may or may not be a known factor. You may be aware of the inheritance you can expect from your parents or grandparents or you may have no idea. You may have won a lawsuit and expect a major settlement at some point in the future, but aren't sure what will be left when the appeals are exhausted. Or, you could be one of the lucky few that actually wins a lottery.

In most cases you can't plan for a windfall, but you may be able to get a better handle on what inheritance you could expect from a family member's estate. No question, this can be a very hard discussion to start, but it is important to discuss finances especially with your parents just in case they become unable to handle their finances at some point in the future. If your parents have a sizeable estate, it is important to be certain they have worked with a financial advisor that has estate-planning expertise.

Your Asset Allocation

Now that you have a better understanding of the various retirement savings programs and other assets that might help you build your retirement nest egg, let's revisit the assets chart we prepared as part of Chapter 4 (see page 50).

Review your assets and put a mark next to any asset that you think you will have at the time of retirement. Now let's build a new chart that will help you figure out your current asset allocation with the holdings you expect will be available at retirement. If you can, it's best to build this in a worksheet program, such as Excel or Lotus 1-2-3, so you will be able to sort the information in various ways and let the program calculate your numbers. Any asset that you include that is collateral for a loan (such as your home, which is mortgaged)

INTEGRATING YOUR RESOURCES

▶ ASSETS INVENTORY

Asset Category	Market Value/ Asset Name	Dividends Date	or Interest	Basis/ Cost to Sell	Date Purchased	Years Held
....	....	....	....	....	....	....
....	....	....	....	....	....	....
....	....	....	....	....	....	....
....	....	....	....	....	....	....
....	....	....	....	....	....	....
....	....	....	....	....	....	....
....	....	....	....	....	....	....

should be listed at its value minus liabilities. For example, if your home's market value is $250,000 and you have a mortgage totaling $200,000, only put $50,000 in the current market value column.

You also should determine why you are holding these assets. To simplify things, let's group them in three categories in the "Purpose" column: growth, safety, or income. In the next chapter, we'll take these a bit deeper after you understand the various risk factors and type of investments. The following is your new chart.

▶ ASSETS ALLOCATION

ASSET	PURPOSE	TYPE OF ACCOUNT	CURRENT MARKET VALUE	PERCENTAGE OF HOLDINGS
....	....	....	....	....
....	....	....	....	....
....	....	....	....	....
....	....	....	....	....
....	....	....	....	....
....	....	....	....	....
....	....	....	....	....
....	....	....	....	....

Once you've filled out the first four columns, total your current market value and then calculate the percentage of holding each investment represents. We'll analyze this one other way by grouping your assets according to "Purpose." If you are working with a spreadsheet program, copy your chart and then sort your holdings by the "Purpose" column. Make sure to copy your chart so you don't throw off the "Percentage of Holdings" numbers. Instead, we'll use that column to calculate the asset allocation by purpose.

Now, total the assets you hold for each of the three purposes: growth, safety, or income. Just to be sure you understand what we're doing, we've put together the following sample.

INTEGRATING YOUR RESOURCES

▶ ASSETS ALLOCATION

ASSET	PURPOSE	TYPE OF ACCOUNT	CURRENT MARKET VALUE	PERCENTAGE OF HOLDINGS
Stock Mutual Fund	Growth	401(k)–Husband	$20,000	
Stock Mutual Fund	Growth	IRA–Wife	$10,000	
Company Stock	Growth	ESOP	$5,000	
Subtotal	Growth		$35,000	38.9%
Value Mutual Fund	Safety	IRA–Husband	$10,000	
Money Market Fund	Safety	Joint	$30,000	
Subtotal	Safety		$40,000	44.4%
Bond Mutual Fund	Income	401(k)–Wife	$15,000	
Subtotal	Income		$15,000	16.7%
Total			**$90,000**	

Is your portfolio heavily weighted in one area? Do you think you may need to shift assets to be more properly balanced? We'll now take a closer look at these questions in our next chapter on investing basics.

For more information on this topic, visit our Web site at www.businesstown.com

Investing Basics

Cash Accounts

Now that we've learned all about the ways you can save for retirement and have a good idea of where you stand financially today, let's look at how you can effectively make that money grow for the future. Long-term investing is not only learning how to pick the top growth stocks or the safest bonds. What you really need to learn is how to mix the different types of investment vehicles so you can grow your money without taking unnecessary risks: in a nutshell, diversity.

Before getting started you should try to understand your investing personality. You need to figure out how much risk you can tolerate and still sleep at night. You also need to think about how much time you want to spend researching investment alternatives. All of these factors play a critical role in the investment choices you ultimately select for your portfolio.

First, let's discuss the alternatives. Basically, there are three ways you can save: cash accounts, stocks, and bonds. You can mix these up a bit using some types of mutual funds.

Cash accounts include regular savings accounts, certificates of deposit, and money market funds. In many cases, these types of accounts can be deposited with full insurance on your assets through the Federal Deposit Insurance Corporation (FDIC) up to $100,000. Be careful, though; some money market accounts are not insured by the FDIC and there are some banks who choose not to participate in the insurance program.

If you choose to seek out the highest interest return, you will likely find cash savings alternatives that are not insured. Even if not insured, they could still be a relatively safe place to park your money. What you need to do is research the types of investments an institution is using to generate its returns. Frequently, the best returns are generated using high-risk commercial paper, in other words by providing loans to companies with low ratings. Another frequent place to find high returns is in loans to developing countries. We'll be talking more about risk later. Just keep in mind that just because you are using a cash savings vehicle you may not have the safety you intended.

> Cash accounts include regular savings accounts, certificates of deposit, and money market funds.

Understanding Bonds

Next to cash, bonds are the next safest investment. Basically, these are IOUs the government, a company, or another entity sells in order to generate cash. Bond types include U.S. government securities, municipal bonds, corporate bonds, mortgage and asset-backed securities, federal agency securities, and foreign government bonds.

Initially, the bond is sold at some specific amount called its face value. In exchange for borrowing the money, the entity that issues the bond agrees to pay interest to bondholders, as well as to guarantee to repay the loan in full at some date in the future, which is called the maturity date. The time period between the initial sale of the bond and the maturity date is called "the term."

The promise of periodic interest payments makes this a fixed-income investment. A bond investor that buys a bond on the day it is sold knows he or she can expect a certain level of income for a certain time period and get his or her initial investment back at the end of the time period. The risk a bond investor takes is that the entity issuing the bond may not at some time in the future be able to pay the interest or repay the full loan amount.

Bonds are rated by a number of agencies including Standard & Poor's (S&P), Moody's Investor Services, and Fitch Ratings. Each rating service uses its own alphabet soup to specify the creditworthiness of a bond. The safest bonds are those issued by the U.S. Treasury or a U.S. government agency.

This excellent chart from the Bond Market Association (*www.investinginbonds.com*) summarizes the bond ratings from these key services (see page 264).

Bonds that are considered investment-grade receive Aaa or AAA ratings to Baa or BBB ratings from Moody's or S&P. Speculative or junk bonds ratings vary from Ba or BB to D. Companies or other entities with lower ratings must pay a higher interest rate to get buyers, so their yields will be higher, but so is the risk that investors take.

Average maturity is also a factor in bond return. Short-term bonds have an average life of one to five years. Intermediate-term bonds mature in five to ten years. Long-term bonds have a lifespan of over ten years. To learn more about how bond rating works, visit the

> Next to cash, bonds are the next safest investment.

Standard & Poor's online information library at *www.standardand poors.com/ResourceCenter/RatingsDefinitions.html*.

Credit Ratings			
Credit Risk	**Moody's**	**Standard & Poor's**	**Fitch**
INVESTMENT GRADE			
Highest quality	Aaa	AAA	AAA
High quality (very strong)	Aa	AA	AA
Upper medium grade (strong)	A	A	A
Medium grade	Baa	BBB	BBB
NOT INVESTMENT GRADE			
Somewhat speculative	Ba	BB	BB
Speculative	B	B	B
Highly speculative	Caa	CCC	CCC
Most speculative	Ca	CC	CC
Imminent default	C	C	C
Default	C	D	D

> Older bond prices could rise when interest rates fall because the return on a bond paying a higher interest will be more favorable.

Bonds are bought and sold throughout their life cycle. Bond prices fluctuate as economic conditions shift. For example, if interest rates are rising, bond prices of older issues will drop if their interest rate is lower than the current rate available for new bonds. Conversely, older bond prices could rise when interest rates fall because the return on a bond paying a higher interest will be more favorable. You can learn more about buying bonds at *www.bondsonline.com*.

Stock Basics

The riskiest type of investing is in individual stocks, which is also the type of investment that offers the greatest growth potential. There is no insurance available for stocks, as there is for cash investments, and there are no promises of returning the money you invest, as bondholders are promised. In fact, when you buy stocks, unless you buy them during an Initial Public Offering (IPO), your transaction is not even with the company whose stocks you purchase.

What is a stock then? Stocks are issued as certificates of ownership that entitle you to a fraction of the company. You actually own a tiny percentage of all the company's assets, including its buildings, inventory, furniture, and so forth.

Types of Stock

There are two types of stock: common stock and preferred stock. Common stock comes with voting rights, but you are last in line to claim money for your certificates of ownership if a company goes bankrupt. Preferred stock doesn't usually come with voting rights, but its owners fall ahead of you in collecting leftover assets after the creditors have gotten their share. Also, if the company pays dividends, the preferred stock shareholders have a specific dividend guarantee that is paid first before any dividends are paid to common shareholders. If a company can't make the full dividend payment to preferred shareholders, the unpaid dividends will be tracked and paid out in some future year before common shareholders will get any dividend payments.

Voting Rights

Voting rights don't mean much to most stockholders today. Few have a significant enough share of a company to truly influence any key decision-making. Unless you are someone like Warren Buffett or Bill Gates, you pretty much sit on the sidelines and watch things happen to your stock holdings.

Your Responsibility

As a stock investor, your key responsibility is to carefully research stocks before you purchase them and determine what you think the future growth prospects are for the companies you select. There's a lot of information out there about every major company, but if you've been reading the news lately you can see that even major companies can hide their true value from analysts and

Stock Certificates

We've been talking about stock certificates, but you probably have never seen one. In the past, actual paper certificates were handed out when stock was sold. Today, most of us keep the "certificates" on deposit with our broker or bank that handles our stock transactions (i.e., in "street name"). If you held the certificates yourself, not only would you need to insure their safety so they don't get lost, you also would have to physically take them to your broker or bank to sell them. This could cause great delays in completing your sale.

Learn More about Direct Stock Investing

Direct stock investing takes a lot of time, but you do have the possibility of getting the highest reward if you pick stocks correctly. You also face the greatest loss if your stock choices go belly-up. Before taking the plunge, take time to learn about stock investing and maybe even practice by managing a make-believe portfolio either on paper or using one of the free portfolio sites online.

There are some excellent online resources for learning more about investing with tools for practicing your own portfolio management style. Some of my favorites include Yahoo Finance (*http://finance.yahoo.com*) and CBS Marketwatch (*http://cbs.marketwatch.com*). Dow Jones's SmartMoney University (*http://university.smartmoney.com/*) offers excellent self-directed courses that help you learn more about investing.

investors alike. In fact, in some cases, regulators believe the analysts and accountants may be too closely tied to the companies to be certain that true values are being reported to the public.

If you don't want to go it alone, you have one of two choices. The first option is to find a broker or financial planner who will help you manage your portfolio. Fees for private money management can get high and unless your portfolio is a large one, you'll have a hard time finding a top money manager. The second alternative is to invest using mutual funds. Let's take a closer look at how they work.

Mutual Fund Alternative

Mutual funds pool the money of hundreds of investors to build a portfolio that can include cash, stocks, and bonds, depending on the objectives chosen by the portfolio manager. These investment vehicles are great for small investors who want to participate in the market, but don't have much money to start their portfolio. Mutual funds allow you to instantly buy into a diversified portfolio and slowly build your asset base while you learn more about investing and ultimately decide whether you want to go it alone or continue working with a professional money manager.

Mutual Fund Prospectus

When you buy a mutual fund, the assets you are buying are not only the value of the investments held by the fund, but also the expertise of the portfolio manager. Mutual funds are run according to a set of objectives clearly stated in the mutual fund prospectus, which is a legal document you should review before purchasing any fund. These documents not only include the stated objectives, but also give you a history of the fund's performance and the fund's top holdings as of a specific date. In addition to the prospectus, you should review the quarterly or semiannual reports that give you the most up-to-date information you can find on most funds. Some funds report their portfolio's performance more frequently online. Also, there are calls from various investor groups that require more frequent reporting.

Basically, the objectives will state the fund goal, the types of investments that can be included in the portfolio, and the country or countries in which the fund can invest. These pooled portfolios help the small investor reduce the risks and volatility of investing directly in the stocks or bonds of individual companies. Portfolio managers use two styles of investing: active money management or indexing. Indexing is a mathematical model based on tracking the results of various indexes, such as the popular Standard & Poor's 500, which is a grouping of 500 of the top growth companies.

As an individual investor what you actually own is a pro rata share of the portfolio and you receive distributions in the form of dividends, interest, and/or capital gains based on that pro rata share. You can build your portfolio even more quickly by automatically reinvesting these distributions.

Choosing a Mutual Fund

Choosing a mutual fund can be a daunting exercise. There are more than 8,000 mutual funds from which to choose. Mutual funds fall into four distinct groups: equity funds, fixed-income funds, balanced funds, and money market funds. Equity funds, which account for about 50 percent of the total dollars invested in mutual funds, invest primarily in shares of common stock. Money market funds, which are the next largest portion of the mutual fund pie, account for approximately 30 percent of mutual fund assets. They invest in short-term debt securities of the U.S. government, banks, and corporations, as well as U.S. Treasury Bills. Fixed-income funds, which make up about 13 percent of total mutual fund assets, invest primarily in bonds and preferred stocks. These funds can be either taxable, which include corporate and long-term government bonds, or tax-free, which include municipal bonds. Tax-free bond funds are free from taxes on interest earned, but can be taxed on capital gains. The smallest piece of the pie is in balanced or hybrid funds, which total about 5 percent of the mutual fund universe. These funds invest in a combination of both stocks and bonds.

Choices get even more confusing when you start looking at the objectives of funds. Stock funds mix their assets under varying

Mutual Funds Are Popular

Mutual fund investing is very popular today and a much safer way to take advantage of the higher returns available with stock investing. More than 70 million people were investing through mutual funds with over $6.9 trillion held in mutual fund accounts at the end of December 2001, according to the Investment Company Institute. There are also over 8,000 mutual funds from which to choose, so picking funds can be a real chore. If you take the time to pick the right funds, however, your time needed for monitoring your investment will be considerably less than it is for a portfolio built with individual stocks.

criteria based on the risk of the stock holdings. When you start researching stock funds, you'll find categories such as aggressive growth funds, growth funds, or growth and income funds. We'll take a brief look at the kinds of companies you can expect to find in each of these different types.

Aggressive Growth Funds

Aggressive growth funds are definitely the most volatile type of equity mutual funds. You will usually find these at both ends of the performance line—the top ten performers of the year and the ten worst performers. Their goal is to find assets that will give them maximum capital growth by picking stocks in companies the manager believes has good potential for rapid growth and capital appreciation.

When you invest in this type of fund, be ready for a wild ride. These funds have wide swings up and down and low stability of your principal investment. You definitely must have a strong stomach for this type of investment and a lot of patience. If not, you could end up selling out of the fund at its worst point, when your mutual fund has lost a lot of money and you're too nervous to wait for a rebound. The types of companies you'll usually find in these funds are small emerging growth companies. You may also find a concentration of one or more industry sectors. Some will use speculative strategies, such as short-selling or options, to leverage their results. If you are ready for the roller coaster ride and can afford to assume greater risks, you will find the potential for significant and rapid gains, but also be ready for the potential of huge losses, especially in the short term.

> Seek out growth funds, which are less volatile.

Growth Funds

You may want a fund that has good growth potential, but is not as risky as the aggressive growth funds. For this alternative, you should seek out growth funds, which are less volatile. In these types of funds, you will find managers who invest in common stocks seeking growth rather than current income. Their portfolio holdings are more conservative than aggressive growth funds, because the portfolio will be built using well-established companies within industries with long-term growth potential, rather than small emerging companies.

You can't expect to get much income from these funds. Growth companies usually reinvest their profits and pay low or no dividends. Therefore, these funds are not suitable if you are seeking current income. While their potential for a drop in principal value is less than with aggressive growth funds, their volatility may not be right for you if you cannot assume risk to your principal. But, by taking some risk of a short-term drop in principal, many growth funds have sustained strong long-term performance records.

Growth and Income Funds

Growth and income funds, also known as value funds, have stated objectives that seek both long-term growth and current income. In these portfolios, you will find stocks of well-established companies and most likely significant dividend payments. Value fund managers use dividend yields to offset the volatility that can be found in pure growth funds. Dividends are a stable component of the total returns on these types of funds, while capital returns can fluctuate widely.

There are a number of different investing styles that make up the value or growth and income fund universe. Some managers will concentrate their portfolios in growth and income stocks, or put together a combination of growth stocks, stocks paying high dividends, preferred stocks, convertible securities, or fixed-income securities such as corporate bonds and money market instruments. Others may look for the beaten-down companies that they think have a good chance for a recovery. Still others may be a bit more aggressive and use what are called hedging strategies by investing in growth stocks and then buying and selling covered call options to generate the income side of the portfolio rather than depending on dividends.

There is no doubt that this style of mutual fund management, provided you've picked a good manager, is the least volatile of equity mutual funds. The downside is that they will not have the potential for rapid growth that you'll find in the riskier equity fund types.

> Dividends are a stable component of the total returns on these types of funds, while capital returns can fluctuate widely.

Bond or Fixed-Income Funds

These types of funds can invest in bonds and preferred stocks. They can also be taxable, when their assets are held in corporate or

Ratings for Bond Funds

Bond ratings vary by credit rating agency. In addition to their individual bond ratings, Standard & Poor's uses a similar rating system for bond funds. To give you an idea of how these ratings work, here is a brief description from Standard & Poor's about its rating criteria.

AAAf—The fund's portfolio holdings provide extremely strong protection against losses from credit defaults.

Aaf—The fund's portfolio holdings provide very strong protection against losses from credit defaults.

Af—The fund's portfolio holdings provide strong protection against losses from credit defaults.

BBBf—The fund's portfolio holdings provide adequate protection against losses from credit defaults.

BBf—The fund's portfolio holdings provide uncertain protection against losses from credit defaults.

Bf—The fund's portfolio holdings exhibit vulnerability to losses from credit defaults.

CCCf—The fund's portfolio holdings make it extremely vulnerable to losses from credit defaults.

government bonds, or tax-free, if their assets are in municipal bonds. Even tax-free bond funds may experience capital gains. While the interest earned is tax-free, capital gains are generated when municipal bonds are sold at a profit prior to their maturity date.

As with stock funds, the reason to select a mutual bond fund rather than investing in bonds directly is that you want greater diversity in the types of bonds held in the portfolio. These funds also offer more liquidity, because in many cases you can get your money by writing a check, if the service is offered.

When picking a bond fund, you should research the types of bonds in a portfolio, the creditworthiness of the bonds, and their average maturity date. As previously discussed, all these factors determine the safety of a bond.

Money Market Funds

The safest of all mutual funds is the money market fund, but they also offer the least potential for the growth of your money. Money market fund holdings can include short-term debt securities of the U.S. government, banks, and corporations, as well as U.S. Treasury Bills. These funds have no potential for capital appreciation.

Money market mutual funds have a constant share price of $1. The interest rate they earn fluctuates rather than the share price. They frequently earn more interest than an insured bank account, but you don't have the safety that insurance offers. You may find a better interest rate with a long-term certificate of deposit (CD), but the advantage mutual funds offer is that they are more liquid, making the money readily available to you when you need it. CDs usually limit your access to the money during the term of your investment, while money market mutual funds allow you to write a check on the money at any time. You may find that some money market funds limit the number of free checks you can write each month and will charge a fee if you exceed that minimum.

Hybrid and Balanced Funds

While most of these mutual fund types will hold cash assets at some time, if you don't want to worry about how to mix your portfolio among stock funds, bond funds, and money market funds, there are funds whose objectives are to do this balancing act for you: hybrid or balanced funds.

These funds are usually the least volatile of funds that include stocks and bonds. Their objectives are not to achieve the highest possible return, but to provide stability and some income. You will never find a balanced fund in the top ten funds of the year, but you also won't find it at the bottom of the pack either, unless you've selected an incompetent manager. Usually, the stated objectives will specify a specific balance between stocks and bonds, such as 60 percent stocks and 40 percent bonds or cash.

International Funds

You may want to add an international flavor to your mix. There are international funds within all of these mutual fund types. Basically, you can choose between two types of international mutual funds: world/global funds or foreign funds. The key difference is whether or not they invest in U.S. stocks or bonds, as well as foreign funds. Pure foreign funds do not invest in U.S. stocks. A world or global fund may be less volatile, but if you choose to add an international component to your portfolio using these funds be sure there is not a significant overlap with your domestic stock funds.

Understanding Risks

Throughout this discussion of stocks, bonds, and mutual funds, we've consistently talked about risks. There are lots of different types of risks associated with investing. Let's take a quick look at the major types.

Inflation Risk

Inflation risk usually impacts people who are afraid to take risk. These folks risk the possibility that their money will not be worth as much in the future. You know that the costs of the basics increase every year—housing, clothing, medical care, and food. By investing solely through guaranteed investment alternatives, you

Types of Money Market Funds

You will have three types of money market funds from which you can choose: general money market funds, funds that invest only in U.S. government instruments, and tax-exempt money market funds. General money market funds usually invest in a combination of commercial paper and U.S. government securities. The U.S. government funds invest in money market instruments whose principal and interest is backed by the U.S. government or its agencies. The cost of this guarantee is slightly lower yields than general money market funds.

Tax-exempt money market funds invest in short-term municipal bonds that are exempt from federal income taxes. These types of funds usually offer the lowest return among money market mutual funds because of the tax-free advantage. When deciding whether to use a tax-exempt money market fund or a taxable one, you'll need to compare the after-tax yields for both taxable and nontaxable funds to find out which is best for you.

will not be able to keep pace with inflation and will most likely run out of funds in retirement, unless, of course, you are already a multi-millionaire.

Opportunity Risk

Opportunity risk looks at your tradeoffs. Each time you make an investment, you risk the possibility of missing out on a better use of your money elsewhere. You can choose a stock or stock fund that takes a huge hit and you've not only lost your initial investment, but you also lost the possibility of earning interest had you invested that money in bonds or in a cash-based opportunity. Bonds and cash investment vehicles have the opposite problem. If you invest in long-term bonds and certificates of deposit (CDs), you are most likely to face this situation at some point. For example, if you deposit funds in a long-term CD earning 3 percent interest and interest rates rise to 6 percent, you are stuck earning the lower rate or you'll have to pay a penalty to get out early. Long-term bonds can be even riskier, because you'll take some loss on principal to sell the bond if interest rates are higher than the rate your bond is earning. The value of long-term bonds goes down when interest rates go up. You'll lose principal if you try to sell.

> The value of long-term bonds goes down when interest rates go up. You'll lose principal if you try to sell.

Reinvestment Risk

Reinvestment risk primarily affects fixed-income investments. When a CD's term ends or a bond matures, you have to find another investment alternative for the money. The alternatives available may not be as good at the time you must reinvest. This can be of great concern to retirees because they are more likely to have most of their funds tied-up in fixed-income investment vehicles.

Concentration Risk

Concentration risk becomes a factor if you put all your eggs in one basket. Some investors like to jump on whatever stocks are hot without carefully diversifying their portfolio. When that hot investment type is no longer in favor, a portfolio can drop dramatically in value if your investments are too concentrated.

Interest Rate Risk

Interest rate risk is related primarily to cash and bond investments. Bonds are affected the most when interest rates rise, because their prices fall. Stocks can also be affected, depending on the market reaction to rising or falling rates. When the Fed lowers rates, stocks tend to rally. When the Fed raises rates, stocks tend to fall. Also, company profits can be severely impacted if they carry a lot of debt and interest rates are rising. Consumers tend to slow spending when rates are rising, which can also affect sales and business profits.

Credit or Default Risk

Credit or default risk is the risk that the borrower won't repay an obligation and is primarily related to bond investing. In most cases, unless you are investing in junk bonds, you probably don't have to worry about this kind of risk. A bond fund with a high yield may look very attractive to you, but remember the reason for that higher yield is the risks being assumed because of the low quality assets that are held.

Marketability Risk

Marketability risk relates to the liquidity of an investment. You may not be able to sell your investment when you want to do so. You are most likely to face this risk in trying to sell real estate or the stock of a small company that is not heavily traded.

> If you want to sell a foreign asset when the value of the dollar is down, you could lose additional money just based on that drop.

Currency Translation Risk

Currency translation risk is a risk you will only experience if you are buying investments outside of the United States, because of the fluctuation of currency exchanges. The U.S. dollar's value fluctuates daily against the currency of other countries. If you want to sell a foreign asset when the value of the dollar is down, you could lose additional money just based on that drop. In international investing, you face both market risk and the risk that the value of the dollar will drop against the currency of the countries where assets are held. Most investors face this risk if they invest in international mutual funds.

How Time Impacts Your Investing Choices

Time can either be your best friend when investing or it can be your biggest enemy. If you have ten or more years before needing the money, you can take a lot of risk because you have plenty of time for that investment to recover from any market shock. If you need the money in two years, you don't want to take any unnecessary risk because you don't have time to wait for a market turnaround.

For a short-term horizon, your primary concern should be preservation of principal. The last thing you want to face is selling an asset when it is in a loss position just because you need the money. Don't get me wrong, there will be times when you have to accept your losses and move on if you made a bad investment choice, but you don't want to be forced to do this just because you don't have the time to wait for better market conditions.

Having Patience

Even if you do have the time to wait, it's important to know whether you will have the patience to ride out an investing storm. Many investors who got caught up in the technology stock bubble sold out at the bottom after investing at the top when technology stocks were high. That type of impatience can be more devastating to a portfolio than waiting for a turnaround if you then decide to put everything in safe and insured asset types. Inflation risk then becomes a big factor in your retirement savings future.

There is no doubt that you will face ups and downs when investing in stocks and bonds. You have to learn how to have enough patience to ride out a storm, provided you believe the investment is still a good choice and will recover after the economy improves. Economic cycles are a fact of life and you will see numerous periods of inflation and recession throughout your lifetime.

A good way to learn patience is *not* to watch the market fluctuations daily and make yourself sick. Pick investments carefully and feel confident in your choices and how they fit into your long-term plans. Then make changes if the choice no longer fits your long-term plans. You also want to start shifting to safer investments as you get closer to needing the money.

Fear of Risk

Fear of risk keeps many people away from growth investing entirely. They just can't face the possibility that something could happen that could result in the loss of part or all of their investment. Even the slightest probability of that happening persuades them to keep everything in the bank. Allocating your assets and carefully selecting types of assets depending on your time horizon can minimize risk.

Switching Investments

You may need to switch if you no longer believe a stock's growth potential is a reality. Another reason to switch may be that a mutual fund changes its management strategy and it no longer fulfills a particular asset allocation niche. When management changes, you may want to reassess your holdings in that fund. But, if the stock or fund drops in value because that type of stock or fund is down across the board, you probably want to hold on to it as long as you think your initial reasons for selecting the investment are still valid.

Allocating Your Assets

The best way to minimize risk is to carefully balance your assets among various investment vehicles. Many people think that seeking out the top-performing stocks and mutual funds is the key to successful investing. They are wrong. Many studies have shown that individual investment choices account for only 5 to 10 percent of a portfolio's success, while 90 to 95 percent can be attributed to the way the portfolio is allocated among stocks, bonds, and money market instruments.

Risk Tolerance

There are five key factors in asset allocation: your investment goal, your time horizon, your risk tolerance, your financial resources, and your investment mix. We've talked extensively about setting goals. We've also looked at how the time horizon impacts your investment. We discussed different types of risks, but do you know your risk tolerance? To try to figure that out, here are some questions you can ask yourself:

- Do market fluctuations keep you awake at night?
- Are you unfamiliar with investing?
- Do you consider yourself more a saver than an investor?
- Are you fearful of losing 25 percent of your assets in a few days or weeks?

> Many people think that seeking out the top-performing stocks and mutual funds is the key to successful investing. They are wrong.

If you answered "yes" to these questions, you are likely to be a "conservative" investor. How about these:

- Are you comfortable with the ups and downs of the securities markets?
- Are you knowledgeable about investing and the securities markets?
- Are you investing for a long-term goal?
- Can you withstand considerable short-term losses?

If you answered "yes" to these questions, you are likely to be an "aggressive" investor.

If your answers were mixed between the two groups of questions, then you are probably a "moderate" investor.

Financial Resources

Once you've got a handle on your risk tolerance, then it's time to look at your financial resources. The amount of money you have to invest will be a big factor in the risks you want to take. A small investor just doesn't have the funds to properly diversify a portfolio. In that case a well-diversified mutual fund is your best bet for getting started. Once your portfolio has grown large enough, you may want to take some risk by selecting a more aggressive mutual fund or picking individual stocks.

In Chapter 5, we discussed the returns you can expect from bonds, stocks, and cash and began discussions about how mixing these types of assets can have an impact on your return. Stocks historically have averaged 11.3 percent, bonds have averaged 5.1 percent, and cash deposits have averaged 3 percent. We also learned how to use these numbers to calculate a weighted average for your portfolio.

Now, it's time to use all the information we've learned about asset allocation and test how your portfolio is doing. Let's revisit your portfolio. First, you may want to revise the "Purpose" column to include the various investment types, so you can get a better handle on how aggressive or conservative your portfolio actually is.

Use this information to decide how balanced your portfolio really is and whether that balance matches your savings goals and

> Once your portfolio has grown large enough, you may want to take some risk by selecting a more aggressive mutual fund or picking individual stocks.

your risk tolerance. What chance does your current asset allocation have of meeting your goals? If your gap is huge and you know you can't meet your goals with the current estimated level of return, you must decide whether you can tolerate more risk and try to improve your portfolio's growth potential or revise your goals to a level that more realistically matches what your portfolio can achieve. Another option is to dramatically increase the amount you are saving each year toward retirement to help fill the gap. We'll take a much closer look at using good asset allocation strategy to fill the gap in Chapter 19.

Market Timing versus Buy and Hold Investing

Some investors try to improve their odds of meeting goals, thinking they can increase their portfolio returns by timing the market, but in reality those who have been most successful in investing believe the buy and hold strategy works the best. In fact, billionaire investor Warren Buffett goes one step further. He recommends that one buys good companies and holds them "forever."

Market timers believe that they can buy low and sell high. The problem is that few can accurately time the market. In fact, one study done at the University of Michigan for the period from December 31, 1981, to August 25, 1987, showed that stocks returned an average of 26.3 percent annually. During that period there were ten days when the largest price advances occurred. If you missed those ten days, your annual return would have been only 18.3 percent or a loss of one-third of the market's return. Take out the twenty biggest days and the annual return would have been 13.1 percent or a 50.2 percent loss of the market's return.

You probably are not as perfect at picking stocks as Warren Buffett. So the idea that you hold a stock forever may not work for you. Knowing when to sell your stocks or mutual funds requires regular monitoring of the quarterly reports you receive either from an individual company or from a mutual fund company, depending on the type of investment you select. In the next chapter, we'll explore portfolio management in greater detail.

Buffett Wisdom

In a quote from the Owner's Manual for Berkshire Hathaway stock, Chairman and CEO Warren E. Buffett writes: "As owners of, say, Coca-Cola or Gillette shares, we think of Berkshire as being a non-managing partner in two extraordinary businesses, in which we measure our success by the long-term progress of the companies rather than by the month-to-month movements of their stocks. In fact, we would not care in the least if several years went by in which there was no trading, or quotation of prices, in the stocks of those companies. If we have good long-term expectations, short-term price changes are meaningless for us except to the extent they offer us an opportunity to increase our ownership at an attractive price."

Chapter 17

Managing
the Plans

Monitor Your Investments

Many of us may wish we could do the research, pick our investments, and put our entire retirement portfolio on autopilot. Wouldn't it be nice if retirement investing were that simple? Unfortunately, it's not. Even if you choose to build your portfolio using index mutual funds, which are the simplest way to take advantage of growth stocks, you still need to monitor what is happening with your investment choices, as well as watch to be sure your asset allocation is remaining within your level of risk tolerance. You have to carefully watch your plan statements from your employer and be sure the company is complying with retirement fund rules.

You may think the business press is covering the stock market almost as though it's a sports game—reporting ups and downs with action words that make you want to take action yourself. Don't get caught up in all the hype and respond too quickly to a bad day. Retirement investing is for the long term. Any change to your portfolio should be done with careful consideration of why you initially picked the investment and what has changed that is making you want to reconsider your choice.

Annual Reviews

A good practice is to plan annual reviews of your investment portfolio at which time you check your asset allocation balance and review the performance of your portfolio's choices. If the performance of any of your assets is negative, that doesn't automatically mean you need to pick something else. You should research how other similar assets have done and whether your choice is performing badly compared to the asset type.

For example, if you held growth funds at the time the Internet bubble burst you certainly saw negative returns, but so did everyone else who owned growth funds. What you needed to check at the end of 2000 was how badly your funds were hurt and how did their negative performance compare to others in the same fund category. A good place to find average returns by fund category is Morningstar.com. The same is true about any stock choices. You must compare your picks to others in the same industry.

> Any change to your portfolio should be done with careful consideration of why you initially picked the investment and what has changed that is making you want to reconsider your choice.

You also want to check your asset allocation. For example, if you decided, based on your risk tolerance, that you were comfortable with a balance of 60 percent stocks, 30 percent bonds, and 10 percent cash, you need to run the numbers to be certain you are still in that ballpark. Sometimes, if it's been a stellar year for growth stocks, you'll find this balance to be way out of whack and your portfolio actually has a much greater exposure to growth stocks than you intended. Other times when stocks are down, your bond or cash balance might be high.

Changes Made Outside the Annual Review

Changes to your portfolio outside of your annual review should only be done if your employer decides to change administrators and you must pick new investment choices, or if you find out about a significant change in a mutual fund or stock that is in your portfolio. Obviously, if you held Enron stock and saw its dramatic decline, you would have minimized losses by selling as soon as you realized it was going to fall. In that case, the fall was so swift, you might not have reacted in time anyway. Investors lost billions of dollars during that catastrophic fall.

If you have a lot of individual stocks in your portfolio, you will need to monitor them much more closely than if you invest using mutual funds. If you invest in stocks, you need to keep up on company news and watch company reports as well as reports from analysts and other financial experts.

Mutual Fund Changes

Mutual fund investors need to monitor significant changes in fund managers or fund management strategy. Also, they need to be certain that the fund is actually investing your money based on the portfolio management strategy indicated in the prospectus.

You will receive at least semiannual statements, and in most cases quarterly statements from your mutual fund companies, that will show the top portfolio holdings and performance results. Don't just take a quick look and throw them away. Spend some time reviewing the types of stocks and bonds included in the portfolio and

Three Ways to Adjust Your Portfolio

1. Invest a lump sum of new retirement savings in the type of assets that are below your intended allocation targets. You most likely would be able to do this using an IRA outside of your employer plan.
2. Reallocate your assets by selling the types that exceed their target allocation and buying the types that are low. If the assets are held outside a retirement plan, be certain you understand the tax consequences of exchanging assets.
3. Change next year's contribution allocation in your retirement plan to increase your investment in the types of assets that are low and decrease the portion that goes toward the assets that are high.

Do Not Panic

If you find out there is a major management change for one of your mutual fund picks, there is still no reason to panic. Unlike a stock that is hit with bad news and can drop dramatically in a day, mutual funds take longer to show the effects of a manager change. Even if the manager plans to make a major shift in mutual fund strategy, it will usually take months, or sometimes even years, to buy and sell assets strategically. Just because a fund changes managers does not automatically mean you should sell it. Research the new manager's performance. Most likely he or she managed at least one other fund before taking over yours. Web sites like FundAlarm.com, Morningstar.com, and CBS Marketwatch do cover manager changes and will frequently give you a good deal of information about whether the change is good or bad for the fund.

maybe research some of the companies yourself if you don't recognize them. If you have some questions about investment strategy, do some additional digging to find out what others are saying about the fund. One great Web site for researching more about management changes and other problem alarms is FundAlarm.com (*www.fund alarm.com*). You can sign up for a free monthly e-mail that lets you know when the site is updated. Another good Web site is CBS Marketwatch (*http://cbs.marketwatch.com*), which has excellent coverage of the mutual fund industry.

Monitor Plan Statements and Employer Compliance

So far, we have been talking about the assets held in your retirement plan, but you also need to monitor your employer's compliance with pension plan law to be certain your defined-benefit and/or defined-contribution plans are being managed according to federal law. In Part 3, we reviewed your rights and responsibilities for each plan type individually. Now we'll take a closer look at how to use the reports your employer gives you every year to be certain the company is in compliance and what you can do if you suspect there is trouble.

Summary Annual Report

Each year your company pension plan administrator, whether for a defined-contribution or defined-benefit plan, must give you information about your plan investments. Some companies will just automatically circulate the annual report; others will send you written notice that the report is available and ask you to request a copy if you want one. This is called the summary annual report or SAR. You also have a right to ask for the full annual report and financial statements that are filed with the government once every year. Retirement plans that have 100 participants or more usually file a Form 5500 with the government, and smaller plans file a Form 5500-C/R (filed every three years).

When you get the SAR, it is usually one or two pages long and summarizes the Form 5500 or 5500-C/R that has been filed with the

Internal Revenue Service, which reviews the information and sends a copy to the Department of Labor. The summary will tell you about the plan's investment performance, the total administrative expenses for the year, financial arrangements with individuals or organizations closely related to the plan, and whether the plan has outstanding unpaid loans. All of these items can give you an indication of potential problems if you look at them closely. If any of these items raise questions in your mind, you should definitely request the full annual report from your plan administrator. The administrator does have the right to charge you a fee for the cost of copying of up to 25 cents per page.

If you are in a defined-benefit plan, you have no control over investment choices, while in a defined-contribution you usually do have more control. Even though you don't have any control over a defined-benefit plan, you still have a right to see how the money is invested. Details will be reported in the annual plan.

Administrative Fees

Another key factor that can hurt your pension's future is the application of fees. Most companies will hire third parties to provide some of the record-keeping, investment management, accounting, legal, and other administrative services it needs to manage the plans. Your plan administrator does have the responsibility to be sure these fees and commissions are reasonable. The annual report will show all plan expenses. You can total these expenses and divide that figure by total assets to find out what percentage of these assets are being spent to administer the plan.

Accountant's Opinion

Another key place to check for problems is the accountant's opinion, which should be attached to Form 5500. Larger plans do file a report written by an independent public accountant who reviews the plan's financial statements and lists any major problems he or she finds. The accountant's opinion should be "unqualified." Opinions that are "qualified" or "adverse" will be explained in an attachment. Carefully read, and be sure you understand, any comments written by the independent accountant.

Requesting the Full Annual Report

If you are having difficulty getting a copy, then resend your request in writing using "certified" mail or by other means in which you will have a way to prove when the request was made. Your plan administrator can be fined up to $100 per day if he or she refuses to comply with your request for a copy. Another source for a copy is the U.S. Department of Labor's Pension and Welfare Benefits Administration Public Disclosure Facility. While this should not be your first stop, it does give you a way to get a copy if you are having difficulty. If you suspect problems, you can also get copies of previous years' filings.

Investigating the Problem

If you do suspect a problem, three federal government agencies can step in to investigate: the Department of Labor (DOL), the Internal Revenue Service (IRS), and the Department of Justice. Each has different responsibilities for assuring compliance with federal law.

The Department of Labor gets involved if you think the plan trustees or others responsible for investing pension money have been violating rules. You can write or call the nearest field office of the U.S. Department of Labor's Pension and Welfare Benefits Administration to report a problem. If the DOL does find after an investigation that funds have been mismanaged, they can ask a court to compel plan trustees and others to put money back into the plan. Courts can also impose additional penalties of up to 20 percent of the recovered amount and bar individuals from serving as trustees or plan money managers.

The IRS gets involved if you suspect people have taken advantage of their relationship to the plan, such as taking loans. The IRS can impose tax penalties if unlawful activities are uncovered. If you do expose a problem, you could be eligible for an Informants' Reward of up to 10 percent of the amount collected, but to get this reward you must file a written claim at the time you make the report.

The Department of Justice gets involved if there is a report of embezzlement or theft of pension money, kickbacks, or extortion. If any of these types of activities are suspected, they should be reported to either the Federal Bureau of Investigation or the DOL field office. The Department of Justice will take violators to court, if illegal activities are found. Violators can be fined and possibly even receive prison sentences.

Change Jobs Wisely

Another factor in managing your long-term retirement savings is carefully planning any job switches. There is no doubt you will change jobs several times during your career. The old-fashioned notion of starting with a company after getting out of school and staying there for life is rarely even possible today.

Few companies show that kind of loyalty to employees. At the first sign of economic downturns, many companies begin cost-cutting measures by laying off employees. Knowing they can't depend on a long-term relationship, employees will more easily jump ship if there is any sign of questionable economic conditions. The entire employment arena has turned into one in which everyone is looking out for their own best interest and sometimes shooting themselves in the foot.

Planning to Leave

Of course, if there is a layoff, you just have to make the best of the situation and figure out how to preserve whatever retirement savings you have in the best way possible. But, if you are voluntarily looking to switch jobs or if someone approaches you about a hot opportunity, jump only after considering not only the wage package but also other benefits as well. While health, disability, and life insurance; vacation benefits; and other benefit options are important parts of the benefits mix, we're just going to concentrate on the key things to look at relating to retirement.

If the company has a defined-benefit plan, in most cases, unless you've been there for at least ten years, you will probably be forfeiting any rights to plan. Even if you do collect something at retirement, it will be greatly reduced because as we learned in Chapter 11, the formula is usually heavily impacted by the number of years worked and by the last three to five years of income. By leaving earlier in your career, you most likely have a much lower salary than you will have later in life. Benefits will also be reduced because of fewer years of service.

When planning to leave, the bigger question is how you are vested in any defined-contribution plan or possibly what cash value you may be able to take with you from a cash-balance pension plan. The new tax law passed in 2001 certainly makes it easier for you to switch and take something with you. Let's take a look at how this all works.

Vesting Schedules

There are two types of vesting schedules: cliff vesting and graded vesting. Vesting, as you may remember from our earlier discussion in Part 3, relates to the amount of ownership you have in the company's contribution to your retirement plan.

What to Do If You Suspect a Problem

If you do suspect a problem with your pension fund, your most effective way of reporting that is in writing. You should summarize the problems you suspect and include any supporting documents. You also have the option of contacting an attorney, which you may want to do if you see severe problems and want fast action.

Government agencies have limited resources and aren't able to investigate all claims or the investigation may take a very long time. You may not even have to spend your own money on an attorney. The law does permit the court to award attorney's fees if you win a pension case. You can get a referral to a lawyer experienced in pension law who is willing to represent workers and retirees through a referral service run either by your state, city, or county bar association.

All of this is a lot of work, but if you suspect your pension funds are being mismanaged, it's definitely worth the time. Your retirement future is on the line if the money isn't there when it comes time to retire.

Cliff vesting requires that you wait a number of years before being 100 percent vested. Under the old plan it was five years, but that was reduced to only three years as part of the 2001 tax law. Before the three-year period, you have no vested interest in company contributions and all the money contributed by the company is forfeited if you leave before the end of that vesting period.

Graded vesting is a more gradual route to 100-percent ownership. With this type of vesting, you wait a number of years before vesting starts and then you are vested at 20 percent per year until fully vested. Under the old law, vesting started in the third year of service and you were fully vested after seven years with the company. Under the 2001 tax law, vesting starts a year earlier and you are 100-percent vested in your sixth year with the company.

Evaluate Offers

When considering changing jobs, it's important not only to compare retirement plan options of the old company versus the new company, but also to carefully consider the timing of your job switch. If you are near the anniversary of your hire date, waiting two or three months could be the difference of 20 percent additional vested money. If your company uses a cliff vesting schedule, you could lose all company contributions by leaving just before your third anniversary and 100 percent vesting.

Many folks who got caught up in the Internet craze left stable employment with great retirement benefits to chase the dream of being millionaires. Rather than a stable 401(k) program, many of these folks were offered thousands of options in company stock only to find out they were worthless when Internet companies went bust.

While promises of profit-sharing and employee stock options or ownership might sound great, they don't offer the same security as a company match to a 401(k). While I'm not suggesting that you never consider getting in on the ground floor of a new business that can't afford to offer you a large salary and benefit package, weigh the offer very carefully against what you might be giving up not only in cash but also in other benefits. Just be sure you understand the risks you are taking not only with current employment, but also with your retirement future.

> While promises of profit-sharing and employee stock options or ownership might sound great, they don't offer the same security as a company match to a 401(k).

IRA Rollover Options

If you do decide to switch jobs, don't spend your retirement money unless you absolutely must do so to survive economically. As we discussed in Part 3, the penalties are severe for early withdrawal of your funds. (You can check the withdrawal rules of each of the retirement types in Part 3.)

The good news is that the new tax law made it much easier for you to roll over any vested retirement savings or your own contributions into either your new employer's plan or into an individual IRA. In most cases, it makes sense to roll over the funds into an IRA that you can control rather than one whose investments are controlled by your company. This gives you more flexibility to choose how to invest your money. If you aren't comfortable with making your own investment decisions, you might be better off checking to see if you can roll the money into the new company's plan. Many do allow you to roll over assets from other company plans, but some do not.

Job changes are not the only things that can create a major roadblock to successfully meeting your retirement goals. We'll now take a look at other surprises that can get in the way.

> It makes sense to roll over the funds into an IRA that you can control rather than one whose investments are controlled by your company.

For more information on this topic, visit our Web site at www.businesstown.com

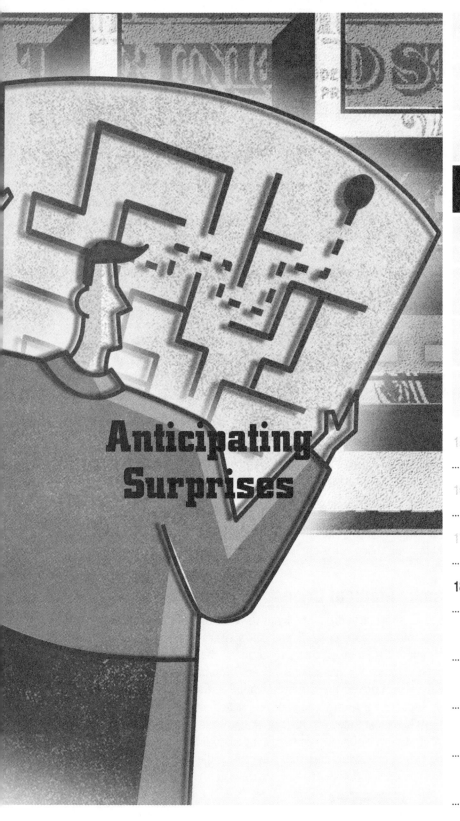

Anticipating
Surprises

Chapter 18

Wage-Earner Disability

You may not realize it, but you have a much greater chance of becoming disabled before sixty-five than dying before that age. Social Security found that three out of ten twenty-year-olds will face disability before age sixty-five. A recent Senate committee found that seven out of ten people between ages thirty-five and sixty-five will become disabled for three months or longer. The Senate also found that one out of seven employees will be disabled for five or more years before retirement.

Even with these known statistics, only 25 percent of employees have employer-sponsored disability plans. If you are depending on Social Security disability to pick up the slack, don't do it. Social Security rejects seven out of ten claims initially. Social Security's disability rules are so restrictive, you literally have to be unable to do any type of work for at least twelve months to qualify for benefits and even then you have to wait six months for the first benefit check. By then, you will most likely have wiped out a good bit of your assets.

When you become disabled, not only do you lose your income, but there is a good chance you will lose your medical coverage at the same time you need that coverage to recover from the disability. The solution is to carry disability insurance, which we'll discuss in greater detail below, but few people can afford the price. Worker's compensation gives some protection if your disability was caused by an accident at work, but statistically only 5 percent of all permanent and total disability cases are work-related injuries.

Family Medical Crises

Long- or short-term disability is not the only thing that can throw a family into a medical crisis. Even if the wage earner is not the person taken ill or the victim of a serious accident, the costs to the family can be dramatic for major illness. Even if you have insurance, there will be things not covered and you could be stuck with huge medical bills, especially if you exceed your coverage limits.

While most times you have to accept what your employer provides in the way of health coverage, if you do have choices, pick the plan that offers deductibles that you can handle in your budget and

> If you are depending on Social Security disability to pick up the slack, don't do it. Social Security rejects seven out of ten claims initially.

be sure you have high maximum lifetime limits. Many companies offer various flexible savings plans to deposit pre-tax money to cover deductibles and co-payments. These amounts can be taken out of your paycheck and put aside for use later in the year. Not only does it help to reduce your tax bill, but it also helps you to minimize the budget impact of a major illness.

Seeking Assistance

In addition to medical costs, there could be lost wages because you or your spouse may need to take time from work to care for the ill family member, whether it is your child, your parent, or other relative. There could also be travel expenses if specialty treatments are needed far from where you live. If catastrophe occurs, you may be able to seek assistance from government programs, such as Medicare, Medicaid, state children's health insurance programs, state catastrophic expense programs, veterans' health care benefits, and hospital charity care programs. Cost of drugs can also take a huge bite out of the budget. Sometimes you can work with your doctor and a pharmaceutical company to get drugs for free or at a reduced cost if the need arises.

You also may be eligible for tax deductions when facing a medical crisis. Unreimbursed medical expenses that exceed 7.5 percent of your adjusted gross income can be written off. If you expect to have large medical bills, you can help ease the pain during the year by adjusting your withholding taxes from your paycheck.

If you are facing a family medical crisis, you can get some excellent information and locate resources for assistance at the Patient Advocate Foundation (*www.patientadvocate.org*).

> You may be eligible for tax deductions when facing a medical crisis.

Monitor the Number of Visits

As you seek treatment for the illness, you'll have to carefully monitor the number of visits allowed under your insurance, especially if you are covered under a health maintenance organization (HMO). Frequently when you are sent to a specialist for treatment, the referral will only allow a certain number of visits before you must go back to your primary care physician for re-evaluation. If you exceed the number of authorized visits, your coverage could be denied and you would have to pay out of pocket for doctor's visits and treatments.

Monitor Your Bills

You also must keep close watch on the bills. You should always seek an itemized bill and be sure you review it for possible errors. Statistically, about 90 percent of hospital bills do contain errors and frequently they are in the hospital's favor. These unnecessary charges can eat away at your coverage limits.

Layoffs/Forced Retirement

As the economic situation worsens, layoffs and forced retirement become issues throughout the United States. Not only is there a loss of income, but people laid off also face the loss of health insurance and retirement benefits.

While you may be able to continue health insurance under the COBRA act, your costs of the coverage will usually be 102 percent above what the company paid. In most cases, the company was paying a large share of the costs, so your monthly health insurance bills will rise dramatically at a time when you no longer have income coming into the house. In fact, what usually happens is people must forego health insurance because they simply can't afford to carry it. In 2001, 2.2 million people lost their health insurance because of layoffs, which was the largest annual increase in the number of uninsured Americans since 1992, according to Families USA. About one-half of these layoffs occurred after September 11, 2001.

For older workers, plans that encourage early retirement sometimes may seem like forced retirement. In fact, the number of age discrimination claims also increases during times of economic instability. When you lose a job after the age of about forty, your chances of finding employment decreases rapidly because companies prefer to pay lower wages to less experienced workers. While age discrimination is illegal, companies get around it by using issues of inadequate job performance or prove that a younger worker is required for successful job performance.

In addition to health insurance, the other major hit is the impact a layoff or forced retirement could have on your retirement savings plan. If you are vested with your company, you will be offered a lump-sum payment, but frequently there are errors in computing

The number of age discrimination claims also increases during times of economic instability.

this payment, as we discussed in Part 3. When you are expecting a sizeable lump-sum payment, it's wise to spend a little money up front and hire an independent retirement specialist to be certain your benefits are being paid accurately to avoid getting less than you are entitled to receive.

Employer Plan Cutbacks/Terminations

Job losses are not the only employer changes that could put a severe dent in your retirement plans. Employers do have the right to cut back or terminate benefits provided they give you adequate warning. Frequently, these warnings are so convoluted that you don't really understand the impact until retirement and then it's too late to fix the problem.

While Congress has passed laws recently to require better disclosure of plan changes to employees, frequently employees don't spend the time figuring out how the change will affect them. This problem is greatest when the employer switches from a traditional pension plan to a cash-balance plan, as we discussed in Chapter 9. Even if you are far away from retirement, be sure to read carefully about any plan changes at your workplace. If you don't understand what has been provided, don't hesitate to question the plan until you do understand what is happening and how it will affect you.

Divorce

No matter which side of a divorce you are on, the impact on your finances for both short-term and long-term needs will be devastating. There is no question every detail of the agreement to go separate ways will have an impact on how much you can save for retirement.

Alimony, child support, health care costs, and other costs of daily living all take a huge bite out of your retirement planning goals. You can minimize all these effects by trying to get past the emotional need to hurt each other and instead trying to work with a divorce mediator to go your own ways with the least damage possible. It's beyond the scope of this book to get into all the economic pitfalls of a divorce, but we will focus on the key things you need to

Age Discrimination No-Nos

Here are the things that are illegal and can be used to file a complaint if you believe age discrimination was a factor in your job loss or denial of a job opportunity:

- Denial of employment on basis of age
- Requirement to retire before age seventy
- Coercion of older employees into retirement by threatening them with termination or loss of benefits
- Firing of older persons because of age
- Denial of promotions, transfers, or assignments because of age
- Penalization of older employees with reduced privileges, employment opportunities, or compensation because of age

If you believe you have been a victim of age discrimination, you can file a complaint with the Equal Employment Opportunity Commission (*www.eeoc.gov*).

do in your divorce decree to protect your rights to an equitable share of the retirement assets, especially if you stayed at home to care for the family.

The Divorce Settlement

A Qualified Domestic Relations Order (QDRO) is the legal instrument used to protect and divide future pension benefits between spouses. If you do want to pull your retirement plan and a QDRO is not on file, a company will ask for a copy of the divorce decree before releasing funds.

When a QDRO requires the separation of retirement assets, money can be withdrawn for you or your ex-spouse and rolled over into a qualified retirement account, such as an IRA, without any taxes having to be paid, provided things are done according to the tax code. These situations are very complicated so don't try to save money by doing it yourself. Seek the help of a qualified tax advisor when trying to divide up retirement assets.

The two key things you must include in a divorce settlement is that the separation of retirement assets is under the tax-free section of the Internal Revenue Code 408(d)(6) and that all transfers of funds are done by "direct" or "trustee-to-trustee" rollover. Once the funds are in your spouse's hands through a proper transfer, your spouse takes responsibility for paying any taxes or penalties due if he or she withdraws the money early.

In addition to retirement savings, you may also be eligible to collect Social Security on your ex-spouse's work record. Generally, you must have been married for at least ten years and cannot remarry before the age of fifty-five to collect on an ex-spouse's record. Check with Social Security if you think you may be able to collect based on your ex-spouse's record.

Tax Returns

Another key financial decision will be whether to file joint or separate tax returns the year before the divorce is final. There are huge tax consequences for filing a return separately and you could lose some major deductions, even the ones you are used to taking

---

Warning— Don't Separate Retirement Funds Early

While it is best to minimize the desire to hurt one another financially, you can go overboard in trying to be helpful and end up with a huge tax hit. Retirement funds cannot be separated tax-free for any reason before the divorce is finalized. You just can't help your spouse with cash flow problems before divorce, even if you plan to give him or her that money after the settlement is in place. If you do, you could be the one stuck with both taxes and penalties as we discussed in Part 3 regarding early withdrawal of retirement savings.

for IRAs. But, if your spouse has not been reporting all income or you believe he or she may be taking improper deductions, you probably want to take the tax hit and file separately. You can be held responsible for your spouse's taxes as well if the IRS questions a joint return.

You must file separate returns once your divorce decree is final even if the divorce is final on December 31. If you are not married on the final day of the year, you should file as single or "Head of Household." To get the more beneficial tax designation of "Head of Household" status, you must maintain the home for at least one child for at least half the year and pay more than one-half the expenses of maintaining that home.

Death of Spouse

The loss of a spouse is not only emotionally devastating, but all previous financial planning will need to be reviewed and revised. After taking care of immediate needs, such as funeral plans, dealing with bills, and beginning to work on estate issues, you'll need to sit down and consider what is best for both your short-term and long-term savings needs.

Things will be a lot simpler if an adequate amount of life insurance is in place, which we'll discuss later. In addition to life insurance, there may be veterans' benefits, other government benefits, private pensions, other cash settlements from your deceased spouse's employer, as well as possible payments from Social Security, especially if you have kids under the age of eighteen or are near to or have reached retirement age. There is so much to be decided at the same time you are trying to overcome grief that it will most likely make sense to seek professional help to get everything in order and be sure you are making the right choices now to meet your long-term financial needs. Once the critical issues are settled, you will need to review your retirement plan and be certain you make all needed adjustments to ensure you won't outlive your assets.

The other thing you don't want to forget to do is file whatever tax forms are necessary. Even if all assets are jointly held, a form must be filed to specify that no tax is owed. Estate tax laws are in

> All previous financial planning will need to be reviewed and revised.

the process of changing over the next ten years, so be certain to ask a tax advisor to review your wills periodically even before the death of a spouse.

The financial impact of remarriage will also be a concern and you could even lose some retirement benefits if you do remarry. Before considering remarriage, be certain to check the rules of your deceased spouse's retirement plans and carefully weigh how the marriage may affect your retirement future. Many seniors today are deciding just to live together to both protect retirement assets and minimize the impact on their children's inheritances.

Minimize the Impact of Surprises

While time is the only thing that can ease the emotional pain caused by many of these surprises, proper planning can definitely ease the financial aspect of a loss. In most cases, you can buy insurance to protect yourself financially. Insurance is basically sharing the risk of some future negative occurrence, such as death, disability, or sickness. You can self-insure and just save a huge chunk of money, but few people have enough money to consider that option. Instead, people share the risk with an insurance company by paying annual premiums. The insurance company hopes to make its money by not having to pay anything based on those premiums or to be able to invest those premiums effectively to make money before having to pay anything out.

Before shopping for insurance, you must make a full assessment of what may be your anticipated need and how much of the risk you want to carry yourself. You can reduce the costs of insurance by increasing your responsibility. This is usually accomplished by increasing your deductibles or your co-payments. For example, with car collision coverage, deductibles can range from as low as $100 up to a few thousand, depending on how much cash you want to put at risk. The higher the deductible, the more you must pay out of pocket after an accident, but the less you will have to pay in annual premiums.

We'll explore the various types of insurance and how you can assess your needs. When you do start shopping, be sure to get several quotes and be certain that the quotes you are comparing are for equivalent levels of insurance. While the price may seem right, when

> Before shopping for insurance, you must make a full assessment of what may be your anticipated need and how much of the risk you want to carry yourself.

you review the fine print, you may find the coverage you seek is not fully included in the cheaper policy.

Life

Life insurance is definitely a must for any family. You may have some insurance at work, but is it enough to cover your needs? How do you determine what those needs are?

When trying to compute a figure, you need to estimate final expenses (including medical bills, funeral expenses, legal fees, and taxes), the payoff of major debt (including credit cards, car loans, and mortgage), some funds for emergency expenses, and money for your children's education. Insure.com has an excellent life-needs calculator (*www.insure.com/life/lifeneedsestimator*) you can use to come up with a number.

Once you figure out how much you will need, you'll then have to pick out the type of policy you want. You can choose term life, whole life, or variable life insurance. For most people, term life makes the most sense because they can afford to buy more insurance at a lower premium. Unlike whole life or variable life, you will not be building up a cash asset. Instead, you will be paying solely for the risk coverage. But, unless you have difficulty qualifying for term insurance, you'll be better off paying less for term and investing the difference.

When picking out term insurance, you should try to get insurance that will guarantee you a rate for a set number of years and allow you to extend that policy before that term with a price adjustment. The longer the guarantee, the safer you will be. As you age, life insurance costs go up tremendously and you could get to the point that you can no longer afford to carry it. The rate guarantee will cost more annually initially, but will be well worth it when you are past the age of forty or fifty.

> As you age, life insurance costs go up tremendously.

Disability

Disability insurance is a much more complicated insurance to select. You may have both short-term and long-term disability at work. If you do, be sure you understand the level of coverage you can expect to get if you should become disabled, how soon that coverage starts, and how long the coverage will last. Many plans will be 50, 60, or $66\frac{2}{3}$ percent of your salary. Waiting periods are usually three to six months for long-term disability, while short-term disability will usually start sometime during the first month.

All policies will have a waiting period before benefits start, usually between sixty days and six months. The shorter the waiting period you select, the higher the premium. Some policies will cover partial disability if you are able to go back to work but must work fewer hours. In these cases, your income will be supplemented.

Whether you are taxed on the disability payment is another critical factor. If the policy is bought by your employer with pre-tax dollars, you will pay taxes on the benefits collected. You can collect disability benefits tax-free if you pay the premiums with after-tax dollars.

While disability will have a huge impact on whether you can continue to save for retirement, you no longer will have to pay premiums. How long you can collect the benefits will also depend on the policy. You can be insured from the time of disability to age sixty-five or you can buy insurance for a set number of years, usually two or five years. Obviously, the longer the protection, the higher the premium will be.

The biggest factor is whether you can afford to buy the insurance. A group disability policy through an employer averages between $150 and $200 per month and many employers pick up at least part of that tab. Private policies can cost five to ten times that amount, depending on the coverage you select, your age, your occupation, your salary, and your health status.

You can buy disability on a "non-cancelable" or "guaranteed renewable" basis. The non-cancelable type cannot be canceled and your premiums cannot be raised once you've taken a medical exam and the policy has been issued as long as you pay your premiums. The guaranteed renewable type protects you against cancellation as long as you pay your premiums, but premiums can be increased. Many policies also have provisions that include periodic benefit increases to allow for raises and costs of inflation.

Health

A major illness can devastate anyone's budget. Paying major medical costs or for health insurance after a job loss are one of the loopholes that even allow you to withdraw money from your retirement savings without paying a penalty. You certainly want to avoid doing that, but sometimes unexpected situations make this a necessity. Your best way to avoid this type of shock to your plans is by carrying sufficient health insurance.

Today, most people are stuck with what their company offers even if it's a poorly designed, minimum-benefit plan. Sometimes you find you must choose between a health maintenance organization (HMO) that covers all the basics, but you're not pleased with the medical services, or a traditional plan that is too expensive for your budget.

When you do reach retirement, you will either have automatic Medicare coverage or you can buy into it. We discussed Medicare and health insurance supplements, such as Medigap, in Chapter 14, so we won't revisit that here. We also discussed long-term care insurance in that chapter, which you should definitely try to make room for in your budget.

Property and Casualty

You probably already have coverage in place for your home and car. Even if you are a renter, you should carry renter's insurance on your belongings. Having to start over with nothing can quickly erase any retirement savings you may have been able to sock away. Another type of policy you may not have considered, but that can protect you from a lawsuit that throws you into bankruptcy, is umbrella insurance. This insurance takes over where your other personal liability policies leave off. For example, if your car policy has a maximum of $500,000 in coverage, a $1 million umbrella policy would pay the difference if damage and injury exceed that total. Without that coverage, your assets could be wiped out. These policies are usually about $150 to $200 per year depending on your coverage choices.

Business Insurance

If you own a small business, you have a lot more to consider when it comes to protecting assets. Incorporating your business can shield your personal assets, but protecting your business assets is

> ### Learn More about Your Health Insurance Rights
>
> While there is not a lot of choice when you do get health coverage from your employer, you're better off than the 39 million Americans with no health coverage at all. Health insurance laws are regulated on a state-by-state basis. Each state has different regulations about what benefits must be offered. Usually, these differences greatly impact the costs of health insurance whether you or your employer pays. If you've been denied coverage, you may want to research laws in your state to be certain that denial was legal. Insure.com has an extensive database where you can begin research at *www.insure.com/health/lawtool.cfm*.

critical to your financial future. Not only must you protect your business assets from fire or theft, but you also face a greater chance that you will be sued by a third party for bodily injury or property damage that could wipe out all that you have built. Also, life insurance becomes more critical because your death or the death of a key employee or partner can cause a business to self-destruct and leave remaining family members with nothing once the taxes are paid.

Business insurance is very complicated and beyond the scope of this book, but if you are a small-business owner, don't forget to check with your insurance salesperson to be certain you have protected your business adequately.

For more information on this topic, visit our Web site at www.businesstown.com

PART V

Retirement Playbook

This part helps you:

- Discuss the parameters for your retirement playbook.

- Learn to manage your savings so they'll still be there when you get to retirement.

- Look at ways to fill the gap, if your goals exceed your means.

- Update your current life circumstances and establish realistic goals.

- Discover retirement asset rip-offs and talk about how to avoid them.

- Determine how much you can withdraw based on the risks of various withdrawal levels.

- Learn how to use assets wisely and minimize the tax bite.

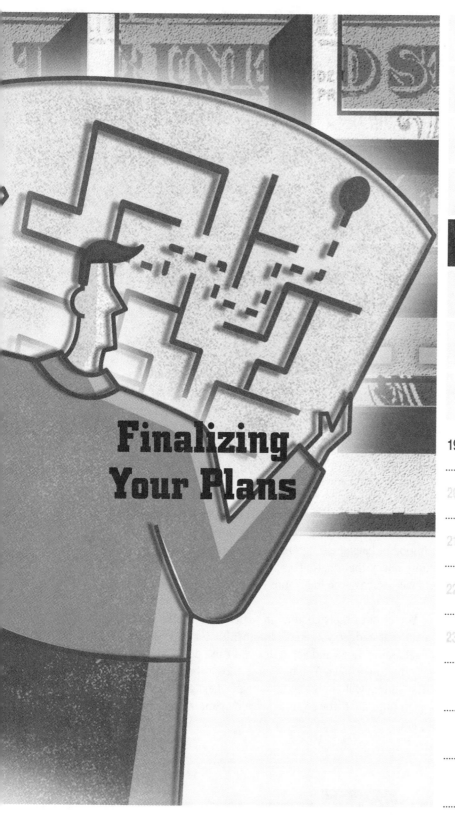

Finalizing
Your Plans

Chapter 19

Designing the Playbook

Now that we've explored the details of all the pieces that make up a retirement plan, it's time to finalize yours. Remember, whatever you put together now is not cut in stone and can be easily revised if your goals and dreams change. What you are doing now is developing a foundation upon which you can build as you step through the various phases of life.

Just as you would plan a strategy for any game, the game of life also has a set number of parameters that will affect how you develop that strategy. Time, retirement activities, and the basics of daily living all play a part in the parameters you'll develop for your playbook.

Time Frame

For retirement, your time frame is critical to determine how much you'll need, how soon you'll need it, and for how long you'll need that money. If your retirement is thirty years away, you've got lots of time until you'll need the money and can take a considerable amount of risk to build your nest egg. If you are only ten years away from retiring, not only will you have less time to build that nest egg, you also need to take less risk so you can be sure you won't lose what you have already built.

Another key aspect of time is how long you think you will live in retirement. You certainly don't want to run out of money when you are no longer able to make more. You can increase your likelihood of having enough through retirement by buying an annuity policy that guarantees you a set payment for life, but the costs will increase the lump sum you will need to buy into that policy.

You're not simply coming up with a budget and saving money to meet that budget, you are dealing with a lot of parameters that are just assumptions and estimates you can't definitely quantify before the time comes. You must just accept the fact that retirement planning will always be taking your best guess and sticking to the plan until life throws you a curve ball and it's time to revisit the plan.

> You don't want to run out of money when you are no longer able to make more.

State of the Economy

Not only is time a factor, but the state of the economy can also be a major benefit or deterrent to your success. A severe recession can put a huge dent in your savings growth and that could be compounded by an unexpected job loss. Inflation can send interest rates skyrocketing, which might help your savings grow more quickly, but will also increase how much you will ultimately need. Rising interest rates could increase your debt costs and cut into what you are able to save.

With all these thoughts in mind, take the time now to revisit your retirement dreams and your retirement budget. Have our discussions shifted your thinking about those plans already? If so, revise your plans and budget and refigure your retirement gap using the Ballpark E$timate worksheet from Chapter 6. When finished you should have a monthly number of additional savings you will need to fill that gap.

Filling the Gap

The first line of defense for filling that gap should be your employer-sponsored plans, especially if an increase in your contribution will increase the amount of money your employer will contribute as well. It's one of the easiest ways to get help for building your nest egg. You may be thinking, "I just can't save another penny." That may be true today, but when you get your next raise think about putting at least part of that percentage increase into your savings accounts.

You can also fill the gap by revisiting your budget and finding ways to live more frugally. You may find it a bit painful to cut back spending now, but not only will it help you save for retirement, you will also be helping yourself get ready for life on a fixed-income. We discussed a number of strategies in Chapter 7. Revisit those now that you have a better idea of just how much you need.

Before making any choice to spend money on a major purchase, consider the impact this purchase could have on your long-term retirement needs. Don't always act on your first impulse, but begin

---

Get Control of Your Consumer Personality

Economists believe people have a "propensity to consume," which means that you will always spend in the same proportion to what you are spending now. As your income goes up, if you save only 5 percent of your income, that savings rate will stay the same. For example, if you are earning $40,000 a year and save 5 percent or $2,000, you'll still save only 5 percent or $3,000 if your income climbs $20,000 to $60,000 per year.

Fight that urge to spend as your income increases, and you can more easily fill your retirement gap without making a significant lifestyle change. Rather than buying that brand new car or a more luxurious home, learn to control your consumer personality and prove the economists wrong. For example, if you are saving 5 percent now and get a 5 percent raise, increase your saving by 2 percent and increase your spending by 3 percent.

to take a more thoughtful approach to spending priorities and what you'll be giving up in the future in order to enjoy that new toy now.

Increasing Income

If you get your savings to the maximum level possible and you have your spending under control, your only other option for filling the gap is increasing income. You may want to consider taking a second job or starting a small business on the side to increase the amount you have available to save. Another option may be to go back to school and retrain for a better-paying job.

After exhausting all possibilities for generating more savings, if you still have a significant gap, your only choice will be to revisit your retirement game plan and find ways to reduce your needs. Many people are doing that by deciding to work longer or to work at least part time in retirement. Others are reducing their budget by deciding to sell their home when they reach retirement, find housing that is smaller and costs less, and fill the cash gap with the profits of the sale.

If work is your only option, or the option you prefer to cutting back now, then think about what you would like to do in retirement. Hopefully, you won't need to earn as much money and can think about reducing stress levels and finding work that you would enjoy. Maybe you can turn a hobby into an earning opportunity. All this will be much more possible if you develop a strategy early and work toward the goal.

Take some small steps to begin saving.

Don't Give Up

Your possibilities for filling your gap are limited only by your imagination and your ability to seek alternatives. Don't give up too easily. All might seem lost now as you look at the numbers. If so, take a break from the disappointing news and revisit the plan later. Take some small steps to begin saving. Consider options for increasing your income. You may find once you get the ball rolling, new opportunities you never considered will come your way. Sometimes just setting your mind on a goal and a dream can help you take small steps to make it all possible.

Catch-up Time

Once you reach the age of fifty, you do have one last opportunity to rapidly close the gap. You can save intensively thanks to the 2001 tax law that allows you to make catch-up contributions in just about every type of retirement savings vehicle you own. For full details on how this works, review the chapters in Part 3 about the specific retirement plans you hold. Here is a summary of the additional contributions you can make once you reach fifty.

		Catch-up Contributions	
Year	IRA	401(k), 403(b), Section 457, SAR-SEP	Simple IRA
2002	$500	$1,000	$500
2003	$500	$2,000	$1,000
2004	$500	$3,000	$1,500
2005	$500	$4,000	$2,000
2006	$1,000	$5,000	$2,500
2007	Beginning in this year, all catch-up contribution levels will be indexed to inflation.		

Your employer does have the option to match these catch-up contributions, but it is doubtful that many will choose to add this cost to their benefit package.

Asset Allocation Strategy

We discussed the importance of asset allocation in Chapter 16, now we'll discuss how you can apply that strategy to filling your retirement gap. You may think that just increasing your return by 1 percent really won't do much, but you are wrong, especially if you have time on your side.

First let's take a look at what just 1 percent can do. The following chart shows how much a $1,000 investment grows at various earnings rates over ten, twenty, and thirty years.

> You may think that just increasing your return by 1 percent really won't do much, but you are wrong, especially if you have time on your side.

Growth of $1,000 Investment			
Earnings Rate	**10 years**	**20 years**	**30 years**
3%	$1,344	$1,806	$2,427
4%	$1,480	$2,191	$3,243
5%	$1,629	$2,653	$4,322
6%	$1,791	$3,207	$5,744
7%	$1,967	$3,870	$7,612
8%	$2,159	$4,661	$10,063
9%	$2,367	$5,604	$13,268
10%	$2,594	$6,728	$17,449
11%	$2,839	$8,062	$22,892

You can easily see how both earnings rate and time can be on your side when building a portfolio. If you have twenty years to go until retirement, your money can earn an extra $663 per thousand by just increasing your earnings rate from 6 percent to 7 percent. If you have a $50,000 portfolio, that could mean an additional $33,150 in savings. Increasing your earnings rate by another percent to 8 percent could mean an additional $791 per thousand or a total of $1,454 per thousand. A $50,000 portfolio would grow an additional $39,550 or a total of $72,700 more with an 8 percent return rate rather than a 6 percent rate.

You can quickly see how tweaking your portfolio just to add an additional 1 or 2 percent to your earnings rate can go a long way to filling your retirement gap. If you can cut your investment costs by just 1 percent, it can make a huge difference in meeting your goals. You may be wondering why we haven't gone higher than an 11 percent return. We're talking about reality here. Over a long period of time the best rate you can expect—unless you've been incredibly lucky and hit the jackpot by picking the next Microsoft and putting all your eggs in one basket—is 11 percent even with a 100-percent stock portfolio.

As mentioned earlier, over any thirty-year period stock earnings have averaged 11.3 percent, bonds have averaged 5.1 percent, and cash deposits have averaged 3 percent. The 1990s may have

> If you can cut your investment costs by just 1 percent, it can make a huge difference in meeting your goals.

gotten you to believe that 20 percent growth was sustainable, but the sobering 2000s are certainly showing you the other side of stock investing—in some years you will take a loss to offset those phenomenal gains. Here is a second chart to show you returns that are realistic expectations, depending on various common asset allocation choices.

Return Rates by Asset Allocation	
Asset Allocation	**Average Rate of Return**
90% stock, 5% bonds, 5% cash	10.68%
80% stock, 10% bonds, 10% cash	9.85%
70% stock, 20% bonds, 10% cash	9.23%
60% stock, 20% bonds, 20% cash	7.86%
40% stock, 40% bonds, 20% cash	6.62%
30% stock, 40% bonds, 30% cash	5.52%
20% stock, 40% bonds, 40% cash	5.50%
10% stock, 40% bonds, 50% cash	4.67%
50% bonds, 50% cash	4.05%

You can use these average returns to help you figure out the best asset allocation for your portfolio. If you are using the online version of the Ballpark E$timate worksheet (*www.asec.org/ballpark*), you can adjust the budget numbers to reflect a different real rate of return than the 3 percent assumed in the worksheet. The 3 percent rate of return in the worksheet is adjusted for inflation, so you must adjust these rates of return by the inflation assumption you expect. A 3 percent inflation rate would mean that a 10.68 percent return would be only 7.46 percent after inflation. If you will be in a 25 percent tax bracket, that return drops to about 6 percent as you begin to withdraw money and pay taxes on it, if you have been using tax-deferred retirement savings vehicles. You can figure out the real rate of return after inflation using this formula:

Earnings Rate / Inflation Rate = Adjusted Growth Rate

> You can use these average returns to help you figure out the best asset allocation for your portfolio.

While the Ballpark E$timate worksheet might assume an adjusted growth rate lower than the one you expect to earn, accepting the lower rate can't hurt you. The worst that can happen is that you end up saving more than needed. Knowing this could be the case and remembering how easy it is to rework the numbers, an annual review of how you are doing can help you adjust for any differences in both your savings success rate as well as your earnings rate on your savings.

If it turns out that the Ballpark E$timate is too conservative and you are exceeding your goals, it is a lot easier to decide to save less than to find a way to save more. A few years down the road, if you feel confident you are exceeding your goals, plan an extra vacation or buy some major item you've been putting off to reward yourself for all your hard work. Whatever you decide, don't put off measuring your success each year. A stock market drop like we saw after the technology stock bubble burst can quickly offset one or two good years.

Performance Assessment and Adjustments

Once you've got your portfolio rolling, you will need to revisit it annually to see how successful you've been at meeting your goals. How you calculate your success will depend on how you've decided to invest in the first place. You may have decided you want to build your own portfolio of stocks, bonds, and cash or you may have chosen to work with a mix of mutual funds. Each type of investment alternative has different ways of compounding your gains.

Stock gains can be attributed to dividends paid and capital gains based on the increased value of the stock. But, don't forget, there could also be capital losses based on the drop in stock value. To figure out how well a stock investment has done for you, you'll need to calculate the gain, total return, annual return, and average annual return. Here are the formulas you'll need:

Current Market Value – Cost of Investment = Gain in Value

Get a Second Opinion

You can get a second opinion on how successful your portfolio might be with a service on the Internet developed by Pulitzer Prize winning economist Bill Sharpe. As cofounder and chairman of Financial Engines (*financialengines.com*), he developed an incredible tool that you can use to track your retirement portfolio and keep an eye on how close you are to meeting your retirement goals. Once you take the time to put in all your numbers, you get an extensive report that lets you know the chance of meeting your goals under various economic conditions.

The Financial Engines Web site also provides comprehensive investor education as well as "Investor Scorecards" that rate the mutual funds you hold. These services are free, but if you want advice on how to reshape your portfolio or if you want alerts about your portfolio's holdings you will have to pay an annual fee.

This is just a paper gain unless you actually plan to sell the investment at the current market value. If it's done poorly, don't panic because it's only a paper loss and could recover.

To figure total return to date, use this formula:

$$\text{Dividends} + \text{Gain in Value} = \text{Total Return}$$

Once you know your total return, you can calculate your percent return using this formula:

$$\text{Total Return} / \text{Cost of Investment} = \text{Percent Return}$$

Your final step will be to divide your percent return by the number of years you held the account to determine your average annual return using this formula:

$$\text{Percent Return} / \text{Number of Years Held} = \text{Average Annual Return}$$

You can figure the return for mutual funds essentially the same way, but in most cases your annual statements will give you a summary of your fund performance.

If you buy a bond when issued and plan to hold it for its full term, the rate of return is the interest stated on the bond. If you bought mid-term, you then need to calculate its yield to figure your average annual return. To calculate a bond yield, use this formula:

$$\text{Annual Interest} / \text{Cost of Bond} = \text{Yield}$$

You may not want to go through these calculations each year for each of your investments, but you should definitely do this for any investment you think may be underperforming. Even if you find the investment is not doing as well as you had hoped, you may not want to sell it, but it is time to review why you bought it and whether it still satisfies your initial investing goals.

You not only have to look at the performance of your individual stock, bond, or mutual fund choice, but you also need to compare it to other like investments to see if it is performing above, below, or at

> Your annual statements will give you a summary of your fund performance.

the same level of similar investments choices. If its performance is considerably below similar choices, you probably do want to consider selling it and replacing it with a better pick. The best way to decide that is to find out the specific reasons for underperformance and whether you think the investment can recover over the next year.

As you review your holdings each year, you should take the time to test your asset allocation and review the performance of key holdings. Remember, the most important aspect of portfolio management is maintaining the proper balance. We'll now move on to the considerations you need to make as you get closer to your actual retirement date.

For more information on this topic, visit our Web site at www.businesstown.com

Chapter 20

Pre-Retirement
Planning

Revisit Your Plans

You may think that you can start your pre-retirement planning a year or two before your exit date, but if you are wise, you'll start the process about ten years before that date. By giving yourself that much extra time to finalize your plans, you can do a reality check to be sure your retirement goals match your current financial and health status and still have the time to fix any problems that might get in the way of attaining your dream retirement.

Becoming Organized

If you have been doing an annual checkup, your ten-year plan review should be relatively simple and you are probably not going to have to spend much more time on your plan than you have been dedicating to it annually. But, let's face reality—most people are not that well organized, especially when a life crisis gets in the way.

Don't feel bad if you are in the majority of the population and put together retirement goals when the mood struck you and then placed them in the closet until you really needed them. You'll still have time to revise those plans and develop something that can realistically match your current goals as well as your financial means and health status. How much you'll have to revise those plans will depend on how far you have detoured from your original financial goals and what other life challenges may have gotten in the way.

What You See Is What You Get

The good news about reaching age fifty-five and being ten years away from retirement at age sixty-five is that you can start counting on the reality of your numbers. Most companies, even if they plan to revise their corporate pension benefits, will exempt employers fifty-five or older from any changes. You basically have a what-you-see-is-what-you-get scenario unless your company files for bankruptcy between now and your retirement date. Even if your company were to go bankrupt, most likely the federally run Pension Benefits Guarantee Corporation will come to the rescue to secure most of your anticipated benefits.

> Don't feel bad if you are in the majority of the population and put together retirement goals when the mood struck you and then placed them in the closet until you really needed them.

Once you reach the age of fifty, you can rebalance even a portfolio that's heavy in company stock. You don't have to get rid of all the company stock before retirement, but it is a good idea to keep your exposure below 10 percent of your portfolio. In fact, most asset allocation professionals will say that no individual stock should exceed 4 percent of your portfolio holdings to be truly balanced and risk averse.

Attainability of Original Goal

Your first task as you start the pre-retirement planning process is to test the attainability of your original goal. Does your original plan truly meet your thinking today? If not, rework your retirement dreams using the techniques we discussed in Chapter 2. Whether you change goals or keep the same ones, rework your budget from Chapter 3 to be sure they're still realistic. As you move closer to retirement, the budget will become more of a certainty.

Next, pull together your assets and liabilities as suggested in Chapter 4, so you can get a fresh snapshot of your current situation. Finally, work through the Ballpark E$timate worksheet, discussed in Chapter 6, and see whether you still have a retirement gap or your savings are on target. If you do have a huge gap, Chapter 7 may offer you some good ideas for getting a handle on the situation. Don't forget that you can use the 2001 tax law catch-up provisions we discussed in the last chapter to fill that gap.

Bringing the Plan Up to Date

Once you finalize your goals, it's time to bring the plan up to date. Health can be a big factor in whether your goals are realistic. Another big factor, of course, is financial status. After all the challenges life threw at you, do you still have the financial means to live out your plan?

You hopefully can save aggressively during the remaining ten years because your children are out of the home and you no longer have to worry about their financial needs. But, if your parents need assistance they could affect your last-minute savings plans.

No Idea? Call Out the Cavalry

If you've gotten to this stage and still have no idea of what you want to do, or your plans are in total disarray because of various life crises, it may be time to call in the cavalry. The International Foundation for Retirement Education (*www.infre.org/index.html*) certifies retirement counselors who do more than just look at the numbers. They help you consider the psychological and emotional issues that may be getting in the way of your making a decision. The foundation is supported by the National Association of Government Deferred Compensation Administrators (NAGDCA) and the National Preretirement Education Association (NPEA) which, together, manage and administer more than 150 retirement plans for over 10 million American workers and are based at Texas Tech University.

If you have a huge gap and don't think you have any chance of filling it, you will need to accept reality and rethink your plans to better reflect financial means. You may decide to work longer or to work at least part time in retirement. One advantage of making this decision as early as possible is that you can then plan for it and find an opportunity that matches the other aspects of your plans for retirement. You may even be able to work out a phased-retirement with your current employer, where you continue working at least part time in the same job or in a consultancy position. These deals usually take time to arrange unless your employer has a program established. Whatever you decide, don't even consider increasing the risk of your portfolio. Now is the time to begin decreasing its risk.

Investment Restructuring

As you move within ten years of your goal, it is time to begin trading in any aggressive growth stock or mutual funds you hold in your portfolio for something a little less aggressive. The reason to start shifting your portfolio at ten years out is because you never know when the stock market will take a dive. If, at ten years out, you have a strong gain, lock in that gain and shift to something that won't be as hard hit if the economy takes a downturn. Don't sell something that is in a loss position, unless you don't believe it has a chance of recovery before you need the money.

At five years, your time is running out to wait for a recovery. By this time your portfolio should have a maximum of 40 percent in growth related stocks, but don't consider this an ultimatum. Look for your best opportunities to get your portfolio near that allocation. During the last five years before retirement, your allocation goal should be to have between 20 and 30 percent of your portfolio in growth stocks or mutual funds.

You don't want to get rid of all growth potential, because you still could have fifteen, twenty, or thirty years in retirement and don't want to outlive your money supply. Holding at least 20 percent of your assets in growth stocks or mutual funds makes good sense through most of your retirement, but the type of growth stocks or

> You don't want to get rid of all growth potential, because you still could have fifteen, twenty, or thirty years in retirement and don't want to outlive your money supply.

mutual funds you hold should not be in assets that have a great chance of risking your principal. Even though no stocks or mutual funds are insured, there are many options to help you choose more stable companies or less risky mutual funds.

When you do retire, you could move all funds into safe investments or decide to buy an annuity that would guarantee you a set income for life. Research your options, carefully consider the costs of any of these choices, and pick the one that best fits your financial situation, your health status, and will allow you to sleep at night.

Business Liquidations

If you own a small business, you should begin thinking about your exit about ten years before retirement. Are you planning to sell it to someone or just liquidate the assets? Are you thinking of turning it over to a family member or partner and expecting the business' continued earnings to help you finance your retirement?

Whatever the choice, you need to start moving in that direction as early as possible during the last ten years before retirement. If you start planning before ten years, that is even better. If you have chosen a partner or family member to take over the business, it's important to let others know your choice and begin turning over management of the business well before your exit. Not only will it let you have more confidence that the new manager will run the business well, but it will also prevent any power struggles later if your heir apparent is well ensconced in the position. Many small businesses fail because the founder or owner never picked a successor and the ensuing battles for power destroyed what otherwise could have been a successful transition.

> If you own a small business, you should begin thinking about your exit about ten years before retirement.

Buy/Sell Agreement

If you do have a partner in your business, you will need to put a legal mechanism in place called a buy/sell agreement, which protects both of you when one decides to leave the business or dies. These agreements specify how the business will be dissolved or continued after one partner is gone.

A buy/sell agreement is a must when you start a business with a partner or group of partners. How you structure this agreement will be determined by the strategy that could be best for you tax-wise at the time of sale or dissolution.

One of the key reasons for putting this agreement in place is to protect you and the business when one of the partners dies. Partners will usually take out life insurance policies based on these agreements to be sure there will be enough money to carry out the terms of the agreement after the death of a partner. Life insurance proceeds can be used to buy out the business and pay any taxes that could be due. Many small businesses end up having to close their doors because provisions were not made for covering taxes or a partnership agreement and the surviving owners were forced to liquidate to cover taxes or buy out the family members of a deceased or disabled owner.

Installment Sale

If you are the sole owner and know you want to sell, then you've got lots of things to think about regarding how you will finance the sale. You can sell the business in one lump sum or over a series of periodic payments, called installments. One big advantage of using an installment method is that you won't be hit with having to pay all the taxes due on the sale in one year. The risk you take is that the business could be run into the ground and you may never see the money.

Even if you don't want the risk, you could be stuck using an installment sale, especially when the economy is not good and bank financing is hard to come by. An installment sale doesn't guarantee you won't have a huge tax bill the year you sell. Not all assets of a business can be deferred by using installments. Inventory, accounts payable, and any property you've owned for less than a year will not be eligible. Basically, anything that you would normally report as current income on your tax return will still be taxed in the year of sale even if you use an installment sale method.

Installment sales are most beneficial if your business has been around for a long time and you have built considerable value in intangible assets, such as goodwill. Also, if you own a considerable number of assets for more than a year that have increased greatly in value, an installment sale can ease the tax bite when you want to sell the business and retire.

Earnout Arrangement

If you plan to stay in the business as a consultant or employee, you can also structure the sale with an earnout arrangement. This will allow you to continue getting cash flow from the business. The way these arrangements are structured, you usually can specify a payout of additional money provided the business reaches certain preset goals. Sometimes these arrangements can help you ultimately get more for your business, but they only work if the business succeeds. You must also be certain you designate who will be responsible for reviewing the books and how performance will be measured.

Medical Needs

Another key concern before retirement is how you will meet your medical needs. If you are one of the lucky few that has health insurance as part of their retirement package, be sure you understand what type of coverage is included. You may even find it is possible to shift to a different type of medical insurance before retirement that will be better for you when it's time to retire. Usually, you have to make the decision to change coverage five years before retirement.

For example, if you are currently saving money by using a health maintenance organization (HMO), but have definitely decided to move somewhere else for retirement, you may want to shift to a plan that would be usable where you want to retire. Most often, a traditional medical plan where you pay deductibles and co-payments is the most flexible. Many companies and the federal government require employees to have held the type of insurance they expect in retirement for at least five years. This prevents employees from shifting to more expensive coverage just before they retire.

While you most likely will have Medicare in retirement, company policies help cover the cost of supplemental coverage such as Medigap. Employee retirement health coverage benefits usually decrease the cost of carrying supplemental coverage in retirement.

> Sometimes these arrangements can help you ultimately get more for your business, but they only work if the business succeeds.

Unfortunately, these benefits are not guaranteed and may not be there when it's time for you to retire.

Long-Term Care Insurance

If you are between the ages of fifty-five and sixty and haven't made arrangements for long-term care insurance, don't wait any longer. Long-term care insurance rates get considerably higher once you reach age sixty and skyrocket after that time. By the time you reach fifty-five, you should revisit your life insurance needs. You may find you can reduce that cost because you don't need as much life insurance now that your children are grown and your residence is primarily paid off. The extra money you save by having a lower life insurance face value may be used to help finance long-term care insurance.

Life Insurance

Deciding what to do with your life insurance if you have a whole life insurance policy with cash value rather than a term policy can be a much more complex decision. Always seek professional advice if you want to make an insurance change and be certain the change you are making is the best one for you and your spouse or heirs. But, remember, as we discussed in Chapter 14, be sure to get a long-term care policy that has a premium level guaranteed for life.

Avoid Retirement Asset Rip-Offs

As you get closer to retirement and your nest egg blossoms, you will find you become the victim of fraud attempts to get a piece of your carefully planned retirement pie. The best way to avoid any of these scams is to be certain you understand exactly what you are getting for your money and how much the service, policy, or investment advice is going to cost you.

Investment Schemes

Investment schemes that promise you high-interest returns, insurance schemes that promise you immediate cash for your policy,

> The extra money you save by having a lower life insurance face value may be used to help finance long-term care insurance.

or reverse mortgage schemes that promise you regular monthly cash payments for your home can be a good opportunity, but frequently are fronts for a fast-talking salesperson looking to make a commission. If you are considering something like a viatical settlement, a high-interest bond fund, or a reverse mortgage, seek advice from a fee-paid financial advisor who does stand to gain financially from whatever decisions you make.

We covered how reverse mortgages worked in Chapter 7 and we reviewed investment opportunities and their risks in Chapter 16. As you get closer to retirement and have more in your portfolio, it is even more critical that you carefully research any place you are considering depositing your money. If the investment sours or is a scam, it will be much harder for you to recover from the mistake. You just don't have the time to make up for mistakes by saving more money once you are near or in retirement.

Viatical Settlements

We haven't talked about one of the newest schemes: viatical settlements. Basically, these agreements buy out your interest in a life insurance policy, if the policy has a cash value. You get cash up front and the company buying the policy collects when you die. The amount of cash you can get is usually more than the insurance's cash value, but less than the face value. If you have been paying into the policy for years and no longer want to make the payments or just can't make them because of illness, it might make sense to sell that policy. Sometimes you will find it is better to take the cash offer of a viatical settlement rather than let it lapse, especially if the cash offer is more than you would get by just cashing in the policy and taking out your cash balance. Some seniors have found this is a helpful way to finance long-term care policies with a lump-sum payment or to buy an annuity.

But beware, there are many companies out there whose only desire is to rip you off, so this is not a decision to be made without the help of a good advisor. An advisor can help you determine if the offer is a good one or if another option would be better. Another key consideration is your surviving spouse or heirs, who will end up with less cash using this option.

> If you have been paying into the policy for years and no longer want to make the payments or just can't make them because of illness, it might make sense to sell that policy.

Annuities

We've discussed annuities several times and these are one option you can consider at the time of retirement or several years later. Basically, what annuities do is guarantee you a set number of payments for the rest of your life, the rest of your life and that of your spouse or other designated survivor, or for a set number of years. There are numerous payout options you can consider when you set up the annuity. At retirement you are typically buying what is called a lump-sum or single payment annuity. Basically, what you do is decide to put all or part of your retirement nest egg into the annuity with the promise that you'll get it back based on the payout arrangements you choose.

Annuities do have fees that are usually higher than you must pay a financial advisor to manage your portfolio, but they also give you lifetime guarantees a financial advisor can't offer. Annuities are usually invested in for safety and their returns are usually set at levels below what you can earn managing the funds yourself. The key for you to decide is whether you want the responsibility for that management or if you would prefer the safety of the guarantee.

Either way, you need to carefully consider the fees you will pay and how much you can be sure to get. Remember that once an annuity payment is set, there is no increase for inflation, so your income will truly be fixed to that amount no matter what your future needs are. Fixed annuities have no chance of ever going up. Variable annuities do have the possibility of offering you increases later in life, but if the investments do poorly you can also end up with lower payments.

> Remember that once an annuity payment is set, there is no increase for inflation, so your income will truly be fixed to that amount no matter what your future needs are.

Federal Programs

About three months before retirement you should make an appointment with the Social Security Administration to apply for benefits. In fact, it can't hurt to make an appointment and sit down with a Social Security specialist six months before retirement to review your options and discuss the application process. When you apply for Social Security, your application for Medicare will be completed at the same time. If you decide to collect Social Security at a later time, don't forget you must apply for Medicare at age sixty-five.

Seeking Advice

You may decide to go it alone in retirement and manage your funds, but even if you do you would still be wise to sit down with a financial planner who specializes in retirement at least once to get a second opinion on your plans. An uninvolved third party can review your plans and make sure the decisions you are making are well designed and give you a good chance of not outliving your assets.

When you seek out a financial planner be sure you pick one who is fee-based rather than commission-based, so you know whatever products he or she recommends are not chosen primarily because of the money he or she could earn in commission by making the sale. If you do end up working with someone whom friends have highly recommended, who earns commissions on what he or she sells, be sure that all commissions to be earned are clearly specified so you know how biased the recommendation could be. You may agree with all the recommendations and go forward, but you do so with full knowledge of the choices and how much the advisor stands to gain. Remember, commissions come out of money that would otherwise be invested for your future.

> An uninvolved third party can review your plans and make sure the decisions you are making are well designed.

For more information on this topic, visit our Web site at www.businesstown.com

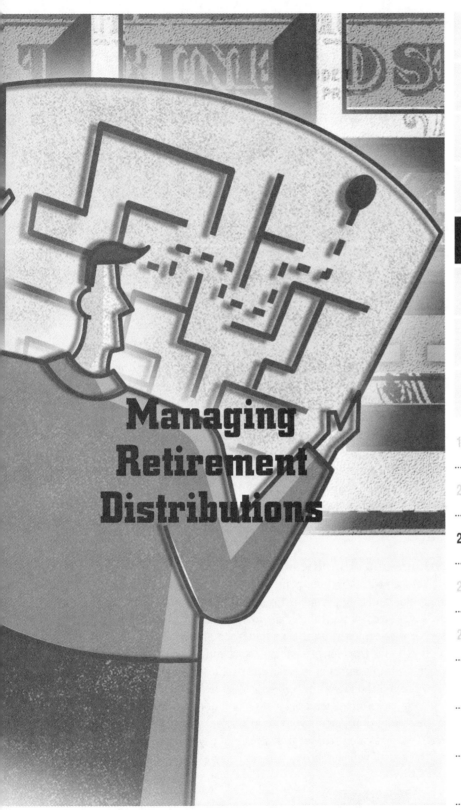

Managing Retirement Distributions

Withdrawal Landscape

When you finally get to the point that you are ready to retire, you will probably have a combination of "official" retirement assets in numerous tax-qualified retirement plans as well as assets outside these plans, such as investments and cash savings. Most financial professionals have a basic rule of thumb when planning what to withdraw first: use up the assets outside retirement plans before drawing down on the retirement funds.

If you have a pension plan from your former employer, you will start getting some payments from that plan after retiring and, most likely, you'll start collecting Social Security. Other than those two items, the money saved through defined-contribution plans and IRAs is better left untouched until you absolutely need them.

The reason to use the non-retirement money first is that the money in retirement funds is sheltered from taxes until withdrawn, while you must pay taxes on earnings from savings and investments outside your sheltered retirement plans. Most of your retirement assets will probably be in tax-deferred savings and it is assumed that the longer you live in retirement the lower your income will be. It is better that the money withdrawn be withdrawn at a lower tax rate. The Roth IRA should be the last asset to be withdrawn because it has no withdrawal requirements and it is the best type of IRA for your heirs to inherit. We'll review the IRA withdrawal rules shortly, but first let's look at pension and annuity withdrawal methods.

Pensions and Annuities

You can withdraw your pension in a lump sum or take it as an annuity guaranteeing payments through retirement. The big decision here is whether you want the company to manage your pension assets or if you think you can do a better job of it yourself.

If you take the money as a lump sum, you can take immediate payment, set up a series of installments over a set number of years, or you can roll the money into an individual IRA. The lump sum is calculated based on an actuarial assumption of how long you will live and the stream of payments you can expect during your lifetime. A present value is calculated for that stream of payments to determine what the size of your lump sum will be. There are frequent errors in this calculation, as we discussed in Chapter 11. If you are taking a lump sum, review the problems discussed in that chapter and consider having a professional review the payout plan.

The greatest advantage of choosing the lump-sum option is that you can use the money in whatever way you want and whenever you want. The biggest question if you take a lump sum is what will you do with the money to manage it better than you think the company might have done. You will need to pay taxes on the money withdrawn, so to minimize your tax bite you should roll the funds into an IRA and defer taxes, unless you need the money immediately for some reason.

The more common way to take your pension is to use an annuity, which will guarantee you payments for life or over a set number of years. Most companies will provide a counselor to review your annuity options as part of a retirement planning process. Once you make your choice, you will be stuck with it for life, so be sure you understand your options. Pension plan annuities usually do not have an inflation adjustment, so the payment level will be fixed for life.

Three Annuity Withdrawal Options

1. **Single Life**—This option will provide payments over your lifespan. Folks who are single, divorced, or widowed and don't need to worry about providing a cash stream to anyone other than themselves will choose this option. This type of annuity will offer the highest monthly payment during your lifespan. If you are married and choose this option, you will need your spouse's permission. If you die before your spouse, your spouse will get no money.

2. **Joint and Survivor**—This option will provide payments over your lifespan plus the lifespan of your surviving spouse. You can designate the percentage your survivor will receive. Options are usually 100 percent of your benefit or a reduced amount, such as 50 or 75 percent of the payment. The larger the percentage you select, the lower the initial payment will be. Most planners estimate that a survivor will need at least 75 percent of your payment to maintain a similar lifestyle in retirement.

3. **Term Certain**—This option can be a single life or joint life annuity coupled with a guaranteed minimum payment period of five, ten, fifteen, or twenty years. The way this works is that if you choose a ten-year option, you will be guaranteed payments for life. If you die after the ten-year period, the payments will stop at death if you choose a single life annuity, or at the death of the designated survivor if you choose a joint life annuity. If you (and your designated survivor, if joint) die before the ten-year period is up, your beneficiary will continue receiving payments for the remainder of the ten years.

Other Retirement Assets

Unless you are one of the lucky few with a pension, most of your retirement benefits are savings in a 401(k), 403(b), Section 457, Keogh, or IRA. If your savings are in an employer-sponsored defined-contribution plan, you most likely will be required to roll over the money into a personal IRA. Few companies will continue to manage the money of retirees. The rest of your retirement savings will most likely be in some type of IRA.

Unless the money is sitting in a Roth IRA, you must start withdrawing your money when you reach age 70½. If you are still working, you can delay your withdrawals until you stop working. If you don't take the required minimum distribution (RMD), you can be penalized a 50 percent excise tax on the money not distributed. The Roth IRA has no required distribution schedule.

The RMD used to be a complicated series of withdrawal options, but luckily the IRS simplified those beginning in 2002. Here is a chart from the IRS that shows you how to figure the RMD based on life expectancy figures.

> Unless the money is sitting in a Roth IRA, you must start withdrawing your money when you reach age 70½.

	Required Minimum Distribution Factors		
Age	Life Expectancy Divisor	Age	Life Expectancy Divisor
70	26.2	85	13.8
71	25.3	86	13.1
72	24.4	87	12.4
73	23.5	88	11.8
74	22.7	89	11.1
75	21.8	90	10.5
76	20.9	91	9.9
77	20.1	92	9.4
78	19.2	93	8.8
79	18.4	94	8.3
80	17.6	95	7.8
81	16.8	96	7.3
82	16.0	97	6.9
83	15.3	98	6.5
84	14.5	99	6.1

This chart might look confusing, but it's really not difficult to calculate the RMD:

$$\text{Total Assets in Retirement Account} / \text{Life Expectancy Divisor} = \text{Required Minimum Distribution}$$

Just to be sure you understand how this works, let's work out an example together. If you are doing this on your own portfolio, add up all your IRA assets in tax-deferred accounts. You should not include assets held in a Roth IRA. For this example, we'll assume you are calculating the withdrawal at the age of seventy-five and that your total remaining assets are $500,000 in your IRAs. Your RMD would be $22,936 ($500,000 / 21.8) that year. This would be equivalent to 4.59 percent of your portfolio. You can calculate the RMD for each IRA individually, but it's not necessary. In fact, you can withdraw all of your RMD from any one of the IRAs or any combination of IRAs you hold.

The old rules are still around and under certain estate planning scenarios you may still want to make use of one of those. This is especially true if you want to designate a beneficiary that is considerably younger than you in order to provide money for children or grandchildren. By naming the younger beneficiary, you can minimize how much you take out. Check with an estate planner if this is one of your goals for your retirement savings to be sure you are doing things right and minimizing the tax bite.

You do not have to name a beneficiary before starting to withdraw the funds, which used to be the rule. In fact, under the old law, once you named a beneficiary you could not change the name. But, you should name a beneficiary as soon as possible for inheritance purposes. You can always change the name if you change your mind.

Seek Advice

We'll review all the rules and give you some basic data to work with as part of your planning process, but it is recommended that you seek professional advice especially at the initial planning phase before you start making withdrawals. You should also ask the professional to review your asset allocation choices and be certain they will support the withdrawals you plan without leaving you short of funds. This is the most critical phase, when you no longer can correct a mistake just by saving more money. Not to be melodramatic, but a mistake at this stage could leave you penniless.

How Much Should You Withdraw?

Now that you know what the minimum requirements are for withdrawal, we'll take a look at the maximums you can withdraw so you don't outlive your assets. This is when things really get complicated. There are so many unknown factors that contribute to this decision.

You need to know how long you will live and how much your portfolio will earn. You also need to factor in the chance that you will experience a major illness that could drain these funds more quickly than planned. As with all aspects of retirement, we'll have to make assumptions and best guesses.

To help you for planning purposes, see the chart on page 325, which was based on data from a study of historical returns between 1926 and 1995 by Philip L. Cooley, Carl M. Hubbard, and Daniel T. Walz for the *American Association of Individual Investors' Journal,* published in February 1998. You can read the study entitled, "Retirement Savings: Choosing a Withdrawal Rate That Is Sustainable," which also looks at other variables for calculating portfolio longevity success, online at *http://aaii.com/promo/mstar/feature.shtml.* The full study does look at other options for determining portfolio success rates. Other options do not adjust for inflation and some consider only the historical returns between 1946 and 1995.

You will see that not only must you consider the number of years you will live in retirement, but you must also factor in the asset mix for your portfolio and what the likely return on that mix will be. The authors of the study considered various asset mixes and what level of risk you may want to take as you decide the percentage you will withdraw from your portfolio each year. The higher the percentage you withdraw, the riskier it gets.

Let's compare this chart to the IRS minimum distribution for a seventy-year-old with $500,000 in total IRA assets. The life expectancy factor for a seventy-year-old is 26.2. The RMD would be $19,084 (500,000 / 26.2) or 3.8 percent. Based on this chart, the retiree could be 90 to 100 percent certain of not outliving assets even if he or she lived another twenty-five years until the age of ninety-five with an asset mix of 25 percent stocks and 75 percent bonds.

If the retiree believes he or she will live another thirty years to age 100 and wants a 90 to 100 percent chance of not outliving assets at a 4 percent withdrawal, the asset mix would have to be a bit riskier with 50 percent stocks and 50 percent bonds. Remember, this 100-year-old will have to manage the portfolio over thirty-five years. If you are expecting that long a retirement, you definitely want to include

> You will see that not only must you consider the number of years you will live in retirement, but you must also factor in the asset mix for your portfolio and what the likely return on that mix will be.

How Much Can You Withdraw Without Outliving Your Assets?

Inflation Adjusted Withdrawal Rates as Percent of Initial Portfolio Value

Asset Mix	Chance of Success	Number of Years in Retirement			
		15 Years	20 Years	25 Years	30 Years
100% stocks	90–100%	6%	4%	4%	4%
	75–90%	7%	6%	5%	5%
	Less than 50%	11%	8%	7%	7%
75% stocks	90–100%	6%	5%	4%	4%
25% bonds	75–90%	7%	6%	5%	5%
	Less than 50%	10%	9%	8%	7%
50% stocks	90–100%	6%	5%	4%	4%
50% bonds	75–90%	7%	6%	5%	5%
	Less than 50%	10%	8%	7%	7%
25% stocks	90–100%	5%	4%	4%	3%
75% bonds	75–90%	6%	5%	4%	3%
	Less than 50%	9%	6%	5%	5%
100% bonds	90–100%	5%	4%	3%	<3%
	75–90%	5%	4%	3%	3%
	Less than 50%	7%	5%	4%	4%

more growth in your portfolio. But as you can see from the chart above, there is little advantage to making the portfolio any more risky by increasing the stock portion of the portfolio to 75 percent.

At first glance, you may think the government is forcing you to take more risk at age seventy-five, when you must withdraw 4.59 percent of your portfolio, but in reality that's not the case. Remember that your portfolio will continue to grow at some rate between the ages of seventy and seventy-five. Let's take a look at the impact on a $500,000 portfolio over a six-year period, with the minimum required distribution taken each year at two sample rates of return adjusted for inflation.

First, let's assume the portfolio is invested with 40 percent in stocks, 40 percent in bonds, and 20 percent in cash. Based on our calculations in Chapter 16, the rate of return would be 6.62 percent and adjusted for a 3 percent inflation rate would be 3.51 percent. Here's what happens to the portfolio over a six-year period beginning at age seventy with withdrawals taken on the first day of the year.

- Age 70 withdrawal: $500,000 / RMD Factor 26.2 = $19,084
  Balance after withdrawal: $480,916
  Balance after 3.51 percent returns for year: $497,796

- Age 71 withdrawal: $497,796 / RMD Factor 25.3 = $19,675
  Balance after withdrawal: $478,120
  Balance after 3.51 percent returns for year: $494,902

- Age 72 withdrawal: $494,902 / RMD Factor 24.4 = $20,283
  Balance after withdrawal: $474,619
  Balance after 3.51 percent returns for year: $491,278

- Age 73 withdrawal: $491,278 / RMD Factor 23.5 = $20,905
  Balance after withdrawal: $470,373
  Balance after 3.51 percent returns for year: $486,883

- Age 74 withdrawal: $486,883 / RMD Factor 22.7 = $21,449
  Balance after withdrawal: $465,434
  Balance after 3.51 percent returns for year: $481,771

- Age 75 withdrawal: $481,771 / RMD Factor 21.8 = $22,100
  Balance after withdrawal: $459,671
  Balance after 3.51 percent returns for year: $475,805

Most of the money taken out of the portfolio over the six-year period would have been out of the earnings on the portfolio.

You can see that with an inflation adjusted average return of 3.51 percent, a person would actually only spend down $24,195 of his or her principal, even though a total of $123,496 would have been withdrawn. Most of the money taken out of the portfolio over the six-year period would have been out of the earnings on the portfolio.

Next, we'll run the same calculations for a less risky portfolio that is invested with 30 percent in stocks, 40 percent in bonds, and 30 percent in cash. Based on our calculations in Chapter 16, the rate of return would be 5.52 percent and adjusted for inflation would be 2.45 percent. Here's what happens to the portfolio over a six-year period beginning at age seventy with withdrawals taken on the first day of the year.

- Age 70 withdrawal: $500,000 / RMD Factor 26.2 = $19,084
  Balance after withdrawal: $480,916
  Balance after 2.45 percent returns for year: $492,698

- Age 71 withdrawal: $492,698 / RMD Factor 25.3 = $19,474
  Balance after withdrawal: $473,224
  Balance after 2.45 percent returns for year: $484,817

- Age 72 withdrawal: $484,817 / RMD Factor 24.4 = $19,870
  Balance after withdrawal: $464,947
  Balance after 2.45 percent returns for year: $476,338

- Age 73 withdrawal: $476,338 / RMD Factor 23.5 = $20,270
  Balance after withdrawal: $456,068
  Balance after 2.45 percent returns for year: $467,242

- Age 74 withdrawal: $467,242 / RMD Factor 22.7 = $20,583
  Balance after withdrawal: $446,659
  Balance after 2.45 percent returns for year: $457,602

- Age 75 withdrawal: $457,602 / RMD Factor 21.8 = $20,991
  Balance after withdrawal: $436,611
  Balance after 2.45 percent returns for year: $447,308

> This increase is not primarily because of the IRS's RMD factor.

You can see that with an inflation adjusted average return of 2.45 percent, just a 1.06 percent difference, a person would actually only spend down almost double the amount of the principal—$52,691. This increase is not primarily because of the IRS's RMD factor. The total withdrawn is actually slightly less—$120,272. The key factor is that a larger proportion of the withdrawal each year is coming from principal rather than earnings on that principal.

This comparison gives you a good idea of how important your asset allocation mix is during retirement. Your asset allocation not only has an impact on how long your money will last, but also on how much you will be able to withdraw each year.

Revisit Annually

You can see from this one comparison, that you can't just put your portfolio on autopilot even during retirement. You need to continue your annual reviews of your portfolio and its performance.

During retirement you are more concerned about preservation of principal rather than growing that principal, but growth must also be a factor. Carefully balancing the needs of preservation of capital and growth can help you sustain a good income from your savings throughout retirement.

In addition to reviewing your portfolio's performance each year, you'll need to factor in your health status and your lifespan expectations. As you age, you will have a better idea of how much longer you think you may live. No question it will still be based on estimates and assumptions, but you can make those guesses with a lot more knowledge of how things are actually progressing.

While you can't save more during retirement, you can stretch out the life of your portfolio by changing its asset allocation or reducing your withdrawal percentage. You are in control and it's up to you to make the money last.

Tax Ramifications of Withdrawals

Unless you are withdrawing funds from a Roth IRA, they will be taxed at your current income tax rate. You may remember that those rates are in a state of flux until 2006, but at that time, rates are expected to be 10 percent, 15 percent, 25 percent (27 percent in 2002), 28 percent (31 percent in 2002), 33 percent (36 percent in 2002), and 35 percent (39.6 percent in 2002). With all this uncertainty about tax

> During retirement you are more concerned about preservation of principal rather than growing that principal, but growth must also be a factor.

rates and their expected downward direction, it makes sense to delay paying taxes on money for as long as you can.

Another factor to consider is state taxation. You'll find there are considerable differences depending upon which state you live in during retirement. If you are thinking of moving to another state in retirement, definitely check out their rules on state taxes for retirees.

Income taxes are not the only thing you should factor into a tax investigation; you should review sales taxes and what may be exempt, as well as gasoline taxes. Some states do not tax pension money or Social Security, while other states do include these payments in state tax calculations. The deductions allowed for medical costs and federal taxes can also greatly affect your tax bill.

Estate Planning

If you have considerable retirement savings and definitely want to leave a portion of your retirement assets to your heirs, then you should coordinate your requirement distributions with your estate plans. Estate planning is definitely beyond the scope of this book, but we will review some key factors that you should consider.

One way to give your heirs the remaining funds in retirement assets after your death is to name your estate as beneficiary, but you can stretch out tax deferrals even longer for your heirs by properly naming them as beneficiaries to your IRA and using a mechanism called the "stretch IRA." By not naming your beneficiaries individually on your IRA, your heirs will usually have to withdraw all IRA funds over a five-year payout period. Also, by naming beneficiaries on the IRA this keeps the asset outside of probate and exempt from the costs associated with settling the estate.

Another vehicle that can protect the assets for your heirs is life insurance. Life insurance is used commonly in estate planning to cover the costs of taxes and probate expenses. Whether there will be estate taxes at the time you die is still a moving target because even the changes passed by Congress "sunset" in ten years and revert back to the old rules.

Roth IRA Benefits Your Heirs

Your heirs can get the greatest benefit if your funds are held in a Roth IRA and left for the money to grow in that tax-free environment. After you die, your beneficiaries withdraw the money tax free, but they can decide to leave it in the Roth and only take out the required minimum withdrawal based on their age. Using this technique, your heirs can have a tax-free annuity for their lifespan.

If your spouse is the beneficiary, inheritance should be handled differently. Your spouse can transfer the IRA to his or her name and never be required to take out money or can take money as needed.

So Now What?

Hopefully, you are not totally confused as you finish reading this chapter. You can tell that planning to withdraw your money is a complicated decision that impacts not only you, but your spouse and your heirs as well.

Take advantage of any free retirement planning seminars offered by your employer. You may want to take a course in managing retirement portfolios offered as an adult education course at your local community college. Learn all you can, come up with a basic idea of what you want to do, and finally review your plans with a certified financial planner (CFP) or certified public accountant (CPA) who specializes in retirement planning.

> Review your plans with a certified financial planner (CFP) or certified public accountant (CPA).

For more information on this topic, visit our Web site at www.businesstown.com

Living on a Fixed Income

Chapter 22

Making Ends Meet

You've finally made it to retirement. You now get to learn about the joys of living on a fixed income. No longer will you be able to think that maybe the next raise will help you meet your budget needs. The measly cost of living increases you can expect in Social Security will probably not cover your increasing costs for medical care and food. If you are one of the lucky few that has a pension from your workplace, you won't see any raises there either.

Your first step when you actually get to retirement will be to develop a budget based on realities. First, figure out how much money you are actually receiving each month now that all the red tape is complete and checks are flowing into your bank account. Hopefully your estimates were close to what you actually get, but until the checks actually appear you can't be sure.

Where Will the Money Come From?

The National Commission on Retirement Policy reports this breakdown of income sources for retirees:

- **Low Income**   Social Security: 88.8%
  Pensions: 2.3%
  Assets: 6.1%
  Earnings: 1.7%
  Other: 1%

- **Middle Income**   Social Security: 74.7%
  Pensions: 8.3%
  Assets: 11.6%
  Earnings: 3.7%
  Other: 1.7%

- **High Income**   Social Security: 21.1%
  Pensions: 24.3%
  Assets: 23.3%
  Earnings: 28.8%
  Other: 2.4%

As you can see, retirees with the highest income have little dependence on Social Security. Their largest chunk comes from earnings with pensions as their second largest contributor to retirement income.

Developing a Detailed Budget

Now it's time to develop a detailed budget. Use the budget form in Chapter 7 to try to account for every penny. There won't be a lot of leeway for that miscellaneous spending. Once you've got the budget done, post it in a convenient place to remind yourself of your promises. Monitor your actual spending for the first few months and see how closely your proposed budget matches how you really spend your money. Revise the budget to match your actual use of the money.

Be sure to leave room in your budget so you can set aside money for travel or other periodic entertainment. That way when opportunities arise, you have the cash and won't risk building up credit card bills you just cannot pay. Also, set aside some emergency cash for those unexpected expenses.

If you are finding you are exceeding your budget each month, get things under control quickly and find ways to cut back before things spiral into major debt problems. If you live alone, you may want to seek a roommate to help make ends meet. You will find this not only helps the budget crunch, but also offers you companionship if you don't like living alone. Many religious organizations have matching programs to help folks find housemates. You may want to room with another senior or you could decide to take in a younger person, who not only can help meet expenses but may help with some of the tasks of caring for the home.

Working Again

Until as recently as 2000, when President Clinton signed the Senior Citizens Right to Work Act, seniors were penalized for working when collecting Social Security. That was part of Social Security's design, and the Retirement Earnings Test (RET) was part of the law since it

Seeking Assistance

If you are in the low-income group, you may be able to seek assistance from the federal government using the Supplemental Security Income program. Other state programs may also be available. Each state is different, but if you want to get an idea of what could be available, stop by the Senior Link Age Line to view the programs offered in Minnesota at *www.tcaging.org/senior.htm.*

was originally passed in 1935. Today, the only workers who could lose Social Security benefits if they go back to work are people who retired before their normal retirement age. Once you reach your normal retirement age (sixty-five to sixty-seven depending on when you were born), you can work without any penalties.

If you did retire early, you will be subject to the RET. After earning a certain amount of income, Social Security payments are reduced. Here's how it works. A Social Security recipient who is subject to the RET has a certain portion that is exempt from RET. Once the person earns more than the amount exempted, Social Security withholds $1 for every $2 of earnings. This penalty is slightly reduced during the year the retiree reaches his or her normal retirement age.

In 2002, the threshold a younger retiree could earn is $11,280. If 2002 is the year you will reach sixty-five (normal retirement age), then the earnings threshold is $30,000. Both thresholds will be indexed to the national wage index beginning in 2003.

If you are wondering what all this will mean to your pocketbook, we'll work through a couple of examples together. First let's see what happens to an early retiree. For example, a retiree at age sixty-three who earns $20,000 will experience this reduction in benefits:

> Social Security Benefit = $700/month ($8,400/year)
> Earnings up to $11,280 = No Adjustment
> Remaining $8,720 reduces benefit by $1 for every $2 of
>   earnings = $4,360 Withheld
> Amount Paid to Beneficiary = $4,040
> Total Income from Social Security and Work = $24,040

This does get much more complicated for the retiree who is going to reach normal retirement that year. Now let's look at what happens to a sixty-four-year-old retiree who reaches normal retirement age (age sixty-five in this case) in August of the year. He earned $60,000 throughout the year (or $5,000 per month). The earnings from August to December are not subject to the RET. His Social Security benefit is $1000 per month. Here's how his earnings would be figured.

> If you did retire early, you will be subject to the RET.

Earnings subject to RET

January through July (7 months) = $35,000

Earnings Exempt = $30,000

Remaining $5,000 reduces benefit by $1 for every $3 earned =
$1,667

Benefits due January through July = $7,000

Benefits withheld = $1,667

Benefits paid

January through July = $5,333

August through December = $5,000

Total Benefits received = $10,333

This early retiree would earn $60,000 and also receive $10,333 in Social Security benefits for the year.

You may be wondering what counts as income. For the purposes of the RET, only wages earned by working for someone else or self-employment income counts. Non-work income is not counted,

Going Back to Work Could Increase Your Benefits

You could benefit from going back to work, especially if you had years of low or no earnings. Earnings are added to your work record even if you have already started to collect benefits. If you earn more during retirement than you did during low- or no-income earning years, the new earnings could mean that your monthly benefit amount will increase. The AARP found in 1999 that 1.66 million primary beneficiaries aged sixty-five and older got an increase in their monthly benefit during 1995, which is the last year for which information is available. The average increase was $15 per month.

We'll look at an example so you can see how this works. Let's assume a woman began working out of school and earned $7,000 per year in 1958. We'll assume she was twenty when she started working and retired at age sixty-four in 2000. She got married and decided to have a family two years after she started working. She stopped working at age twenty-two for twenty years while she raised a family. She then went back to work for twenty years.

She had twenty-two years with earned income and twenty years with no income. Since Social Security averages the thirty-five highest years, thirteen of the years used in this calculation are $0. If she works even part time after the age of sixty-four, that part-time salary will be higher than the $0. Social Security will automatically recalculate and adjust her benefits as appropriate.

which includes government or military benefits, investment earnings, interest, pensions, annuities, and capital gains.

The RET is used once you are already collecting Social Security. The first year you retire has different rules. The first year has a special monthly earnings test. If our retiree earning $60,000 was retiring that year rather than earning that money in the middle of an early retirement, his benefits would not have been cut. More likely than earning the same amount each month, the new retiree would probably have earned most of that money before retirement. We'll assume he earned $56,000 before retirement and $4,000 after retiring. In the first year of retirement, up to the first $940 of earnings per month are exempt, so there would be no cut in benefits for this retiree.

Social Security bases its benefit reduction on an earning estimate you provide at the beginning of the year. If, during the year, your earnings change, you will have to report the difference. If you end up earning less, your monthly benefit could be too low. But even worse, if you underreported you could end up owing the government money.

Minimizing the Tax Bite

Even though you are in retirement, you don't get to retire from paying taxes. Each year you have to test whether your Social Security benefits will be taxable. If your base amount of earnings is above the tax-free level, you will have to pay taxes on those benefits. First, let's look at the base amount. As with every other age, your base amount depends on your filing status. Here are the IRS base amounts:

- $25,000 if you are single, head of household, or qualifying widow(er)
- $25,000 if you are married filing separately and lived apart from your spouse for all of 2000
- $32,000 if you are married filing jointly
- $0 if you are married filing separately and lived with your spouse at any time during 2000

Once you've exceeded the base amount, your benefits could be taxable. If you do file a joint return, you and your spouse will have to combine your incomes and retirement benefits to complete this comparison. Even if your spouse is not retired and not collecting benefits, you still must add your spouse's income to determine if your benefits are taxable.

If the only income you receive is Social Security, you most likely won't have to pay taxes unless you and your spouse are receiving near or at the maximum level of benefits or you are married filing separately. You may not even be required to file a tax return. But, if you do have income in addition to benefits, you will probably be stuck filing a return even if none of your benefits are taxable.

Each year you receive benefits you will get an SSA-1099 form from Social Security. If you are collecting on more than one Social Security record, such as your own work record and on the work record of your spouse, you will receive more than one form. The form will state all the benefits you received from Social Security and any adjustments to those benefits. If you are a railroad retiree, you get an RRB-1099 instead.

How Do You Know If You Will Have to Pay Taxes?

As with all other tax tests, the IRS has developed a worksheet. You can use the following worksheet to figure the amount of income to compare with your base amount. This is a quick way to check whether some of your benefits may be taxable.

A. Write in the amount from *box 5* of all your Forms SSA-1099 and RRB-1099. Include the full amount of any lump-sum benefit payments received in 2000, for 2000, and earlier years (if you received more than one form, combine the amounts from box 5 and write in the total):

A. ....

Note: If the amount on line A is zero or less, stop here; none of your benefits are taxable this year.

> Each year you receive benefits you will get an SSA-1099 form from Social Security.

B. Enter one-half of the amount on line A:

B. ....

C. Add your taxable pensions, wages, interest, dividends, and other taxable income and write in the total:

C. ....

D. Write in any tax-exempt interest (such as interest on municipal bonds) plus any exclusions from income (shown in the list under *Exclusions*, earlier):

D. ....

E. Add lines B, C, and D and write in the total:

E. ....

Note: Compare the amount on line E to your base amount for your filing status. If the amount on line E equals or is less than the base amount for your filing status, none of your benefits are taxable this year. If the amount on line E is more than your base amount, some of your benefits may be taxable.

As long as your income is not above $34,000 (if single) or $44,000 (if married filing jointly), no more than 50 percent of your benefits are taxable.

The good news is that as long as line E is less than your base amount, you don't owe any taxes on your Social Security. If you exceed the base amount, then you will have to fill out an eighteen-step worksheet to find out what portion of your benefits are taxable. As long as your income is not above $34,000 (if single) or $44,000 (if married filing jointly), no more than 50 percent of your benefits are taxable. Don't panic, you won't have to pay a 50 percent tax; rather, only 50 percent of your benefits would need to be included as taxable income at your current tax rate.

You can earn too much in retirement and end up with higher taxation on your Social Security benefits. In fact, you could be taxed on as much as 85 percent of your Social Security benefits. The more you exceed the base amount, the greater proportion of your benefits will be taxable. You can get full details about the taxation of Social Security in IRS Publication 915, "Social Security and Equivalent Railroad Retirement Benefits." You can access it online at *www.irs.gov/prod/forms_pubs/pubs/p915toc.htm* or call for a copy at 1-800-829-1040.

Taxable Income

You're probably wondering just what is taxable income during retirement. It's really not that different than how income was taxed before you retired. Taxable income can include compensation for services, interest, dividends, rents, royalties, income from partnerships, estate and trust income, gain from sales or exchanges of property, and business income of all kinds. One key difference in retirement is that you do not need to report any income amounts for supportive services or out-of-pocket expense reimbursements if you are involved in certain volunteer programs, including the Retired Senior Volunteer Program (RSVP), Foster Grandparent Program, Senior Companion Program, and Service Corps of Retired Executives (SCORE).

Let's take a brief look at the type of income you will probably need to calculate for tax purposes in retirement, including retirement plan distributions, purchased annuities, railroad benefits, and military benefits.

- Retirement Plan Distributions—We've discussed the taxable aspects of each of these plans in great detail in Part 3, so unless your retirement plan income is from a Roth it will be included as income. Types of plans that will have distributions to be included in this calculation include IRAs, 401(k)s, 403(b)s, SEP-IRAs, SIMPLE IRAs, Keoghs, and traditional pensions.
- Purchased Annuities—If you purchased an annuity from an insurance company, bank, or mutual fund group, your payments from that annuity will be taxable.
- Railroad Retirement Benefits—We haven't discussed these unique pension programs, but if you were a railroad employee, your benefits are different from the rest of us.

Taxes Withheld from Social Security Benefits

If you expect to have a tax bill at the end of the year, you can avoid that by requesting that taxes be withheld from your Social Security benefits. You do this by filling out a W-4V with Social Security on which you can elect to withhold 7 percent, 15 percent, 28 percent, or 31 percent, depending on your expected tax obligations. Since you are living on a fixed income, the last thing you need is a tax surprise on April 15.

Railroad employees have two tiers of benefits. Tier 1 is equivalent to the Social Security benefit anyone earning at the same level for the same number of years would have received. Tier 2 benefits match the taxation rules applied to any qualified employer plan, such as a 401(k), and are fully taxable.

- Military Retirement—Pay based on age and length of service is fully taxable. Some military and government pensions based on disability from active service in the Armed Forces are not taxable. Check the taxable status of your benefits with your military payroll office.

There are some things that are not taxed. Most of these are things that would not be taxed even if you were not retired:

- Compensation for sickness or injury, such as workers' compensation, is not taxable.
- Benefits you collect from an accident or health insurance policy are not taxable as long as you paid the premiums or the premiums paid by your employer were included in your gross income.
- Payments from long-term care insurance contracts generally are not taxable.
- Compensation for permanent loss or loss of the use of part of or function of your body is not taxable.
- Life insurance proceeds paid after the death of an insured person is not taxable unless you bought the rights to those proceeds, such as through a viatical settlement.
- Veterans' benefits from the Department of Veterans Affairs are not included in gross income.
- Payments you receive from a state fund as a victim of a crime are not taxable, but you cannot deduct as medical expenses any expenses reimbursed by the fund.

There are some senior assistance programs that do not result in taxable income. These programs are designed to help you cope on a fixed income, so at least the government doesn't tax you for those benefits. These programs include mortgage assistance, help with energy bills, and food benefits from the Nutrition Program for the Elderly.

> There are some senior assistance programs that do not result in taxable income.

Remarriage Strategies and Precautions

Remarriage when living on a fixed income could put a dent in your earnings estimates. Some of your pension benefits being collected as part of your divorce settlement from your ex-spouse could end with a remarriage. Social Security payments might also be affected, depending on how long you were married to the person whose work record your benefits are based upon. Be sure you understand the impact a marriage may have on whatever benefits you are currently collecting. The complications of remarriage and retiree benefits have encouraged a lot of people to just live together when retired.

Another roadblock you face if you are considering getting married as a retiree is the impact your marriage may have on your estate. To protect the rights of your children and other heirs, you should check with your estate planner to be certain any marriage will not negatively impact all the wishes you've already made for your estate. This roadblock has also helped to encourage the increased rate of seniors living together rather than getting married.

> Be sure you understand the impact a marriage may have on whatever benefits you are currently collecting.

Living Frugally

To boil it down, the key thing to learn when living on a fixed income is to learn how to live frugally. You can almost make it a game to see how good you are at finding the cheapest way to do something you want to do. Each dollar you save will be one you can use on something else you need or want. While living frugally is a good habit to get into throughout your life, when you live on a fixed income, it almost needs to become your daily mantra so you don't outlive your assets.

You may find it easier to change to a more frugal lifestyle by picking a frugal buddy. You and your friend can work together to find ways to cut costs. It's always easier to make a life change if you have someone else to help you.

For more information on this topic, visit our Web site at www.businesstown.com

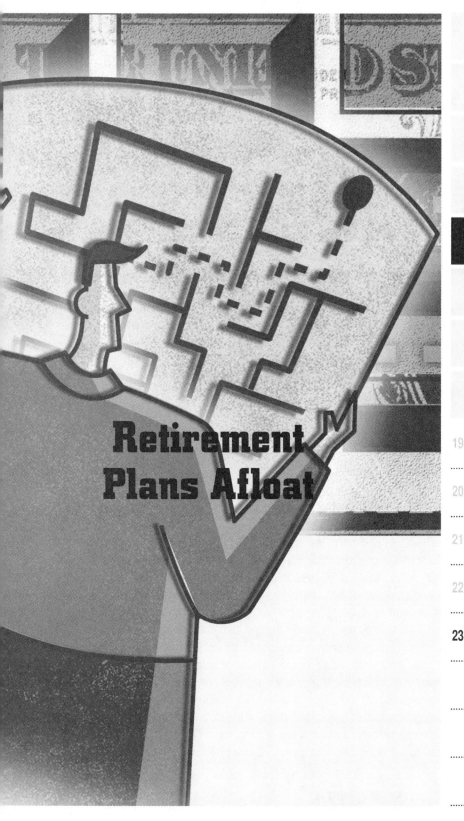

Retirement
Plans Afloat

Portfolio Panic

No matter how carefully you plan, sometimes everything just falls apart. When it happens just as you are ready to retire, it may seem as though all is lost and there is nothing you can do. You'll first need to work through the process of grieving for that loss until you finally get to the stage of hope and can begin figuring out how to put the pieces back together.

One just needs to mention the name Enron and the idea of portfolio panic for thousands of employees quickly comes to mind because stories have been so widespread about the 401(k) plan assets losing 94 percent of their value from their high of $2.1 billion. You may be thinking that's an isolated case and it just can't happen to me, but unfortunately Enron is not unique.

Major retirement savings losses happened at other big-name corporations too, including Lucent, Polaroid, Global Crossing, International Paper, and Dow Chemical. In fact, in most of these cases employee retirement fund programs were locked down during the worst of the stock price drop and employees were unable to sell their company stock to minimize the loss.

> Major retirement savings losses happened at other big-name corporations too, including Lucent, Polaroid, Global Crossing, International Paper, and Dow Chemical.

Court Rulings

Lawsuits have been filed by employees and few have been successful. Shortly after the Enron story broke, the *Wall Street Journal* published an account of a lawsuit filed by Morrison Knudsen Corporation employees. Morrison Knudsen was an engineering and construction company that filed for bankruptcy protection in June 1996. It was based in Boise, Idaho. After a four-year court battle related to the stock losses employees faced in their retirement plans, the employees got nothing.

The *Wall Street Journal* reported that the catastrophe started in 1994 when the company announced an unexpected loss. The next day the stock dropped 25 percent and kept falling until the bankruptcy announcement in February 1996. Morrison Knudsen's 3,500 employees had $75 million invested in a 401(k) and employee stock-ownership plan. In both plans the employees were required to hold the company stock until the age of fifty, but a change in rules allowed for more diversification in 1995. Ultimately, the court ruled the employees were out of luck and could not collect anything from the company for their losses because the 1996 bankruptcy reorganization plan released the company's officers and directors, as well as the company itself, from responsibility for the losses, according to the *Wall Street Journal* report.

Claims against the plan's trustees, T. Rowe Price and Mellon Bank Corp., are still pending because they weren't debtors. The trustees' defense strategy is that they were custodial trustees and were just following company orders. So who is ultimately responsible? The employees who are left holding what's left of the bag.

The story doesn't bode well for Enron employees. Newspaper reports are filled with stories of married couples losing as much as $800,000 or $900,000 in their retirement plans because both worked for Enron. The *New York Times* reported on the devastation at an Oregon utility company that was acquired by Enron just four years ago. After workers lost hundreds of thousands of dollars, the utility called in grief counselors to help them recover their lives.

Reports on the Enron Fiasco

Employees are angry as they read stories about executives cashing in millions of dollars in stock options, while employees were stuck with no option to save their own plans because they were locked out from making changes in their retirement assets. The Enron fiasco has been followed internationally. In fact, one of the most graphic stories was in the British newspaper, the *Guardian*. Angelina Leno, a mid-level employee at Enron for twenty-six years, summed up the employees' anger very well in the *Guardian* report: "They lied to us, they deceived us into thinking that this was the greatest company. And they repeatedly lied to us. When we had our employee meetings it was, 'The company's doing great, we're doing fabulous, we're going to get that stock back up, don't worry.' Now I can understand why, at the last employee meeting with Ken Lay, someone asked him if he was on crack. At the time I thought, God, how can anyone say something like that?"

Leno told the *Guardian* she had more than $500,000 worth of Enron shares before the collapse. She said her broker advised her to sell her shares at the beginning of 2001, when the stock was around

> Employees were stuck with no option to save their own plans because they were locked out from making changes in their retirement assets.

$84, but she instead believed Kenneth Lay and others who told employees the shares would rise to $125. Leno says she is left with a $1,200 per month unemployment benefit, a $500 mortgage payment, and health insurance costs of $500 per month for her and her daughter. She said in *The Guardian* report: "I thought I was going to have a comfortable retirement. I sacrificed all these years to put money towards that. We didn't take vacations; I put everything I could into the account, thinking that in the end I'd be able to enjoy life like I wanted to. I planned to retire in three years. Now I stand to lose my home and my credit. We were the icon of America. The seventh largest company in the world, and Ken Lay brought it to that.

Stages of Grief

Not everyone will experience all the stages of grief and many will experience the stages in a different order than the one listed here. In fact, it is not uncommon for someone to pass through a stage more than once.

- Denial and Shock—At first retirees may be in shock as they try to figure what to do with themselves, especially if plans were not made prior to the exit date. If the retirement was unexpected because of loss of employment, shock and denial are even greater factors.

- Anger—While it may seem odd that anger plays a part, especially if the retirement was carefully planned, major life changes will do that to you even when they are planned. Expect the anger and seek help if it overtakes you. Anger will definitely be a greater factor if the job loss was just before retirement and was unexpected.

- Bargaining—Many people pass through this stage by bargaining with their deity, promising to do various things to get something they desire in retirement. Your church or synagogue leader could be a major help through this stage, as well as all of the others.

- Depression—Retirement is a major loss, even if you don't initially think of it that way. A person can feel isolated and could withdraw resulting in depression. Many times a person's social life is centered around his or her work. The best way to avoid or minimize depression is to be certain your retirement plans do not leave you isolated.

- Acceptance—This is when you finally get to the point of accepting the change.

- Hope—As the pain of the loss becomes less painful, you can begin to re-plan the future and look forward to the times ahead.

It was because of him. Greed took over. These guys were rich and they just wanted to get richer and richer."

Retirement Rage

You probably are not finding it takes much effort to understand the retirement rage that Enron employees are feeling. In fact, anger is one of the stages a person who is grieving for a major loss will definitely need to work through. Grief counselors say it takes eighteen to twenty-four months to fully recover from a major loss. Retirement is no exception, and, even without experiencing the financial devastation employees like those at Enron are facing, just the transition from career to retirement can send a person on the journey through the stages of grief—denial, anger, bargaining, depression, acceptance, and hope.

As you work through the stages of grief, you must find people you can talk with about the problem. You can start with family members and friends, but most likely seeking the help of a grief counselor or your religious leader will help you move through these stages more easily and more effectively, bringing you much closer to a solution when your grieving process is done.

You can also seek out support groups for recent retirees either through your network of former employees, your church or synagogue, or through the recommendation of a professional counselor. The support of others working through the same process can help you fight the feelings of loneliness and depression.

Eating well and maintaining a good exercise program is definitely key to recovery not only for your physical health, but also to keep yourself mentally strong. Once you are feeling strong enough, it will be time to get back to the work of planning your future. Trying to make plans before getting to acceptance and hope will likely prove impossible.

> As you work through the stages of grief, you must find people you can talk with about the problem.

Getting Back on Track

Even if you are starting out on a poor footing, it doesn't mean you have to stay there. Remember, retirement can last as long as twenty to thirty years. Your imagination and your determination got you this far and it's time to call on these strengths again.

You may be left with nothing but Social Security and Medicare, but at least these safety nets are still in place. Build on this foundation and look for ways to make ends meet. No doubt you will have to find work to supplement Social Security. If you do have some savings left, try to leave that money for your later years when you are no longer able to work.

If you own a home with a significant amount of equity, you will need to think about selling it, buying something less expensive, and saving the rest. You can also consider a reverse mortgage, but be sure to review the risks involved that we discussed in Chapter 7.

You may also have cash value in a life insurance policy. You could consider a senior viatical settlement, but tread carefully if you choose this option. Don't go it alone. Work with a professional who can help you find the best option for this asset.

The U.S. Securities and Exchange Commission investigates new fraud causes daily.

Avoiding Frauds and Scams

So far, we've talked mostly about problems with employer-sponsored retirement plans. These are not the only retirement assets in which you could lose all your money. Frauds and scams can take a huge chunk as well.

The U.S. Securities and Exchange Commission investigates new fraud causes daily. Fraud schemes, called affinity fraud, that focus on a particular group, such as seniors, are some of the most difficult to uncover because the targets are frequently friends of each other and don't even realize they are getting other friends in trouble. We'll take a close-up look at one Texas case to give you an idea of how these work. This scheme was promoted as estate and financial planning services between 1992 and 1999. A court injunction halted the fraudulent investment scheme on September 9, 1999. Here are excerpts from the SEC report:

> The Commission's Complaint charges that approximately 100 elderly individuals were fleeced of some $2.5 million

in the scheme. Under the guise of providing estate and financial planning services, the defendants solicited information about the senior citizens' assets and investments. Upon obtaining this information, the defendants encouraged the senior citizens to liquidate their legitimate investments, including bank certificates of deposit and other safe investments, and to invest the proceeds in phony promissory notes promising higher rates of return. In fact, according to the Commission's complaint, the issuers of the notes had no real business or did not exist and the defendants misappropriated, or stole, most of the elderly investors' funds.

According to the Commission's Complaint, [fraud perpetrator] purchased and used mailing lists to target elderly individuals in north and west Texas for investments in so-called "guaranteed" and fully-collateralized "promissory notes." In order to solicit senior citizens, [fraud perpetrator] used Southwest to disseminate literature designed to alarm the elderly recipients with claims that the Texas probate process was lengthy, complicated, and expensive and to suggest that Southwest could provide "estate planning services," "living trusts" and "revocable trusts" to overcome the identified problem. When the targets of the mailing responded, they were urged by [fraud perpetrators] to liquidate legitimate, safe investments, to withdraw IRA monies and to invest in FMS, Liberty, or Enterra in order to achieve a higher rate of return.

Investors were told their investment would be used to fund business ventures, including short-term, high-interest notes, bank cards, resort projects, and short-term, interim mortgage loans, all of which did not exist. Instead, investor monies were used by [fraud perpetrators] to make interest payments to earlier investors ("Ponzi payments"), pay exorbitant sales commissions, purchase several parcels of real estate, acquire and operate a pawn shop, make payments on personal credit cards, and to construct a residence and lake home.

> Investors were told their investment would be used to fund business ventures, including short-term, high-interest notes, bank cards, resort projects, and short-term, interim mortgage loans, all of which did not exist.

Affinity fraud, such as the one described above, exploits the trust and friendship of groups that have something in common. Seniors are frequently the targets of this type of fraud. They tend to intensify the problem because they will look to others in the group before seeking legal help or reporting to government agencies. This complaint talked about a common tactic called "Ponzi" or pyramid schemes. The way this works is that early investors do receive gains and inform friends about their success. These schemes give early investors a false sense of security and trick new investors to join the scheme. In most of these schemes, the fraud perpetrators are stealing money for their own use. The scheme

How to Avoid Being a Victim in an Affinity Fraud

These excellent suggestions are provided by the SEC on their Web site (*www.sec.gov*). Their recommendations are good basic rules to follow before making any investment:

- Check out everything no matter how trustworthy the person is who brings the investment opportunity to your attention. Never make an investment based solely on the recommendation of a member of an organization, or religious or ethnic group to which you belong. Investigate the investment thoroughly and check the truth of every statement you are told about the investment. Be aware that the person telling you about the investment may have been fooled into believing that the investment is legitimate when it is not.

- Do not fall for investments that promise spectacular profits or "guaranteed" returns. If an investment seems too good to be true, then it probably is. Similarly, be extremely leery of any investment that is represented to have no risks; very few investments are risk-free. Generally, the greater the potential return an investment offers, the greater the risks of losing money on the investment.

- Be skeptical of any investment that is not fully documented in writing. Fraudsters often avoid putting things in writing, but legitimate investments are typically always in writing. Avoid an investment if you are told they do "not have the time to reduce to writing" the particulars about the investment. You should also be suspicious if you are told to keep the investment opportunity confidential.

- Don't be pressured or rushed into buying an investment before you have a chance to think about—or investigate—the "opportunity." Just because someone you know made money, or claims to have made money, doesn't mean you will too. Also, watch out for investments that are pitched as "once-in-a-lifetime" opportunities, especially when the promoter bases the recommendation on "inside" or confidential information.

collapses when the supply of new investors dries up, frequently resulting in the loss of all funds.

Unfortunately, seniors are considered good targets by many different types of fraudsters. Fraud schemes can include lottery scams, telemarketing rip-offs, home repair scams, credit card fraud, identity theft, and charity scams. You can find out more details about all the different types of fraud and good resources for dealing with them at SeniorCitizens.com's Web site (*www.seniorcitizens.com/scams/*).

> It's important to know the details of what can go wrong so you can run quickly in the other direction if you even suspect a problem.

Time to Move On

Hopefully, you will never find a need to use the information in this chapter, but it's important to know the details of what can go wrong so you can run quickly in the other direction if you even suspect a problem. If you do believe you are caught up in a fraud, don't hide in embarrassment. Report the possibility as quickly as possible to try to minimize your losses.

Your retirement planning journey has come to an end and it's time to move on and get your own plans in line. Good luck with your planning and have a wonderful retirement.

For more information on this topic, visit our Web site at www.businesstown.com

Index

STREETWISE® BOOKS

New for Fall 2002!

Complete Business Plan with Software
$29.95
ISBN 1-58062-798-6

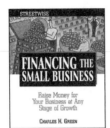

Financing the Small Business
$19.95
ISBN 1-58062-765-X

Landlording & Property Management
$19.95
ISBN 1-58062-766-8

Project Management
$19.95
ISBN 1-58062-770-6

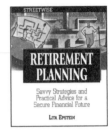

Retirement Planning
$19.95
ISBN 1-58062-772-2

Also Available in the Streetwise Series:

24 Hour MBA
$19.95
ISBN 1-58062-256-9

Achieving Wealth Through Franchising
$19.95
ISBN 1-58062-503-7

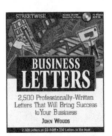

Business Letters w/CD-ROM
$24.95
ISBN 1-58062-133-3

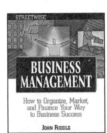

Business Management
$19.95
ISBN 1-58062-540-1

Complete Business Plan
$19.95
ISBN 1-55850-845-7

Customer-Focused Selling
$19.95
ISBN 1-55850-725-6

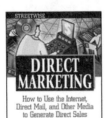

Direct Marketing
$19.95
ISBN 1-58062-439-1

Do-It-Yourself Advertising
$19.95
ISBN 1-55850-727-2

Finance & Accounting
$17.95
ISBN 1-58062-196-1

Get Your Business Online
$19.95
ISBN 1-58062-368-9

Adams Streetwise® books for growing your business

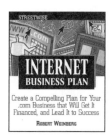

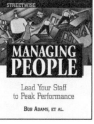

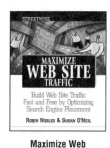
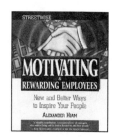

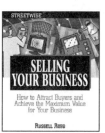

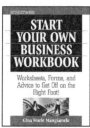

FIND MORE ON THIS TOPIC BY VISITING
BusinessTown.com
The Web's big site for growing businesses!

- ☑ **Separate channels on all aspects of starting and running a business**
- ☑ **Lots of info on how to do business online**
- ☑ **1,000+ pages of savvy business advice**
- ☑ **Complete Web guide to thousands of useful business sites**
- ☑ **Free e-mail newsletter**
- ☑ **Question and answer forums, and more!**

businesstown.com